MAPPING NESHNABÉ FUTURITY

Critical Issues in Indigenous Studies

Jeffrey P. Shepherd and Myla Vicenti Carpio
Series Editors

ADVISORY BOARD
Hōkūlani Aikau
Jennifer Nez Denetdale
Eva Marie Garroutte
John Maynard
Alejandra Navarro-Smith
Gladys Tzul Tzul
Keith Camacho
Margaret Elizabeth Kovach
Vicente Diaz

MAPPING NESHNABÉ FUTURITY

Celestial Currents of Sovereignty in Potawatomi Skies, Lands, and Waters

BLAIRE MORSEAU
FOREWORD BY GRACE L. DILLON

THE UNIVERSITY OF ARIZONA PRESS
TUCSON

The University of Arizona Press
www.uapress.arizona.edu

We respectfully acknowledge the University of Arizona is on the land and territories of Indigenous peoples. Today, Arizona is home to twenty-two federally recognized tribes, with Tucson being home to the O'odham and the Yaqui. Committed to diversity and inclusion, the University strives to build sustainable relationships with sovereign Native Nations and Indigenous communities through education offerings, partnerships, and community service.

© 2025 by The Arizona Board of Regents
All rights reserved. Published 2025

ISBN-13: 978-0-8165-5314-3 (hardcover)
ISBN-13: 978-0-8165-5313-6 (paperback)
ISBN-13: 978-0-8165-5315-0 (ebook)

Cover design by Leigh McDonald
Cover art: *Copper Skinned People* by Cole Redhorse Taylor
Typeset by Sara Thaxton in 10.5/14 Warnock Pro with Lulo and Helvetica Neue LT Std

Publication of this book is made possible in part by the proceeds of a permanent endowment created with the assistance of a Challenge Grant from the National Endowment for the Humanities, a federal agency.

Library of Congress Cataloging-in-Publication Data
Names: Morseau, Blaire, author.
Title: Mapping Neshnabé futurity : celestial currents of sovereignty in Potawatomi skies, lands, and waters / Blaire Morseau.
Other titles: Critical issues in indigenous studies.
Description: Tucson : University of Arizona Press, 2025. | Series: Critical issues in indigenous studies | Includes bibliographical references and index.
Identifiers: LCCN 2024037626 (print) | LCCN 2024037627 (ebook) | ISBN 9780816553143 (hardcover) | ISBN 9780816553136 (paperback) | ISBN 9780816553150 (ebook)
Subjects: LCSH: Potawatomi Indians—Social life and customs. | Potawatomi Indians—Intellectual life. | Indian philosophy—Great Lakes Region (North America)
Classification: LCC E99.P8 M59 2025 (print) | LCC E99.P8 (ebook) | DDC 977.004/97316—dc23/eng/20250129
LC record available at https://lccn.loc.gov/2024037626
LC ebook record available at https://lccn.loc.gov/2024037627

Printed in the United States of America
♾ This paper meets the requirements of ANSI/NISO Z39.48-1992 (Permanence of Paper).

CONTENTS

List of Illustrations vii
Foreword by Grace L. Dillon ix
Preface xiii
Acknowledgments xix
List of Abbreviations xxiii

Introduction: Wayfinding 3
1. Neshnabé Ke: Indigenous Landscape, Memory, and Meaning 39
2. Keno'magéwen: Native Science and Ways of Knowing 61
3. Méndokaswen: Ecology and Spiritual Doings 89
4. Bkanathmownen: Indigenous Science Fiction and Neshnabé Futurity 111
Conclusion: Neshnabé Futurisms 139

Glossary 157
Notes 161
Bibliography 177
Index 191

ILLUSTRATIONS

1. "Nokomis Tends the Land with Waters in Hand" by Elizabeth LaPensée — 4
2. Map of traditional Potawatomi homelands — 6
3. A group of Potawatomi people at the 1929 tribal council election in Hartford, Michigan — 36
4. Map of crude oil and natural gas pipelines on the U.S. side of the Great Lakes region — 47
5. Round Oak's Chief Doe-Wah-Jack — 58
6. Michigan logging practices in the early twentieth century — 106
7. Map of known Potawatomi place-names in Michigan, Indiana, Illinois, and Wisconsin — 147
8. Potawatomi star map by Bmejwen Kyle Malott — 152

FOREWORD
Aanish naa Niinitamawind, "We are the Medicine"

In *Mapping Neshnabé Futurity: Celestial Currents of Sovereignty in Potawatomi Skies, Lands, and Waters*, Blaire Morseau offers readers a profound reimagining of Indigenous futures rooted specifically in the ancestral knowledges and ongoing Indigenous sciences of Potawatomi peoples such as the wonderful practice of turning "toxic" milkweed into health-giving soup. To do so indicates how this original Potawatomi person *mashkikiike*, Anishinaabemowin for "s/he makes medicine." Although this practice was revived a decade ago, many elders then remembered their own folx making milkweed soup in the early spring in this similar manner long ago, once they were watching the introduced process. So, this beautifully illustrates how intergenerational knowledges are never a hierarchy of top-down or elders to little ones in a one-way direction but rather that communities exchange and intermingle and learn from each other.

This work is not just a book; it is a living map, an invitation to navigate the interconnectedness of sky, land, and water, and to contemplate what sovereignty looks like when it is grounded in the teachings of our ancestors and in the relational accountability we Indigenous peoples tend to nurture with all multisited places that Potawatomi peoples, ranging from Mexico to mainly the Great Lakes region, are renewing, the significance of Water Walks, some for over 1,000 miles at a time, and other ecological restorations. *Ke-no'magéwen*, the Potawatomi word used for teaching, is quite literally "the earth demonstrates" so that teaching, learning, and the many multiple species is tied directly to our *Mizzu-Kummick-quae*, "Mother Earth" (here, in Anishinaabemowin aka 'Nish). These current practiced Water Walks reveal how we sister nations of the Anishinaabe, Potawatomi, and Odawa *wii zaagitoonaawaa nibi*, "continue to love the water" in a truly 'Nish-spoken *diba'igan-gaagini*, "forever time." It also reflects *nibi wabo endi ahn Aki Miskwe nibi Wabo*, or "to the water–water healing song–any water–anywhere."

Elder Marie Dixon also shares the more theoretical/figurative meaning of this song: "As women, we carry in us the life of giving waters of Mother Earth" and Blaire's own stories of motherhood and her son bring together that doubling sense that threads throughout this book, a better understanding of futurities in both creative and practical every day moments, ones that are not foreclosed to a singular Futurity but rather to a rich tapestry of many possible futurities.

In that sense, as Blaire points out, the Potawatomi word for these demonstrations of Earth and her teachings and learnings are environmental, place-based, and open to forms of innovative environmental and climate justice activism always entwined with storytelling. Since the Great Lakes region where many Potawatomi citizens live provides 20 percent of the world's fresh water supply and, even, perhaps, more significantly, provides 95 percent of the fresh water in the United States, Blaire's own personal accounts of Water Walks and political acts are intertwined with storytelling of futurities and, even, *bkanathmownen*, a new word Blaire brings up as coined by Potawatomi citizen Kyle Malott "to describe stories that take an alternative perspective on things, in other words, speculative fiction." In fact, lately, futurities/futurisms/futures often are intrinsically speculative fiction—those wonderful experimentations with science fiction (many forms exist now globally!), horror (a growing trend with many forms of Indigenous horror being published or streamed now), and the fantastic/fantasy (this final form used, for instance, by Oji-Cree Two-Spirit Joshua Whitehead in his edited collection *Love After the End: An Anthology of Two-Spirit & Indigiqueer Speculative Fiction* [2020]) to address the spiritual, ceremonial ways of living without giving away too much of the spirit-centered ceremonies that should remain within most Indigenous communities worldwide. Blaire also makes sure to share what she can openly about *mnedo* or spirit beings and even their own roles in mitigating and adapting to extreme global climate weirding without sharing too specifically about these spirit beings, and Potawatomi ceremonies that are sacred or, in 'Nish wording, *aadizookanaan*, sacred teachings/stories/ceremonies that should remain solely within each community and tribal nation/band. This she does quite dexterously, a very tricky aspect in what can be shared in print with all human persons.

I point this out about Blaire's astounding work here since her book reflects the latest trends of moving away from under the "umbrella" of Indigenous Futurisms, instead speaking more directly to Potawatomi ways of knowing, being, and speaking. This trend has become more obvious with edited anthologies of BILPOC (Black, Indigenous, Latinx, and Peoples of Colour globally)–centered futurities/futurisms/futures that are more explicitly bringing in one's own tribal nation along with one's own language and dialects of that nation. Geographer and Mvskoke Nation citizen Laura Harjo's *Spiral to the Stars: Mvskoke Tools of Futurity* is a sampling of futurities with that same theoretical leaning and practice, focused here on Myskoke cartography and mapping. Not only is this happening in academia as decolonizing and restorative Indigenous-centered ways revitalize academic institutions, perhaps, especially in Indigenous studies minors, majors, masters, PhDs, and, sometimes, departments, but this is also happening in Indigenous creative circles. For instance, Koori and Lebanese Mykaela Saunder's *This All Come Back Now: An Anthology of First Nations Speculative Fiction* (2022), along with her own critical work in Goori futurisms, reveals this significance of writing about one's own specific tribal and First Nations peoples, languages, and revitalizations. What stands out about Blaire's work here is that she fuses both analyses of short and feature films like Cree Nation Danis Goulet's *Wakening* and *Night Raiders* and science fiction literature such as Potawatomi Carey F. Whitepigeon's *Daughters of Dawn and Darkness* along with carefully reflective everyday living practices at all times such as Water Walks, demonstrations, and language camps, or, as she suggests, "how Neshnabék communities experience environmental inequality and utilize traditional knowledge systems in **both creative and polit-**

ical ways [my bolding here]." So, both "taking the fiction out of science fiction" and explicit waterways along with acknowledging and exploring "theoretical waterways" occurs!

Blaire's work highlights the enduring connection between Neshnabé people and the cosmos, a bond reflected in their narratives, ceremonies, and languages. The celestial currents of our Anishinaabe/Potawatomi/Odawa existence are far more than constructs; they are practical and ethical guides, directing us toward a future where Indigenous self-determination is not a passive or abstract idea but a living, breathing reality—one that flows through the very elements of the Earth itself.

Through the pages of this book, Blaire critically but creatively invites the audience to envision a future where the teachings of our ancestors are woven with the possibilities of tomorrow. Potawatomi, Anishinaabe, and Odawa peoples have always understood that our survivance is not dependent on placating the forces of domination but rather on our ongoing relationship with the personhoods of bodies of water, and the many realms of skies. In this work, Blaire charts not only a path of resistance but also a path of revitalization, ensuring that the Neshnabé people continue to be the stewards and sovereigns of the lands and waters that they have always known as home.

By examining stories tied to the skies, lands, and waters of Potawatomi homelands, we are invited to walk alongside Blaire, as she guides us through the complex terrain of Indigenous futurity, sovereignty, and the celestial forces that continue to shape our existence on this planet. This is not merely a book about the past; it is a call to action, to reimagine the future and embrace the transformative power of our connections to the natural world.

As you turn these pages, remember that Blaire Morseau's mapping of Neshnabé futurity is a road that leads us forward, back to the stars and waters, into a future where Indigenous knowledges and sciences remains not only relevant but central to the world we create together. Listen and enjoy this *wabeno*, "healer and charm maker's" *inaendumoowin*," "imagination" as Blaire invites us all to *nimidi*, "dance together."

Grace L. Dillon

PREFACE

In the beginning, no one asked me to write this book. The truth is that I struggled a lot doing all the work that comes with publishing one's first monograph, in some of the same ways any junior scholar might. I struggled not just because I birthed, nursed, raised, and cared for my son while doing research for this book and completing graduate school. I struggled not just because I started three new positions, each requiring out-of-state relocation during the COVID-19 pandemic, but also because I faced many internal doubts regarding the validity of my work. One of the many doubts inhibiting the hundreds of hours of labor involved in writing this book included thoughts such as: Perhaps someone who spent more time growing up in the community would have been a better author for this book. Will my community think I'm trying to situate myself as some sort of expert? What right do I have to take up this much space? Despite these reservations, as the momentum of my investigations grew, others encouraged me to publish my research because non-Native "experts" have been publishing dubious, sometimes outright false, and often harmful narratives about Neshnabék for centuries. And I published this book because it is important to have more Indigenous perspectives on futures that include us and our knowledges to ensure spiritually fulfilling and politically generative space is made for our children. I offer this book as a small contribution to the immensely important work others in our community are already doing and will continue to do, including language revitalization, ecological restoration, tribal leadership, caring for our babies, inspiring us with their art, healing us with ceremonies, and so much more.

A Note on Language

For those unfamiliar, linguists situate the Potawatomi language within the larger Algonquian family in North America, related to other languages (sometimes referred to as dialects) such as Ojibwe and Odawa, and to a lesser degree Cree.[1] The similarities in language can be seen on the land itself with towns in the Midwest sharing place-names with locations as far away as New England. Saugatuck, Michigan, is one example, having a sister town in Massachusetts and meaning "place of the mouth of the river."[2] Unlike the Ojibwe, Odawa, Cree, or even the Massachusetts language, Potawatomi is known for vowel deletion. Some Anishinaabé studies professionals might notice a profound lack of double vowels in the Indigenous language written here. This is not a mistake. In this work I apply *Bodwéwadmimwen* (Potawatomi language) words and phrases to prose and summaries of participant observation notes.[3] This method assists in anthropological theorization.[4] I use the established orthography and writing system espoused by the Pokagon Band of Potawatomi Indians, a federally recognized Native American tribe in southwest Michigan and northern Indiana. The writing system was first developed by the Forest County Potawatomi, a federally recognized tribe in Wisconsin.

In nearly all instances, I use the Potawatomi spelling for a word or phrase instead of the Odawa or the more popular Ojibwe spellings. While all three languages are closely related, important differences exist between them. Bmejwen Kyle Malott explains in our co-authored chapter of *As Sacred to Us* that the Potawatomi language has Sauk and Myaamia influences that set it apart from northern dialects used by Ojibwe communities.[5] Because of the regional specificities and traditions of language use that are so intractably bound to individual and collective identities for tribal members, language politics plays a large role in the configuration of community—the Pokagon context is no exception. I've heard many stern corrections for those who mispronounce the word *ktthe* (roughly pronounced "k-chuh") in the common phrase *ktthe migwėtth* (meaning "thank you very much") where one uses the Ojibwe pronunciation "chi" migwėtth. "*Chee?!* What is chee?" Ever the linguistic faux pas in Potawatomi contexts. The only time I use the Ojibwe spelling instead of Potawatomi is in "Midéwiwin," because I am referring specifically to the Midéwiwin Three Fires Lodge in Bad River, Wisconsin. Midéwiwin is the official spelling of their organization. "Mdwéwen" is the spelling of the word in Potawatomi, which refers to the sound an instrument makes. With the Mdwéwen or Midéwiwin Society, there is an implied reference within the structure of the word to the sound the ceremonial Little Boy Water Drum makes when played.

Finally, the reader will note that I use Anishinaabé (Anishinaabék, plural) and Neshnabé (Neshnabék, plural) somewhat interchangeably. While very similar and, indeed, having the same root meaning, Anishinaabé is the more common Ojibwe spelling for "the true humans" or "the original people," while Neshnabé is the Potawatomi spelling.[6] I use the Potawatomi spelling most often, while Anishinaabé is used for tribal affiliations spelled as such or when used in quotations by another person. Please note that some prominent citizens in the Pokagon Band, including some spiritual leaders and scholars, have strong feelings about the interchangeable use (or the *not* interchangeable use) of Anishinaabé and Neshnabé, and that, when referring to a Potawatomi person, one should always use Neshnabé or *Bodwéwadmi*, but never Anishinaabé. It becomes difficult, however, when multiple tribes share a story, political movement, or system of beliefs that includes Potawatomi people but may not be exclusive to them. For this reason, I use Anishinaabé—the most common spelling in the body of literature I cite and in community use—as an endonym to refer to a larger group of all three related tribes.

Further complicating the matter, Potawatomi people often colloquially use "Neshnabé" to refer not just to other Potawatomi folks, but as a synecdoche to all Native peoples across North America. An example is "Those Neshnabés down in the Southwest" referring to Diné (Navajo) or Pueblo communities.[7] To avoid confusion, I use the terms Potawatomi, Neshnabé, or Bodwéwadmi in this book to refer to a person or idea that is specifically Potawatomi. Anishinaabé is used where concepts apply to all three tribal groups known as the Three Fires Confederacy (Potawatomi,

Odawa, and Ojibwe). Names for all other tribes are the individual's endonym used by them in the past or the official name used by the tribe's government where the participant is enrolled.

Cultural Note

In Neshnabé cosmology (certainly extending in length and complexity beyond what this work can represent), bundle items used to conduct ceremony, and even stories, are seen to be animate beings in certain contexts. As a result, they must be protected as one would protect one's family members. For this reason, there are protocols of secrecy and humility in how, when, or if one shares knowledge. Because of the important work that Neshnabé ceremonial leaders are doing in reclaiming space and place in the Great Lakes region by revitalizing ecologies and resisting controversial natural resource management projects, it was necessary to describe the basic purpose behind some forms of ceremony. However, ceremonies, bundle items, and the traditional stories and teachings that accompany these ceremonies are privileged knowledge. It was not and will never be my goal to explore these teachings to serve anthropology or the academy more broadly. As a Neshnabé researcher, I believe it is important to respect the integrity of those teachings. So, I am intentionally vague about certain aspects of ceremonial doings. However, I respect the role that this ceremonial knowledge and the political work that activists and Indigenous ecologists are doing enough to explore it with the detail and attention that scholarly work deserves. So, while I focus on the actions of Midéwiwin society members, this is not a project on religion or spiritual beliefs except in the ways they inform public-facing activity.

On a related note, there are also restrictions on speaking the names of spirit beings out loud. Multispecies ethnographies already investigate the dialectical relationships between humans and other-than-humans. This work does the same, but with the inclusion of the space Neshnabék share with "mythological" beings.[8] These entities include: *Bgwëtthnënë* ("he/she who lives naturally," a bigfoot-like being), *pa'isêk* ("little people," known for stealing items and sometimes children), *mémégwésiwêk* ("those whose faces swing [referring to their long beards]," dwarf-like beings), and *windego* ("one who is thought of as dirty," a giant cannibal-like being). There are seasonal restrictions on talking about some of these other-than-human beings and relatives and telling certain stories that include them. These stories and teachings are reserved for the wintertime, or as some would say when snow is on the ground. Michael Wassegijig Price (Wikwemikong First Nations) claims that this traditional seasonal restriction might not correspond to the Gregorian calendar with winter stories told between the winter solstice in December and ending in mid-March, but rather to when the Wintermaker constellation is visible in the night sky (usually the months of January to March).[9] This protocol is meant to prevent Neshnabék from attracting malevolent beings or circumstances because of "gossiping" about *mnedowêk* (spirit beings). It protects Neshnabék from offending the spirits when they talk about them. So, stories about them or those who use their names are only told when they aren't around: in wintertime. With that said, I also know that my ancestors made pictographs etched in birch bark and made petroglyphs on boulders that depict these spirits and conjure stories. These pictographs don't go away in the wintertime. They're observable all year long. So, I reasoned that while there were certain times of the year I could not talk about mnedowêk out loud, I should safely be able to write about them in this text while honoring cultural protocols.

—*Blaire Morseau*

ACKNOWLEDGMENTS

Ktthe migwètth (many thanks) to all my relations. This book would not have been possible without the generosity of those who shared their knowledge with me, those who enabled me to have the time and space to research and write, and all those who supported me in ways large and small. To all those who have traveled with me, your support has been like a constellation in the night sky, a guiding light in my pursuit of goals. In expressing my deepest appreciation, I extend my heartfelt thanks to each individual and the larger community that has contributed to the realization of this work.

Thanks to my supportive husband, John Mirage Morseau, who always knows how to make me laugh when it's most needed; and my son, *Wgema Nimki Ankwet* / Miksani James Morseau, for being patient in the years I spent in front of my laptop instead of playing with you. The unconditional love and support of both of you have guided me through every challenge. *Gdëbanenën* (I treasure you both).

A special declaration of gratitude to my parents, Dr. Joseph James Caldwell and Theresa Anne Maina, for loving and supporting me. The foundation they have provided has also left an indelible mark on me, both mentally and spiritually. I am forever grateful for the incredible parents they are and the immense love they have given me.

Ktthe migwètth to my father-in-law, Gregory Smith, and my mother-in-law, Lucinda Graverette-Smith. I appreciate you both for many things, but I'd like to specifically acknowledge Lucinda for taking me to ceremonies and sharing your perceptions, memories, and experiences with me. While I don't quote you at length in this work, your wisdom and experience certainly provided the framework for much of it.

Thank you to my dear friends Holly Brause and Katie Hoeppner, and all the women in the Anthropology Writing Group during our graduate education at the University of New Mexico. A second emphasis goes to Holly, who revised several early iterations of this manuscript and provided valuable feedback. And migwètth to my cousin, Erin Topash Burggraf, for keeping me accountable to my writing schedule.

Thanks to the Pokagon Potawatomi language specialists Carla Collins and Bmejwen Kyle Malott, who enthusiastically and freely shared their *Bodwéwadmimwen* (Potawatomi language) linguistic knowledge with me. I would like to thank the elders and traditional knowledge keepers for keeping me grounded with their loving and wise teachings. And thank you to all those who took part and supported this research through formal interviews, oral histories, and informal visits, specifically Valerie and Keith Smith, Violet Snowball-mba, Kevin Daugherty, Majel DeMarsh, Rhonda Purcell, Rebecca Williams, Jason S. Wesaw, Marcus Winchester, Andy Jackson, Roger LaBine, Michael Wassegijig Price, Michael Zimmerman Jr., and many others. Your voices sang this book into existence. Any missteps in this work are mine alone.

I would like to acknowledge my mentors and colleagues in the Native American Studies Indigenous Research Group (NASIRG, aka Native Nerds) at the University of New Mexico where I completed my doctoral work: Dr. Tiffany Lee, Dr. Lloyd Lee, Michelle Paulene Abeyta, Esq., Chad Abeyta, Esq., and Dr. Geneva Becenti. I especially thank Dr. Beverly Singer for your guidance and support. The Indigenous community on campus gave me the sense of belonging I longed for while away from home.

I would like to say many thanks to the following agencies and organizations for their support: the Wenner-Gren Foundation, the American Philosophical Society, and the Society for Ethnobiology for funding various phases of this research. My sincere gratitude goes to the Hibben Fellowship at the University of New Mexico Department of Anthropology for supporting my early graduate studies. Finally, I want to acknowledge and thank the American Indian and Indigenous Studies Pre-Doctoral

Fellowship at Michigan State University for their funding support during the writing phase of the dissertation, which provided the foundation for this book.

My heartfelt gratitude goes to my committee chair, Dr. Les Field, for his knowledge and guidance and for being so open to crafting science-fictional analyses with me, and to my dissertation committee members, Dr. Lea McChesney, Dr. David Dinwoodie, and Dr. Sonya Atalay. I hope each of you can recognize how your scholarship and experiences inspired and aided me in this journey.

ABBREVIATIONS

AIM	American Indian Movement
APA	Administrative Procedures Act
CBPR	community-based participatory research
CRM	cultural resource management
DAPL	Dakota Access Pipeline
DHI	digital heritage item
DNR	Department of Natural Resources
GIS	geographic information systems
NAGPRA	Native American Graves Protection and Repatriation Act
NCAI	National Congress of American Indians
NEPA	National Environmental Policy Act
NHPA	National Historic Preservation Act
NRM	natural resource management
PINI	The Potawatomi Indian Nation, Inc.
TCK	traditional cultural knowledge
TCP	traditional cultural property
TEK	traditional ecological knowledge
TK	traditional knowledge
THPO	Tribal Historic Preservation Officer
VAWA	Violence Against Women Act
WIPO	World Intellectual Property Organization

MAPPING NESHNABÉ FUTURITY

INTRODUCTION
Wayfinding

Beneath a velvety night sky and undulating Milky Way serenading spirit songs from beyond this physical world, *Nokomis*, the Ojibwe spelling for grandmother in *Anishinaabémowin* (*Nokmis* in Potawatomi), carries a copper pail near a meandering river (figure 1). She is wearing a purple ribbon skirt and leather moccasins. There is a wigwam nearby and copper-colored elk tracks that dance around on the earth, reminiscent of the story of Skywoman dancing on the turtle's back—a story Neshnabé[1] peoples share with their Haudenosaunee relatives. Celestial figures in the sky and floral elements near the ground elegantly frame the doings of grandmother. In Neshnabé cosmology there are at least three parts to the Universe.[2] There is the upper world with sky relatives such as Grandmother Moon, the stars, and powerful Thunderbirds; there is an underworld sometimes represented by water, copper, and a notorious though not necessarily malevolent Underwater Lynx or Panther (whom we call *Nambezho*); and, finally, there is the earthly realm humans occupy.[3] These spheres of existence are incorporated in the work of art by Métis/Anishinaabé artist Elizabeth LaPensée included here. Nokomis is carrying a copper pail of water because she is a Water Walker—an activist and traditional leader from the *Midéwiwin* (Medicine) Lodge using ceremony and political demonstration to call attention to various environmental issues related to water. She does this by conducting a women's

FIGURE 1 "Nokomis Tends the Land with Waters in Hand" by Elizabeth LaPensée (Métis/Anishinaabé), 2017. Courtesy of the artist.

water ceremony, cleansing local waters with one of our most important medicines—cedar—as well as with her prayers, walking miles with the blessed water as it sloshes around in copper pails. This carries her medicine and the prayers of activists imagining and working to actualize a better world, one that understands and respects the fact that without clean water there is no life. She walks and prays for the water, and finally pours the contents of her pail into another body of water to activate her prayers, causing them to ripple throughout time and space.

A dark sky with hints of stars and the Milky Way galaxy as seen from the perspective of Earth forms the backdrop of Nokomis's work. The Anishinaabé people use the terms *jiibay kona* and *thibékan* in Ojibwe and Potawatomi languages, respectively, to describe the Milky Way as the "spirit path." This represents the belief that we travel across this sparkling expanse of stars in celestial canoes after passing away. LaPensée is a well-known Indigenous futurist, and her artwork prompts disorienting temporal projections of indigenous experiences through film, video games, and graphic design. "Nokomis Tends the Land with Waters in Hand" provokes viewers to go beyond distortions of Indigeneity deployed by early salvage ethnographies and representations of Native people in Hollywood movies—misrepresentations that placed us in the past and primitivized our cultures. She breaks these colonial depictions through Indigenous speculative fictions told in traditional stories, imagined by participating in ceremony and activism and activated by being on the land and in the waters. Traditional stories and prophecies, together with ecological revitalization and political demonstrations, are forms of what I call "Neshnabé futurity" or imagined landscapes of possibility centered on ethical relationships with the earth, dreamed in ceremony and in storytelling, and put into action by Neshnabék taking part in community activities from picking milkweed to ricing and taking part in water walks—activating Indigenous futurity.

The Pokagon Band of Potawatomi Indians or *Pokégnék Bodwéwadmik* where I am an enrolled citizen is a federally recognized tribe in southwestern Michigan and northern Indiana.[4] At the time of European contact, specifically with the French in the mid-1600s, our traditional lands (see figure 2) included western Michigan, hugged the southern and western shores of Lake Michigan, and stretched all the way up to central Wisconsin and south into Illinois.

As in any worthwhile intellectual investigation, there is debate about the specific borders of Potawatomi territory often understood within a Western cartographic lens of strict boundaries versus the possibility—and indeed more likely arrangement—of permeable traditional territories overlapping those of other Indigenous groups such as the Ojibwe, Menominee, Illini, Peoria, and many others. This cartographic representation of Potawatomi homelands is limited because European contact captures only a snapshot in time. Potawatomi peoples were moving around throughout the northeast corridor and the Great Lakes before and after European contact. As a result, cartographic maps that depict our "traditional homelands" are a single still frame from our larger narrative. Some stories place Potawatomi peoples all the way to the shores of the East Coast (New Brunswick, Nova Scotia, and Maine), through the Saint Lawrence Seaway, to the south and the north of *Mshigmé* (meaning "big body of water" in Potawatomi, referring to Lake Michigan) into present-day Illinois, Wisconsin, and parts of Canada. Indigenous groups

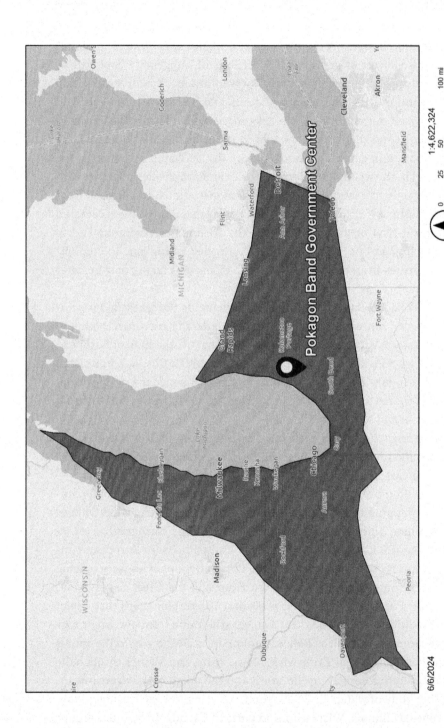

FIGURE 2 Map of traditional Potawatomi homelands, created by the author, 2024.

frequently share traditional homelands and territories with other groups, whether because of seasonal movement or longer-term diaspora migrations. Unlike settler frameworks of territory that dispossess to name and claim for themselves, in choosing to reference this map it is not my aim to rob other tribes of their lands or claim Potawatomi as sole stewards of the region. Instead, I use this map as a tool for orienting readers who may be unaware of Potawatomi homelands and tribal community locations.

Much of this book proposes new ways in which to understand the dynamism of Potawatomi society with a lens toward potential futures without caricaturing our communities; in doing so, we also have to be careful not to essentialize the past or assume that one can practice historical upstreaming to grasp the motivations and worldviews of our ancestors. I mention this because this political move is pervasive in Native American and Indigenous studies—even by our own people. While the intentions of these scholars are to strengthen tribal sovereignty, what they end up doing is inventing two-dimensional fantasies of our cultures and sometimes even dispossessing other Indigenous communities from their lands. With all that said, the traditional Potawatomi diaspora was organized along clan and familial lines. Villages would travel seasonally, break off, or combine with other tribes depending on the needs of the larger Indigenous community throughout the Great Lakes. Citizens of the Pokagon Band of Potawatomi Indians are descendants of the Potawatomi, Odawa, Ojibwe, and Miami individuals who lived within Leopold Pokagon's villages in the early 1800s, and who would later take on a singular Potawatomi identity.[5] The anglicized surname Pokagon from which the tribe gets its name comes from Leopold's earlier moniker, *Pekégen*, meaning "rib."[6] Pokagon became his and his descendants' surname and Leopold his first after he was baptized as an older man. He was a notable leader, having been a young Ojibwe boy adopted by Potawatomi Chief Topinabe in the late 1700s and ultimately marrying Topinabe's daughter, Katesse. Later in life, Leopold successfully negotiated a provision in the 1833 Treaty of Chicago that allowed some Neshnabé groups to stay in the Great Lakes region during the Removal era in the United States around the 1830s, though removals happened continuously before and after the Indian Removal Act of 1830. Fast forward to the twentieth century: the descendants of Leopold's village were excluded from the 1934 Indian Reorganization Act like other Michigan-based tribes because of lack of funds (during the Great Depression). The Pokagon Band managed to sustain a cultural and political identity despite years of predatory lending by local whites who were well aware of Indian annuity payments that in due course led to the loss of Pokagon private property in Silver Creek Township. They held ceremonial and social gatherings, maintained a tribal council, and fought for federal recognition or more accurately "federal reaffirmation," which finally occurred in 1994. Today the Pokagon Band is part of the larger Potawatomi Nation, which in the U.S. includes four federally recognized Potawatomi Bands in Michigan, one in Wisconsin, one in Kansas, and one in Oklahoma.[7] The last two Bands are descendants of those Potawatomi groups who were geographically farthest removed in the mid- and late 1800s, while the first five Bands are those who could remain in or near our original Potawatomi homelands, also known as *Neshnabé ke*. Besides several First Nations in Canada, these seven Bands in the U.S. are usually referred to as the Potawatomi Nation.[8] In fact, recently in summer 2023 at the annual Gathering of Potawatomi Nations, tribal council members voted in favor of forming a twelve-nation Potawatomi Confederacy that includes communities in Canada, representing citizens in the tens of thousands.[9]

Michigan, or *Mzhigénak* in Potawatomi, translates to "the place that has been clear-cut," though most folks cite the alternative Potawatomi word, *Mshigmé*, or "big body of water," as the origin of the state's name. I include these conflicting translations because in my fieldwork I found that some elders from the Forest County Potawatomi tribe in Wisconsin insist that Mzhigénak embodies the very real lived histories of violent resource extraction that shaped and scarred the Great Lakes landscape in the nineteenth and twentieth centuries. While it is not my aim to conduct a thorough spatial-linguistic analysis and determine the etymology of place-names in the Great Lakes, as will be shown throughout this text the stories attached to these names are meaningful in the minds of the participants I interviewed.[10] This informed the major axioms of my research questions, which centered on: How do nation-building projects centered on ceremonial practices and the re-proliferation of *Bodwéwadmimwen* (the Potawatomi language) disrupt settler colonial futures? How does Neshnabé environmental activism and recent ecological revitalization projects undertaken by the Pokagon Band of Potawatomi in particular on and near tribal lands in the Great Lakes region map imagined landscapes of possibility? And in what ways do these actions help us better understand Indigenous futurities in other contexts?[11]

The answers to these questions were ensconced in meditations of Anishinaabé cosmology and "poetics of dwelling."[12] Place is felt, imagined, lived in, and, for Neshnabé peoples, a relative. This work outlines how a community protects a relative and imagines a future together in the face of ongoing settler colonial violence and dispossession. Neshnabé ke—as a series of spaces for mobilizing these futures—must be seen beyond any one tribe's reservation, "tribal trust land," or "fee simple," etc. Not only are these parcels of land an inconceivably reduced pittance compared to ancestral territories, but even the everyday lived realities of tribal citizens are experienced in and between diverse contexts of intertribal relations—at round dances, powwows, naming ceremonies, fasting camps, and hundreds of other gatherings, big and small. Every summer Potawatomi peoples make their kinship-nourishing rounds visiting friends and relatives at powwows and language immersion camps in the summer, round dances in the winter, and sweat lodge, Big Drum, and Midéwiwin ceremonies all year long. Not to mention sugar bush, ricing, and fasting camps, drum group practices, regalia-making classes, storytelling events, youth council meetings, and conferences, just to name a few. There is no singular field site upon which to visit and "study in." The field site is the people. And the people move—a lot.

The ties that bind these gatherings, multi-sited environmental movements, and ecological revitalization projects were part of a larger theoretical focus on "Indigenous futurisms," a term coined by Anishinaabé scholar Grace Dillon.[13] While Dillon was the first to name the cultural and literary asterisms of Indigenous works of science fiction, I find Kristina Baudemann's definition interesting for theorizing the phenomena of my fieldwork. Considering Indigenous futurism as more than stories alone, Baudemann defines them in an appropriately open-ended way as any "Indigenous storying about the future."[14] Her work, like many others on Indigenous science fiction and futurisms, has focused primarily on film and art. However, the above research questions culminated in everyday contexts in what I identify as "Neshnabé futurisms," or the everyday lived activities of Potawatomi peoples that imagine and mobilize reclamations of space and place in more desirable futures and on our own terms—not simply imagine them, though imagining is an important step. These expressions of Neshnabé futurity include traditional prophetic stories, present-day ecological revitalization projects, and ceremonial political demonstrations by Midéwiwin Women's Water Walkers. Like Chippewa scholar Danika Medak-Saltzman, I found that while recent Indigenous-made media from video games to films, art, and novels invite us to imagine alternatives to colonialism, oppression, and structural inequality, these media are connected to the more explicit political activism from movements such as Idle No More, Standing Rock (NoDAPL), and Midéwiwin Women's Water Walks. The artwork is in relation to the advocacy work in a reciprocal and mutually reinforcing current of Indigenous liberation movements.[15] While water ceremonies have been conducted by Indigenous peoples in the Great Lakes since time immemorial, Water Walks are a more contemporary demonstration manifested in response to decades of extreme dispossession and environmental degradation. In the early 2010s, the Pokagon Band of Potawatomi Indians began organizing Women's Water Walks after visitors from another Neshnabé community passed by Pokagon lands. These visitors were en route to walk the entire circumference of all five Great Lakes to bring attention to issues of pollution and harmful resource extraction affecting the water. Midéwiwin teachings informed these walks about women's responsibility to protect water. While I present more detail on Water Walks later in this chapter, for now, I situate them within the larger context of environmental devastation in the Great Lakes.

In addition to the political advocacy demonstrated by Water Walks, the Pokagon Band is investing in revitalizing ecologies in and near tribal lands in southwest Michigan. But a long history of Indigenous disenfranchisement from the environment also informed these contemporary articulations of ecological revitalization. Since at least the early 1800s, many Neshnabék stood witness to the unprecedented ecological, political, and social changes occurring around them. For Native American communities in the Great Lakes region, after the War of 1812 European alliances ended and American expansion into their territories began. The Potawatomi established lucrative trade relationships with the French during the seventeenth and eighteenth centuries and later, though to a lesser extent with the British in the early nineteenth century. But, after Pontiac's Rebellion, Tecumseh's Rebellion, and the War of 1812, the Americans, unlike the French or the British, were not as interested in trade with the Great Lakes Native communities as they were with their land and resources.[16] As a result, Natives experienced extreme dispossession during the late 1800s. A denial of the important roles that Native Americans played in European and American history, their removal West, environmental clearcutting, archeological destruction, and Native American grave robbing also occurred. Traditional Potawatomi place-names were overwritten by foreign, English-language ones, and sometimes even settler-invented *Indian-sounding* ones.[17]

The Great Lakes region of North America is one of the most important sites for considering climate change and Indigenous resistance. The largest freshwater resource on Earth, the Great Lakes hold 20 percent of the world's fresh water and supply 95 percent of the fresh water in the U.S. Today the region is undergoing what Brian Walker and David Salt refer to as adverse "ecological regime shifts," particularly in riverine ecologies and forests.[18] These transformations have been provoked by a multitude of complex historical and contemporary factors, but they disproportionately affect the ceremonial and political spaces of Native American tribes in the region. This disproportion is due, in part, to unequal protection of Indigenous sacred sites and the destruction of ecologies where traditional foods have historically grown, and because Indigenous communities typically live in "expendable" rural areas, vulnerable to pollution and large extraction projects.[19] Beginning in the nineteenth century, American settlers in Michigan used reckless terraforming practices such as the straightening of watersheds or "channelization" to assist assembly and efficiency in the logging industry.[20] These practices facilitated capitalist growth and resulted in the unnatural manipulation, degradation, and exploitation of the natural environment.[21] More recently, a large number of hydrofracking proposals were submitted to the state of Michigan in record-setting state lease sales—a method exempt from Environmental Protection Agency (EPA) oversight.[22] By pumping toxic and many unknown "proprietary" chemicals into the shales to release natural gas, the current method of fracking leads to contaminated drinking water, and precarious disposal methods leave the entire region at risk for spills and cause severe health issues among residents, many of whom are Indigenous minorities.[23]

In response to these issues in the Great Lakes region, tribal communities such as the Bad River Band of Lake Superior Chippewa Tribe in

Wisconsin, as well as the Lac Vieux Desert Band of Lake Superior Chippewa Indians, The Gun Lake Band of Potawatomi Indians, and the Pokagon Band of Potawatomi Indians in Michigan are coordinating and engaging in political mobilization and ecological revitalization projects. Besides traditional advocacy work and legal challenges, some examples of how Indigenous peoples marshal dissent include Neshnabé Women's Water Walks, which stem from the ceremonial Midéwiwin Society Lodge (Three Fires) in Wisconsin, as well as direct environmental interventions such as the re-meandering of local watersheds and the revitalization of wild rice in Michigan.[24] Other examples include the restoration of *nmé* or lake sturgeon, albeit in what Citizen Potawatomi scholar Kyle Powys Whyte calls "our ancestors' dystopia."[25] As an extension of the political advocacy work and the creative work of Indigenous science fiction that imagine alternatives to present contexts, *Neshnabékwéwêk* (Neshnabé women) use ceremonial Water Walks to both heal contaminated waters and publicly expose instances of pollution and hydrofracking in the Great Lakes region.

Initiated by elders from the Midéwiwin Lodge in 2003, Water Walks are ceremonial long walks beginning in the spring of every year. They occur along the shorelines of the Great Lakes and can last several months. With Lake Michigan, a Water Walk is 1,640 miles; however, some Water Walks are shorter, approximately fifteen miles, and occur along smaller watersheds such as the Dowagiac River in southwestern Michigan near the Pokagon Potawatomi reservation. Longer walks are, of course, conducted over the course of days, weeks, and years, while shorter ones such as the annual Pokagon Women's Water Walk are completed in one day. This research was originally inspired by how Water Walkers from the Midéwiwin Lodge may be leveraging themselves politically while revitalizing their relationships to places from which they have previously been dispossessed through removal and ecological destruction. While Water Walks are commonly understood as just a religious practice, *Midés* (a term to refer to members of the Midéwiwin Society) use them to blur the lines between ceremonial and political spaces and reclaim their communities' sovereign rights over the well-being of their traditional homelands.

However, the work of these Water Walkers and the recent projects led by tribal governments in revitalizing ecologies were more than ceremonial or even political mobilization: they were enacting an alternative vision for the future, challenging that of mainstream society that is ineffective in its current fracture between those who express doom over climate change and those who deny its existence altogether. Creative works by Native folks in art and in literature—anything that tells a story—such as the work of LaPensée that opens this chapter and other works of science fiction are directly connected to Indigenous ecological knowledge and Neshnabé mappings of the future. Neshnabé futurisms or futurity is constitutive of public-facing, politico-ceremonial movements such as Women's Water Walks, as well as tribally developed ecological revitalization projects, because they collectively Indigenize a version of the future that, until recently, settler society has imagined *without us*.

On Defining Community

My scholarship is situated within a matrix of works on the Pokagon Band, also known historically as the Catholic Potawatomi from the Saint Joseph River Valley and The Potawatomi Indian Nation, Inc. (PINI). These works include local histories, contracted ethnographies, and newer scholarship.[26] American historians of seventeenth- and eighteenth-century intertribal warfare and European imperialism in the Great Lakes include the well-known historian associated with the concept of the "middle ground," Richard White, and the more locally cherished Benjamin Secunda, who continues to work in behalf of tribes in Michigan through his tribal historic preservation and Native American Graves Protection and Repatriation Act (NAGPRA) efforts.[27] The tapestry of intellectual work also includes that of ethnohistorians of Pokagon political history such as Everett Claspy and Christopher Wetzel, who wrote an ethnography on Potawatomi nationalism.[28] More recent research by Pokagon Potawatomi citizen John N. Low critically investigates how Pokagon Potawatomi identity has been narrated, co-constructed, and reclaimed by Pokagons through urban experience and the reclamation of Neshnabé geographies in Chicago, perhaps most importantly through the perspective of the tribe's own citizens.[29] Cary Miller explores religious political authority in the seventeenth and eighteenth centuries—with many leaders being women from the Midéwiwin Society who have been omitted from official understandings of Neshnabé culture and history by anthropologists.³⁰ Ruth Landes conducted ethnographic research with removed Potawatomi people in Kansas in the mid-1930s, which included rich explanations of where the Prairie Band stood in relation to religious politics from Midéwiwin, to the familial and clan "medicine bundles," drum dances, Christianity, and peyote.³¹ While Landes focused her investigation on the Potawatomi in Kansas, she put their practices and beliefs in relation to the Midéwiwin-practicing communities she researched in Canada previously. Similarly, Thomas Vennum Jr. conducted research on the "Ojibwa Dance Drum," a practice and ceremonial lodge affiliation many Potawatomi peoples have today.³² Both previously cited Potawatomi scholar Whyte and Deborah McGregor, who is Anishinaabé from Whitefish River First Nation in Canada, describe the advocacy work stemming from the Midéwiwin Society as an effective political strategy to address contemporary environmental issues in a larger effort to revitalize social relationships regarding place from which they have been dispossessed.³³ But how might connecting this work with more creative expressions of futurity in Indigenous science fiction and the environmental restoration projects that exist alongside Water Walks advance an understanding of Indigenous futurisms?

Circling back to the discussion of multi-sited analysis, this work departs from traditional ethnographies conducted within what were often assumed to be, but not actual, boundaries of communities (i.e., geographic boundaries, citizenship, etc.). Besides interviews and participant observation, this research employs archival research, ethnohistory, literature, and media studies to understand the unique historical and political contexts that Neshnabé peoples navigate to create their everyday lives in overwhelming climate change while imagining a better future. For the Great Lakes, climate change manifests in the disappearance of traditional food sources, drinking water contamination, and deforestation. Drawing on the anthropology of space and place, the anthropology of knowledge production, and critical Indigenous studies, this research investigates Indigenous political cosmologies and conceptions of the future.

Throughout my research and writing, I recognized that the most fruitful, enticing, and provocative insights came as a result of critically following through on *ideas* and recurring themes that were important to the individuals I interviewed, rather than on tribal affiliation, job title, or participants' geographic location alone. For example, Native science inextricably informed concerns with climate change as understood by Neshnabé peoples (also known as traditional knowledge), prophecies, and by extension conceptions of the future as depicted in Indigenous science fiction film, literature, and art. Instead of restricting interviews to my limited understanding of Indigenous ecological management strategies, traditional knowledge, stories, etc., I privileged the vortices of thought traveled through time and space to be shared in the words of those I met or got to know better, whether this occurred while visiting and helping out at fasting camps, sugar bush, or regalia-making classes. Some social scientists might call this method "snowball sampling." Stated differently, interviews about climate change and political movements easily and appropriately ended as conversations about other-than-human beings who inhabit our world, known as *mnedo* or spirit beings, *their* roles in addressing climate change,[34] and how to understand Neshnabék imaginings of not "the" singular future, but a multiplicity of Indigenous futures. This understanding developed not just through interviews, but through engagement with a diversity of Indigenous-made media recently developed in film, literature, and art such as Cree science fiction filmmaker Danis Goulet's *Wakening* and *Night Raiders* and science fiction literature such as *Daughter of Dawn and Darkness* written by Potawatomi author Carey F. Whitepigeon and *Marrow Thieves* by Métis author Cherie Dimaline.

How, then, to proceed? As a *Neshnabékwé*[35] trained in cultural anthropology and who had set off to understand how ceremony is used in public-facing political dissent, I couldn't unsee or ignore the recent proliferation of Indigenous science fiction media and their propinquity to water protectors and Midéwiwin ceremonial knowledge. While I conducted my research, major science fiction blockbusters came out that echoed the anxieties about climate change that I saw in my fieldwork.[36] These speculative climate fictions and quasi horror stories such as *The Day After Tomorrow* and *Interstellar*, known colloquially as "cli-fi," popularized new framings of the apocalypse—environmental devastation—unlike the genre's earlier villains such as invading aliens or artificial intelligence.[37] If, as some Indigenous scholars have suggested, Native folks relate to ideas of the apocalypse in unique ways because we have already experienced it, were Indigenous science fiction creators simply reproducing these mainstream narratives?[38]

Unbeknownst to me this simple question would serve as a portage for this project that was originally charted for a much different journey. If the answer had been "yes," this book wouldn't exist. But if Indigenous science fiction creators were not simply reproducing mainstream anxieties about climate change, zombie apocalypse, or what have you, and even if they weren't just putting a Native spin on the genre, just what were they up to, then? What were the major differences that characterized their creative work? And what are these media's relationships to lived experience and political action? Because fellow Potawatomi scholar Kyle Powys Whyte chose to put the word "fiction" in parentheses for his article "Indigenous Science (Fiction) for the Anthropocene," I am reminded that without "fiction" we're left with science. Early science fiction from Mary Shelley's *Frankenstein* to H. G. Wells's *War of the Worlds* dealt principally with narratives that speculated on the uncanny futures of Western science in the Industrial Revolution, or at least what concurrent scientific interventions allowed society to imagine was possible—medical science and electricity to perform necromancy in the former and violent alien encounters in the latter. It stood to reason that the most important difference between mainstream or Western science fictions and those dreamt up by Indigenous peoples might lay in cultural frames of reference and ideas about the nature of knowledge. Indigenous science fiction, without the fiction, was simply Indigenous science, also known as traditional knowledge and the myriad of phrases others prefer.[39] Because of these unforeseen epistemological connections between lived experience and political action on the one hand and speculative creative work on the other, in Neshnabé communities the anthropology of knowledge production serves as an important theoretical tradition for understanding the data in this research—the perspectives of participants, the observations of social movements, and the interpretation of creative works. The anthropology of knowledge production frames inquiries regarding Indigenous knowledge about the environment, showing how knowledge is inherently linked to power and subject formation. This body of theory critiques the assumption that scientific inquiry is superior to other knowledge systems, a way of thinking that is ideologically "scientistic" rather than empirically "scientific," by pointing to how knowledge systems are historically situated and politically deployed. Thus it affirms traditional knowledge systems used by Native intellectuals, artists, and activists in my research, highlights the empirical and analytic strengths and achievements of those knowledge systems, and opposes their exploitation.

The anthropology of knowledge production also provides a lens with which to understand natural resource management (NRM) consultation processes that have emerged as arenas of conflict at my research site. In fact, Indigenous environmental activists often begrudged systems and protocols that were ironically designed to help protect the environment because they usually failed to do just that. Section 106 of the National Historic Preservation Act (NHPA) of 1966 and the National Environmental Policy Act (NEPA) of 1969 are policies legislated by the U.S. Federal government and are intended to institute multivocal consultation and outreach requirements for proposed NRM projects. Scholars who work within this tradition, often under the ethics of collaborative anthropologies, such as Ojibwe archaeologist Sonya Atalay, critique these multivocal consultation requirements for their routine inability to address Indigenous concerns.[40] This text builds on the scholarship of knowledge production by investigating how tribes use traditional knowledge systems to reclaim territorial and political space outside inadequate state-mandated consultation requirements. While there is new research about Potawatomi peoples reclaiming traditional knowledge such as the award-winning *Braiding Sweetgrass* by Potawatomi ethnobiologist Robin Wall Kimmerer, my research agenda draws from and expands this body of theory by investigating how Neshnabék communities experience environmental inequality and utilize traditional knowledge systems in both creative and political ways. Traditional knowledge is specifically and strategically deployed by Water Walkers and by tribal natural resource professionals in ecological revitalization projects, and the insistence that Indigenous knowledge be taken seriously is a prerequisite to stopping environmental degradation of their traditional homelands.

Traditional knowledge, or TK for short, is an umbrella term for a system that is unique to each individual community. So, it is necessary to explain just what is meant by "Neshnabé traditional knowledge." Teaching and learning are concepts that are inherently linked to the earth in the Neshnabé worldview and indeed in many Indigenous communities around the world. The Bodwéwadmimwen word for teaching is *keno'magéwen* or "the earth demonstrates."[41] So, it is not enough to theorize knowledge production without understanding the environmental, place-based (not just the social) contexts in which these processes occur. The anthropology of space and place offers a theoretical framework for understanding how Neshnabé Women's Water Walks and tribal ecological restoration projects are used to reclaim political spaces and territorial places. While the anthropology of space and place has often been used to investigate processes of Indigenous identity formations, such as in the highly cited work of Keith Basso, I take an approach similar to those of Cary Miller and Anna Willow, who both effectively use the anthropology of space and place to understand the history of environmental issues in Neshnabé ke—defined previously as Potawatomi homeland.[42] Recent anthropologists' approaches to environmental activism reveals that climate change, deforestation, pollution, and other environmental regime shifts are experienced differently according to race.[43] Anthropologists have also examined how subaltern groups such as Indigenous communities become actors at the forefront of crucial environmental movements around the world.[44] Advancing this academic discussion, this book explores environmental issues in the Great Lakes region framed by the literature of the anthropology of space and place. This orientation leads me to conclude that Women's Water Walks and ecological revitalization projects on tribal lands are important forms of activism that help Neshnabé tribes reclaim both territorial and political space.

Conversely, this theoretical paradigm is critiqued for reinforcing the "spatial incarceration" of the communities anthropologists study in and not taking a broad enough approach.[45] Drawing from ideas about behavior and the built environment, anthropologies of space and place can be overdeterministic and envelop concepts like disciplined places and structures of sociality.[46] For example, Setha Low argues that space encapsulates class struggle and other forms of protest in the urban plaza.[47] Yet, by only viewing valid political activity as those actions that are organized solely in urban public spaces, this case study dismisses an array of other important political processes, desires, and activities that happen in peripheral spaces.[48] Intervening in this body of theory, my findings as a result of participating in Water Walks demonstrate that political action is not only coordinated in singular public places but also in spatially discontinuous phenomenological contexts and rural ceremonial spaces for Neshnabék. For the communities included in my research, for example, political actions happen simultaneously in the Midéwiwin Lodge, on Water Walks, and at ecological revitalization sites on tribal lands, countering the idea that political actors are relegated to particular territories and social, economic, and political spaces—only made legible or effective by picket lines. Taken even further, some have argued that simply being born Anishinaabé is a political act.[49]

While Water Walkers work to increase the visibility of Indigenous issues, critical Indigenous studies is credited with offering an academic space for Indigenous theorists to understand settler colonialism and the multiplicity of ways in which it erases Native presence. The discipline best contextualizes how and why Indigeneity is made irrelevant to dominant settler colonial politics. From the moment an Indigenous colleague of mine in my early graduate career unapologetically exclaimed, "Indians are treated as completely fucking irrelevant," I've been increasingly aware of how right she was. She meant that even when well-intentioned individuals who believe in their politics and values ally with underrepresented groups—ethnic minorities, differently abled individuals, women, minority religious groups, and others—Indigeneity remains wholly oppositional to progressive politics of settler nation states. This is because, while contemporary liberalism usually seeks to represent the interests and hopefully serves the needs of the aforementioned groups, liberal multiculturalism shares a common ancestor with settler colonialism. No matter the angle, it is inextricably tied to the survival of the invading nation that usurped Native lands and lives. The most far-left politics cannot exist outside the settler colonial project. This prevents a meaningful understanding, let alone the development, of politics that are beneficial to Indigenous peoples who are working toward fully actualized sovereignty and land back.[50] Instead, liberal multiculturalism subsumes Indigenous sovereignty within a celebrated veneer of ethnic diversity and the dubious promise of equality . . . one day, and on the settler nation's terms.

Liberal multiculturalism is inadequate for understanding the desires of Indigenous liberation. For this reason, I used critical Indigenous anthropological research in my fieldwork and analytical processes. The scholarship more accurately frames how Indigenous representational authority is integral to sovereignty or the rights of Indigenous communities to represent their own images, histories, lived experiences, and traditional knowledge systems. And it demonstrates how these articulations of sovereignty are directly related to Indigenous peoples' power to make decisions about their communities' futures and the well-being of the environment as tribal nations. These forms of "visual sovereignty," "knowledge sovereignty," and "temporal sovereignty" inform this work, illustrating the specific violences experienced by Indigenous peoples through structures of settler colonialism in the Great Lakes region.[51] This research also details how the exclusion of Indigenous communities is operationalized in Michigan through settler colonial regimes of environmental inequality and constructs a distinctive experience for Indigenous peoples. To these ends, I use a critical Indigenous studies approach defined by scholars such as Patrick Wolfe, Audra Simpson, and Elizabeth A. Povinelli to establish an anthropological framework for analyzing how the processes of reclaiming Indigenous geographies may be accomplished through Water Walks, ecological revitalization projects, and hopes for the future.[52]

What is a Neshnabé community? In a context where tribal citizens might change membership in their lives (because many have ancestors on multiple tribes' rolls), and where social, ceremonial, and political lives of the four Bands of Potawatomi people in Michigan, as well as other Potawatomi communities in Canada, Wisconsin, Kansas, and Oklahoma (not to mention additional Ojibwe and Odawa communities) are intimately bound up in one another, where do "inclusion" and "exclusion" criteria exist?

For this research, I define Neshnabé communities as citizens of Potawatomi nations in the U.S. and Canada, and one in Mexico, as well as some descendant community members who, because of restrictive enrollment criteria or being adopted out, are biologically Potawatomi but not formally enrolled. However, I focused my research activities with primarily Pokagon citizens and Anishinaabé peoples associated with the Midéwiwin Lodge. A demonstration of how this complexity has endured throughout history is articulated in an ethnographic text on the Prairie Potawatomi people written by Ruth Landes in 1970 from research she conducted in Kansas during the early 1930s. While I have previously explained the vast diaspora of Potawatomi peoples throughout the Great Lakes (traditional homelands), into Kansas and Oklahoma (reservations established because of removal), and even up into northeastern Canada, her provocative text further complicated my understanding of our social ties within the larger Potawatomi nation. My third great-grandfather, Tom Topash, was her main informant. Tom and his wife, Mary, were born and raised their family in Dowagiac, Michigan—where the tribe's current government headquarters is now. But after Mary died, Tom went to live with the Prairie Potawatomi people in Kansas, likely because of strong familial ties extant as there were certainly no draws for employment opportunities; even farming would have been more difficult in Kansas than in southwestern Michigan.[53]

Besides the strong kinship ties between Potawatomi Bands, the ethnography disrupts both the larger narrative of Potawatomi conversion to Christianity and the familial one I grew up with—that our families were all Catholic at that point, which is simply not correct. Landes details several informants' attitudes and behaviors toward traditional ceremonial practices including Big Drum and Midéwiwin. As will be explained, beyond ethnographic data gleaned from her scholarship, anthropologists should recognize and respond to the standard framework of inclusion and exclusion criteria based on tribal enrollment alone, at least for Anishinaabé communities.

Similar to the complexities of tribal affiliation, undisputed lines defining what is and what is not Potawatomi culture are lacking, at least in terms of material culture, designs, motifs, ceremonial practices, and more. Of course, Potawatomi peoples have a distinct language and history, and they also maintain traditional stories; they have an uninterrupted political identity despite U.S. and Canadian assimilation policies, and they pass down familiar and clan-specific artistic designs. A passage from Thomas Vennum Jr.'s ethnography about the Ojibwa Dance Drum expresses this complexity well. When making a drum,

> there is scarcely an article incorporated in the instrument or a tool used by him that does not originate from the dominant society: cloth from the fabric store; ribbon, needle, and thread from the five-and-dime; paint, nails, hammer, saw, penknife—all from the local hardware store [...] But regardless of their origin, it is what an Indian *does* with such items and how he combines them that makes the final product so distinctively his own. (Emphasis added by me.)[54]

Whether anthropologists attempt to define (essentialize) or expand ideas about the whole of a community's identity through observation and theorization, they are engaging in what James Elkins calls "mending the zeitgeist."⁵⁵ Georg Hegel (and those who follow the current of this theoretical tradition) is responsible for contemporary understandings of culture or zeitgeist, which can be defined as the sum of the shared norms, beliefs, and worldviews and the expressions of those components through art, language, etc. of a community.⁵⁶ But as Maureen Matthews eloquently explains, drawing from Comaroff and Comaroff in her scholarly work with another Neshnabé community in Canada: "a more useful cultural metaphor might be that of an Ojibwe archipelago, islands of Ojibwe experience amidst a sea of what most native people think of as 'dominant culture' . . . Waves of European understanding and practice . . . wash the beach of each unique Ojibwe reality."⁵⁷

While tribal affiliation and other "research subject" protocols are important for identifying the appropriate participants to answer research questions, as an ethnographer, I travel back and forth between Neshnabé communities identified as Potawatomi, Ojibwe, and Odawa in my interviews and observations. My ancestors formed and strengthened their connections to one another and had complex political organizations based upon their ability to travel the waterways of the Great Lakes region. As a recent article on Great Lakes Indigenous ecology explains:

> The distinct freshwater ecosystem of the Great Lakes . . . [as a] multispecies web of relationships—an ecology crafted by Native Americans in the precontact era—allowed for an impressive system of human movement when coupled with the numerous waterways of the Laurentian watershed.⁵⁸

Therefore, I use the theoretical waterways where the relational threads—whether they be familial, religious, or otherwise—are intimate and appropriate to guide my research travels, experiences, and interviews. The way I have come to understand my research methodology is through "washing upon the shores" of Potawatomi experiences defined by social relationships to place. In George E. Marcus's founding article on multi-sited ethnography, he contextualizes this (then) emerging methodological trend as the outcrop of world systems theory. He explains that multi-sited ethnography is not an attempt to expand the limits of the field site or even attempt to represent a larger holistic whole, but rather multi-sited analysis takes as a point of departure that any society or social context is "in/of the world." As a result, ethnography offers a unique opportunity to see how specific social processes are realized in different spatial contexts through a common structural thread of experience.[59] As Mark-Anthony Falzon succinctly puts it, "The essence of multi-sited research is to follow people, connections, associations, and relationships across space (because they are substantially continuous but spatially non-contiguous)."[60]

How Neshnabé people relate to each other, however, does not completely disregard traditional anthropological constructs, i.e., clan, biological kinship, or in what tribe one is enrolled, either. For example, when meeting for the first time someone in the Pokagon Band or someone from a nearby community, one will often ask "What's your last name? Who's your family?" But the Neshnabé social worlds of relationality, as will be explored throughout this work, are much more complicated and exquisite. This is not to mention the blood politics of ancestry. For example, my enrollment is with the Pokagon Band of Potawatomi Indians. I identify as Neshnabékwé (an Indian woman, Potawatomi spelling).[61] Yet, I know that my very recent ancestors also identified as having Potawatomi, Miami, and Grand River Band Odawa ancestry.[62] I also acknowledge that I am predominantly of settler Scots-Irish ancestry, born with the last name Caldwell (Morseau is my spouse's family name).[63] As a result, my original inclusion criteria that formed the version of this book that started as my doctoral dissertation did not draw artificial distinctions among research participants according to enrollment alone.[64]

As expressed in the preface, this is not a study about religion. In my research I aim to protect Indigenous sacred knowledge within the Midéwiwin Lodge and outside it. As a result, I do not write *everything*. Effectively explained by scholars Eve Tuck (Unangax̂) and K Wayne Yang, as well as Audra Simpson, refusal in the research process is to intentionally decline to record *everything*.[65] Significantly departing from public domain ideologies of knowledge production that assert that information should be as widely accessible as possible, refusal is attentive to the histories of extractive knowledge production, especially research conducted in Indigenous communities. As Tuck and Yang state:

> Settler colonial knowledge is premised on frontiers; conquest, then, is an exercise of the felt entitlement to transgress these limits. Refusal, and stances of refusal in research, are attempts to place limits on conquest and

the colonization of knowledge by marking what is off limits, what is not up for grabs or discussion, what is sacred, and what can't be known.[66]

Opaskwayak Cree scholar Shawn Wilson encourages us to see that research is ceremony and any ceremony is a transformative practice: "if research hasn't changed you as a person, then you haven't done it right."[67] Because I grew not just as a scholar during this research process but also spiritually as a Potawatomi woman who received her Neshnabé name and fasted for the first time, the research and the experiences ensconced here are deeply personal, intimate, and special to me. We receive gifts of insights from multiple sources beyond what is obtained in interviews, observations, or texts. Insights obtained through dreams or serendipity are important to take into account, because doing so honors Potawatomi modes of learning or Indigenous ways of knowing—what is more commonly referred to as traditional knowledge—the focus of chapter 2.

Accountability

Being an Indigenous anthropologist is a peculiar thing. I once heard a colleague in my department at the University of Massachusetts Boston tell the story of how he met his wife. She'd been invited through the grapevine of colleagues they shared to be a part of a panel he'd organized at the American Anthropological Association annual meeting composed entirely of BIPOC anthropologists who did *not* do research in their own communities . . . contrasting the expectation that non-white-identifying anthropologists study social phenomena relevant to their own subjectivities. While I fall under this normative category of intellectual (for now), I do not identify as a "Native anthropologist." Such a term is riddled with problematic power imbalances that stem from Native "consultants" who were employed by white male anthropologists as interlocutors and translators to carry out salvage ethnographic projects. However, as someone who is a part of the community my research focuses on, I am still accountable and have responsibilities to my community that an outsider simply doesn't have—at least not in the same ways.

In the most basic sense, anthropologists investigate the meanings of relationships whether they are political, social, ecological, etc. Entangled in what Clifford Geertz famously termed "webs of significance," anthropologists are an influential part of the relationships they study.[68] I mentioned just how deeply personal this research has been for me. That is not to say that other anthropological works are not as transformative for the researchers. Yet, I know that, as a Pokagon woman with a Pokagon life partner and son, I am necessarily accountable to my community after the conclusion of this scholarship. The relationships that began because of this research and those I built upon in the process inform my everyday practices of being a Neshnabékwé. Being a tribal citizen afforded me some ease of access in the research process, but because of the permanence of my relationships in my "field site," I was often cautious about my reputation and the responsibility afforded me in taking good care of the gifts shared with me by trusting participants. Increased levels of trust means that individuals share more than they may share with non-Native researchers. Elders, friends, and family members may be sharing stories *with me*, not with the readers of my publications. For this reason, as a matter of course I had research participants review their transcripts and offered them the opportunity to redact things they may have changed their minds about sharing and correct any mistakes or things that were misspoken. Finally, I asked participants to review how I contextualized their words in my writing. Consent is an iterative process and ought to be revisited after the ink is dry on the forms.

As an Indigenous scholar working closely with her home communities, I must speak to the idea of belonging—not because I am special or interesting or even all that interested in reflexive ethnography (I am not), but because it has been all too easy for some scholars to grandstand and claim expertise simply because of their identities. While I am an enrolled citizen of the Pokagon Band of Potawatomi Indians, am an active participant in ceremonial and cultural doings in the larger Neshnabé community, and have strong familial bonds with other Indigenous communities in the Great Lakes, I am not unproblematically a "Native anthropologist." I did not grow up on my tribe's reservation;[69] I grew up in New Jersey, but often made trips to my mother's and extended family members' homes in Michigan and Indiana for various tribal and family events. As a result, I am not as "in and of" the Pokagon community as some of the tribal citizens are whom I interviewed and learned from in this research. Therefore, it would be inaccurate to position myself as a

Native anthropologist. I am seen as a member of the community, and my extended family is well known. However, because I did not grow up in the community, I am somewhat of a newcomer. Belonging but not being intimately familiar with one's community since birth is a complexity that I don't think will be fully understood even at the conclusion of this work. (This text, after all, is not about me or even identity per se.) But this place—Michigan—is my home now. My son's umbilical cord is buried here—a traditional Potawatomi practice meant to literally "ground" individuals in their homeland. Indeed, I plan to be buried here as well. There is no "leaving the research site." My life is the site. Furthermore, I also participated in two rites of passage during my research time: my first fast, and receiving my Neshnabé *noswen*, my Indian name. Therefore, I would be remiss to not reflect on the magnitude of Native anthropology, what it means, and how the theoretical tradition has informed my work. I should be clear, however, that while I participated in ceremonies including Midéwiwin, this was not a focus of my research, nor should this be considered "participant observation." I would have done these things regardless of my research focus. But, again, they are spectral insights I acknowledge as part of the process of Potawatomi traditional knowledge acquisition.

The term Native anthropology is a convoluted idea, but Takami Kuwayama provides a basic definition from which to start: an undertaking by an individual to represent their community from a point of view stemming from that community, and usually in the community's language.[70] Regarding language, I am reminded of the polarizing debates within the field of English literature in which Native North American authors play an important role by sharing their stories. Yet are these works that are predominantly or exclusively written in the English language Native American literature, or are they English literature written by Native peoples? In this work I modulate Neshnabé concepts and Bodwéwadmimwen phrases to fit a Western and, more specifically, an English-language framework. I look forward to the day when critical modes of inquiry by Indigenous intellectuals being shared with a wider audience in the language and methods traditional to their communities is not absurdly idealistic, unattainable, or fantastical.

Despite operating within fields of Western academia that were not designed for Indigenous researchers, according to Kuwayama's definition

Native anthropology still effectually challenges traditional anthropological power dynamics and contexts of research.[71] This is because Native anthropologists assume the role of researcher, and not just the researched. The knowledge gained from Native anthropological research also affords the conceptual and political space for confronting long legacies of Eurocentrism and damaging hegemonic discourse about Indigenous peoples. Taken together, the two exigent Indigenous interventions, reclaiming Indigenous representational authority and speaking against settler colonial nationalisms produce a new Native anthropology centered on traditional knowledge systems, refined critiques of settler colonialism, and a view toward social justice.

Beginning in the early 2000s there was an explosion of innovative research published by Indigenous academics. This influx of quality analyses by a new generation of Native intellectuals was and still is an important social movement with profound consequences within and outside the academy. These fresh perspectives and emergent frameworks culminated in a theoretical trend, now a well-established field of interdisciplinary research, critical Indigenous studies. While it would not have been possible without the work of numerous Indigenous researchers over the course of many years (not to mention the establishment of Native studies programs in many universities), the most recent emergence of a critical Indigenous research methodologies movement was largely influenced by Māori scholar Linda Tuhiwai Smith in her seminal text, *Decolonizing Methodologies: Research and Indigenous Peoples*. Her book established a theoretical foundation and served as an essential reference for much of the critical Indigenous research published in the last decade and continues to be a principal text, as reflected in its more recent edition in 2021. Tuhiwai Smith's book is essentially a comprehensive critique of the legacies of Western knowledge production that exploited Indigenous peoples and the structures of domination that we—Indigenous and non-Indigenous—have all inherited. Although anthropological research of at least the past several decades became more reflexive and cognizant of larger relationships of power within research contexts, Tuhiwai Smith's interventions are unique because she addresses Indigenous peoples as researchers specifically instead of mere objects of research. Tuhiwai Smith, unlike many non-Indigenous researchers of the past, was not concerned with simply mitigating the damage of research, but with provoking a systemic change to make research relevant to and useful for Indigenous peoples. Therefore, *Decolonizing Methodologies* is ostensibly a call to reclaim Indigenous representational authority in research in ways that benefit our communities. Tuhiwai Smith explains that research has always been a constituent of European imperialism and the colonization of Indigenous peoples across the globe. Besides giving credence to already racist assumptions about the biological mental faculties and cultural fitness of Indigenous peoples, research, especially anthropological research, later lent to the construction of larger Western institutions that validated certain "ways of knowing" about non-Western societies. This resulted in the unfettered accumulation of qualitative and quantitative data by researchers from Indigenous communities, which were then deployed in ways that were not at all relevant or helpful to the Indigenous peoples who provided them.

What is more, Tuhiwai Smith explains that more and more "experts" used their findings to pathologize and shame Indigenous peoples. This, in turn, led to increases in punitive administrative practices in schools (such as zero-tolerance policies) and inadequate welfare systems. Bad data based on patronizing methods designed to reinforce stereotypes under the guise of "objectivity" ultimately created more points of entry for researchers to study non-white communities in a self-reinforcing loop. "Essentially," Tuhiwai Smith explains, "this has become crisis research, directed at explaining the causes of Māori failure and supposedly solving Māori problems."[72] Therefore, academic research is not an innocent endeavor, but one that is bound up and buttressed by political interests and unequal relationships of power, neither of which has been beneficial to Indigenous peoples. On principle, Native anthropology opposes this exploitative legacy by privileging "indigenous concerns, indigenous practices and indigenous participation as researchers and researched."[73]

Tuhiwai Smith's *Decolonizing Methodologies* inspired an Indigenous methodologies movement as a new generation of Native researchers drew from her interventions and productively responded to her "Indigenist" research agenda. Quoting her directly, Mihesuah and Wilson evoke Tuhiwai Smith's call to create an Indigenous space at the university level, to "Indigenize the academy," to carry out research relevant and useful to Indigenous communities.[74] This is a particularly salient issue since academic gate-keeping such as cronyism is a pervasive way in which research continues to privilege certain assumptions about the world while dismissing or ignoring others. Drawing from investigations on "adverse racism," Keith James explains that even individuals in academia who consider themselves to be very accepting of other groups and negate any discriminatory behavior on their part have been shown in many cases to contribute to informal gate-keeping practices. This is because structured forms of favoritism that serve to maintain particular bureaucratic cultures and practices actually serve to keep minority views and minority peoples out of positions of power.[75] Mihesuah and Wilson make a parallel argument, stating that "[w]hile some herald the need and appreciation for diversity in color and gender, they want conformity in thought and action. They are surprised when we arrive and bring with us diversity of thought, worldview, and values and then horrified when it affects our speech and action."[76]

While anthropological scholarship has productively led to new insights about the political nature of research, influences from disciplines other than anthropology have also helped shape new perspectives and models of ethnographic inquiry. The interdisciplinary field of critical Indigenous studies has influenced anthropology in many respects—from faculty members serving as outside committee members for anthropology doctoral students to ethnographic texts citing deft Indigenous scholars. These examples are the nature of research, so it is no surprise that critical Indigenous frameworks are being productively used in anthropology to produce more nuanced ethnographies. Indeed, Lea et al. propose that critical Indigenous studies can and should "move" anthropology. They call for anthropologists to pivot their ethnographic perspective to one that privileges relationality of Indigenous peoples and colonialism.[77] In *Research Is Ceremony*, Wilson calls for the same thing in what he refers to as "relational accountability."[78] He describes this as an ethical approach—one that takes responsibility for the relationships that are formed within research in ways that are relevant to the community where research is being conducted.[79] One way to accomplish this is to center anthropological analysis away from binarism such as traditional and modern—binaries that have obscured the complex political entanglements between these two groups or forced and erased broader historical perspectives of Indigenous communities and settler nation states.[80] This is part of what I hope readers will take away from the concept of

Neshnabé futurity proposed here—that modernity invents primitiveness of non-European cultures as a temporal self-aggrandizing apparatus. I don't seek to complicate binaries—whether cultural or conceptual—for self-indulgent frivolity, but because these binaries are often inaccurate in representing Indigenous realities and ideas of liberation. Because they are meant to naturalize various modes of oppression, we need a structure outside settler colonialism, and this includes inaccurate anthropological framings of Indigeneity. Indigenous futurisms as an umbrella term and Neshnabé futurity as a specific cultural framework illuminate paths forward.

At the center of critical Indigenous frameworks is a crucial insight about the structure of settler colonialism and how it affects Indigenous peoples in every aspect of our lives. Any analysis within a critical Indigenous framework departs from an understanding that settler colonialism is a structure of domination, not an event.[81] Indigeneity occupies a subject position within a settler colonial society. So, any adequate discussion about Native peoples is invariably a consideration of settler colonialism, or at least it ought to be. Despite similarities in utterance, colonialism and settler colonialism are structurally different. Both are oppressive regimes dovetailing with Western imperial expansion; however, as Patrick Wolfe and Lorenzo Veracini explain, they have disentangled goals: colonialism is inherently exploitative, while settler colonialism is inherently eliminatory.[82] A colonial relationship entails the exploitation of labor from subjects by way of slavery, indentured servitude, or other circumstances that reinforce the unequal position of power between the colonizers and the colonized. Settler colonialism, by contrast, seeks to eliminate Indigenous presence through genocide, assimilation, and overall apathetic attitudes and policies toward Indigenous claims to land and resources in what Wolfe calls "the logic of elimination."[83]

The operative fixture of settler colonialism is its structural nature. For instance, a lay perspective of settler colonialism is understood in terms of its event-ness, as in the colonial period, a genocidal incident, or even the colonial vernacular of architecture. However, as Wolfe explains, settler colonialism is "an inclusive, land-centered project that coordinates a comprehensive range of agencies, from the metropolitan centre to the frontier encampment, with a view to eliminating Indigenous societies."[84] What this means is that there is no end point. Settler colonialism did not happen, it is the criterion on which contemporary Indian policy is constructed, besides the overwhelmingly problematic representations of Indigenous lives, our bodies, politics, and perspectives. Elimination occurs through land theft, genocide (which includes forced removals and assimilation policies), and blood quantum, as well as through environmental degradation, separation of families, and finally, as much of chapter 1 explains, through discursive actions that erase Indigenous connections to place. These machinations of erasure foreclose not only Indigenous presence but claims to land and life. Therefore, any Indigenous "futurisms" are foreclosed.

Futurity

If scholars within the humanities agree on one thing, it is that words matter. They matter so much that they have genealogies and enigmatic meanings within communities we may never be familiar with. For this reason, I want to explain my use of the terms futurism (both singular and plural futurisms), futurity/ies, and futures. I use the terminologies futurity/futurities and futurism(s) interchangeably. I have a personal aversion to the term "futures," not because it is inaccurate but simply because it tends to suggest stock market futures, which can be confusing if used here. While I have noticed that many researchers, including myself, use the term "futurism" and its plural form "futurisms" interchangeably, it has been argued that in Native contexts futurism needs to be plural to honor the multiplicity of potential futures that are imagined and mobilized by the thousands of Indigenous communities around the world.[85] There is no singular Indigenous future because there is no singular Indigenous culture. To this point, anthropologist William Lempert, who studies Indigenous futurisms in North America and Australia, states that "any attempts to develop indigenous futurisms acknowledge the need for a flexible framework that is amenable to the diversity of Native community priorities, histories, and concerns." Further, he says that they must be "grounded in material, social, and psychological community realities."[86]

While Indigenous futurisms, a term coined by Anishinaabé scholar Grace Dillon, is discussed at length in chapter 4, it is worth noting now that futurism (whether singular or plural) is not a neutral term in all contexts. Italian Futurism or *Futurismo* is a well-known early twentieth-century art movement of creative and intellectual works inspired by industry, transportation, and technological innovation in its subject, techniques, aesthetics, and motifs. Despite its rise to prominence around the world and its association with famous artists—their works held in museum collections around the world and sold in prestigious art markets—Futurism's association with fascism is still problematic today.[87] Of the word choices just discussed, I prefer "futurity" and "futurities." Drawing from David Grossman's 2007 lecture, Amir Eshel defines futurity as "contemporary literature [that] creates the 'open, future, possible' by expanding our vocabularies, by probing the human ability to act, and by prompting reflection and debate."[88] Eshel is describing primarily literature here, but the creative, intellectual, and political work I observed in my research are also adequately defined by this quotation. When discussing one community or related body of cultural frameworks such as Potawatomi, Navajo, or others, it makes sense to use the singular. And similar to Indigenous futurisms, when referring to a multiplicity of communities, it stands to reason that "futurities" in its plural form is used.

But why place such an emphasis on temporal vocabulary in the first place? Jonas Fabian wrote a classic text that changed the field of anthropology by challenging social theorists to reconsider their assumptions about the relationship between themselves and the "other," or the people and communities who were the subjects of their research.[89] Ethnographers have always thought about Indigenous peoples in temporalizing ways. Lewis Henry Morgan's *Ancient Society* posited three stages of cultural evolution from savagery to barbarism to civilization, with the last stage conveniently resembling societies of European likeness. The placement of human societies on a linear scale positioned Native peoples in North America as relics of the past—contemporary groups of peoples living as one might expect Western peoples to have lived centuries earlier. Of course, this was an inaccurate and racist hierarchy of organizing humanity that anthropology has long since rejected. As the field of cultural anthropology developed in the U.S., however, salvage ethnographic projects increased. These scholarly and political projects aimed to collect and preserve linguistic evidence and material culture from Indigenous communities with the pervasive assumption that they would not exist in the future. Removing sacred items and family heirlooms, obtaining artwork sold for pittances, and grave robbing fueled the field of anthropology while museums were erected to house and display what they saw as exotic cultural anachronisms to white society. Despite decades of rigorous scholarship and an institutional rebuff of schematizing human diversity in terms of biological evolutionary principles, Indigenous peoples are still affected by these problematic temporalizing theories.

Insolent ideas of "primitive" versus "modern" cultures have permeated peoples' understanding of humanity for decades. These dubious understandings of cultural difference have legitimized policies aimed at "civilizing" Native American peoples, forcing them to resemble white Americans. The calamitous effects of policies of cultural genocide such as Native American boarding schools and land theft because of policies like the Homestead Act of 1862 or the Dawes Act of 1887 on Native Americans cannot be overstated. Starvation and disease in decades of iterative and relentless land theft paralleled many of the years early anthropologists went on their excursions, first facilitated by "explorers" and "pioneers," and federally funded frontier violence. Because much has been published on this topic, the project of this text is not to add to this important discussion. Rather, from the perspective of an Indigenous anthropologist, I am interested in how the concept of Indigenous futurisms has departed from projects typically framed by ideas about cultural revitalization that are bound up with salvage anthropology. I am also attentive to how Indigenous futurisms have made new spaces for Indigenous peoples in the future as a particular form of survivance or what Anishinaabé intellectual Gerald Vizenor famously defined as "an active sense of presence, the continuance of native stories, not a mere reaction, or a survivable name."[90]

Despite the prevalence of more ethical practices in the field today, I agree with Lempert's assertion that "[i]t is not enough that anthropologists have shifted from viewing indigenous peoples as anachronistic relics to engaging the present concerns of contemporary communities. Indigenous futurism is about expanding ethnographic theories and methods to address futures as significant copresent realms of study."[91] Indigenous futurisms is a conceptual rejection of theoretical, institutional, and political projects that placed Indigenous peoples in the past or framed Indigenous peoples as trying to rectify their place in the modern present.

These insights caused me to see not only the value—necessity—of putting Indigenous creative work of futurity, science fiction media, art, and literature in conversation with more overt political advocacy exemplified by Women's Water Walks and environmental interventions such as re-meandering rivers, growing wild rice, and restoring local fauna, but also the need for community-specific theorizations of futurity beyond problematic terminology like revitalization. Remarking on the abundance of new anthropological research on religious movements with Native American communities and some in Africa and Asia in the 1940s and 1950s, Anthony F. C. Wallace defined cultural revitalization as "a deliberate, organized, conscious effort by members of a society to construct a more satisfying culture."[92] Ethnographies centered on refining an understanding of revitalization in language, religion, and even ecology added to the conceptual repertoire of contemporary anthropology in its arguably most formative years in the U.S.—post World War II.[93] As a result, ethnographic data continue to lend to this broad theoretical tradition in anthropology even today.

By framing the sort of work that Indigenous communities are engaged in as "revitalization" that is tied up with salvage anthropology implies a sort of cultural necromancy that continues to foreclose Indigenous existence and agency in the future. It dams the natural meanderings and evolutionary currents of our cultures to one that fits a colonizing gaze. While many Native communities are indeed engaged in deliberate language shift and purposeful proliferation of cultural activities associated with their ancestors (and may even themselves call what they are doing language and cultural revitalization), we need better language to describe these nation-building projects. As Pokagon Potawatomi scholar John Low contends in relation to canoe-building in Neshnabék communities, these practices are not just revitalization or cosplaying tradition; rather, they are material *re-collections*, community-building projects, and ways of strengthening tribal sovereignty.[94] Indigenous futurisms are developed in concert with Indigenous histories, in particular places and politics of refusal of harmful natural resource extraction projects such as pipelines and hydrofracking. In her analysis of the resistance movements by tribes and allies to stop the construction of the Dakota Access Pipeline (DAPL) at Standing Rock and beyond, Shelley Streeby describes the water protectors' various projects as "efforts [to] collectively imagine a different future."⁹⁵ Indigenous futurisms imagine and mobilize projects to actualize alternative futures from those of global warming, rising sea levels, and polluted water in the lakes, rivers, and aqueducts from oil pipelines and hydrofracking.

But what of imaginations and speculations about the future? Because all speculative fiction already imagines potential futures most commonly through literary and visual works, Indigenous futurisms have also been understood through the multiple lenses of Indigenous art, filmmaking, storytelling, and activism. As previously cited, Kristina Baudemann defines Indigenous futurisms as "Indigenous storying about the future."⁹⁶ So, what stories are Neshnabé peoples telling and why?

Many of the contexts in which Neshnabé desires for future generations are dreamed and actualized occur at gatherings. These could be large powwows and round dances or small feasts and beading classes. As places where kinship ties are strengthened, new relationships are formed, and social spirits are nourished, these gatherings are an important part of futurity work. While most of the media, public-facing ceremonial doings, and reclamation work cited in this text are from the last couple decades, I see the ceaseless advocacy and political mobilization of prior generations as forms of futurity as well. Indeed, without our ancestors' actions, we wouldn't be here. For this reason, I include here a photograph of a tribal council election held in Hartford, Michigan, in 1929 (figure 3). A large group of Pokagon Potawatomi people sit and stand close together for a large group photo, some squinting from the sunlight in their eyes, while some small children look away from the camera, likely distracted by something more interesting than the photographer. Many, though not all, of the individuals in this nearly one-hundred-year-old photograph have been identified as the great-, sometimes, great-great-grandparents of present-day Pokagon citizens. On the cusp of the Great Depression, in a time when the future may have seemed bleak, annuity payments for Potawatomi land usurped by the federal government ran dry and it refused to recognize the Pokagon community as a legitimate tribal nation. Our ancestors still organized; they voted, and they carried on for the sake of future generations. Neshnabék futurities extend in both directions—forward and backward in time. After all, the word for ancestors in our language, *ankobthegen*, means both grandparent and great-grandchild simultaneously.

FIGURE 3 Photograph of a large group of Potawatomi people during the 1929 tribal council election held in Hartford, MI. Pokagon Band Center of History and Culture collections. Courtesy of the Pokagon Band Archives.

Summary of Chapters

Neshnabé futurisms are the multiplicity of potential futures imagined and enacted by Potawatomi traditional knowledge and prophesy as observed in Indigenous-made speculative media, eco-politics leveraged by Neshnabé Women's Water Walks, and finally ecological restoration projects on and near tribal lands. More than just maintaining traditional cultural knowledge, resisting controversial environmental issues, or revitalizing ecologies, these actions when taken together form unique versions of alternative futures that position Indigenous peoples at the center. These imagined landscapes of possibility depart from the versions of the future posited by settler society in which Indigenous communities are vulnerable and helpless or are completely irrelevant.

To center an Indigenized, or more specifically Potawatomi, framework to ethnographic theorization, each chapter uses a Potawatomi word to open the arguments therein. In sequence, Neshnabé ke refers to Potawatomi homelands, keno'magéwen means teaching or more accurately "the earth demonstrates/ shows us in the present,"[97] and *méndokaswen* refers to a ceremonial or spiritual doing. Finally, *bkanathmownen* is a new word, constructed with the help of Advanced Potawatomi Language Specialist for the Pokagon Band Bmejwen Kyle Malott to describe stories that take an alternative perspective on things, in other words, speculative fiction.

In chapter 1, "Neshnabé Ke: Indigenous Landscape, Memory, and Meaning," I discuss how space and place is politicized by differential relationships to power, unequal distribution of resources, and the unequal distribution of environmental risk. I highlight how particular narratives of place by settlers, often bogus frontier romance fantasies, advance politics that erase Native presence.

Chapter 2, "Keno'magéwen: Native Science and Ways of Knowing," examines the difference between science and traditional knowledge. Traditional knowledge is actualized in Neshnabé communities, encompassing various iterations and names, and has been politically suppressed in favor of Western science. Complicating this further, some Indigenous traditional knowledge holders may resist mainstream scientific approaches to environmental projects, which have previously ignored or problematically co-opted Indigenous knowledges. I document how consultation has been a well-intentioned but problematic approach to bridging systems of knowledge and attempting to democratize the decision-making process for environmental undertakings. The Pokagon Band of Potawatomi are mobilizing traditional knowledge for future generations through the use of technology and content management systems compatible with Neshnabé cultural protocols.

Chapter 3, "Méndokaswen: Ecology and Spiritual Doings," explores the changing relationships to place for Indigenous communities in the era of human-caused climate change or "the Anthropocene." Ecological revitalization projects being taken up by tribes, such as re-meandering rivers and transplanting wild rice, highlight the complexities of Neshnabé ecology and relationships to other-than-human species. Potawatomi relationships with other-than-human relatives and practices of place-making in the Great Lakes region inform their ecopolitics. This chapter theorizes how projects typically referred to as revitalization embody forms of Neshnabé futurity.

In chapter 4, "Bkanathmownen: Indigenous Science Fiction and Neshnabé Futurity," I explore the multiplicity of ways in which ideas about the future have been developed and disseminated via "mainstream science fiction" media in the mid-twentieth century. These futurisms, based in colonial fantasies of white modernity, were discriminatory to Indigenous peoples, leaving people of color out of the future altogether. Departing from this history, recent changes in representation in mainstream science fiction and wider considerations of other knowledge systems have provided opportunities for Indigenous peoples to creatively explore Indigenous futurisms. The connection between Indigenous conceptions of time and the ceremonial work informed by prophecy in Women's Water Walks is detailed. Chapter 2's foundational discussion of different ways of knowing shows how traditional knowledge informs Indigenous communities' conceptions of the future. Indigenous prophecy operationalizes Neshnabé ecopolitics and deploys alternative conceptions of the future. Midéwiwin Water Walks are argued to be forms of organic intellectualism that reclaim Neshnabé geographies. Finally, in the conclusion I discuss recent community-based counter-mapping projects that reclaim space in the Great Lakes to show how these counter-mapping and place-based Indigenous narratives both in the sky and on our lands reclaim Indigenous space in the future.

CHAPTER 1

NESHNABÉ KE
Indigenous Landscape, Memory, and Meaning

Ke—earth or dirt

Crickets buzz in the early afternoon sun of an unusually hot spring day in Michigan as my son's footsteps crunch the gravel back road of our village. His steps are strong—he's nearly three—but with a still observable uneven pattern from a residual toddleresque stride. He's also stopping every few seconds to greet a butterfly, point at a bird, or ask if we'll find a lion. We're not putting a whole lot of distance between us and our front door. Holding a small woven basket, he intends on collecting rocks. I tell him that we're looking for *nenwesh* instead, milkweed. We come across a neat miniature stalk with four perfectly sized leaves on top, puckering up toward the sun beaming down on us from high in the sky. After we offer *séma* (tobacco), I instruct Miksani to grab the uppermost leaves where they meet the stem and put it in his basket. He's so proud that he forgets about collecting rocks (if only for a few minutes), because he knows we're making a soup with what we gather. I didn't realize it at the time, but as I reflected on this intimate moment collecting traditional foods on my tribe's lands I saw that these actions are an example of what Mvskoke anthropologist Laura Harjo describes as "este-cate sovereignty," or self-determined practices bound up with a community's traditional knowledge that make space for building or strengthening kin relationships in specific Indigenous geographies.[1] As we walk together, greeting the lands that sustained our ancestors, picking the same leaves, it strikes me as particularly apropos that one of the traditional Potawatomi names for the place where we were—Hartford—is *Byankik* in *Bodwéwadmimwen*, the Potawatomi language, meaning "the place we returned to." As will be discussed in chapter 4, a related phrase, *biskaabiiyang*, one of Grace Dillon's Anishinaabé concepts of Indigenous futurisms, is indeed "returning to ourselves."

The first time I heard about milkweed as a traditional Potawatomi food was from stories told by Andy Jackson, an elder in the Pokagon Band and Tribal Council person when we spoke in 2016. Milkweed is a plant that grows in the Great Lakes region and throughout the Midwest of the United States and is traditionally used in soups. For generations, Neshnabé peoples picked milkweed in the early spring before their purple flowers blossom and well before the late summer pods emerge. It is said that ingesting the plant works to clean out one's digestive system after a less nutritious wintertime diet. I see nenwesh growing in patches along country roads in slivers of refuge, wedged between corn fields, hot metal guardrails, and cars whizzing by—somehow seen just about everywhere yet inconspicuous and often ignored by everyone who isn't Potawatomi. "People kept tellin' me they didn't know," Andy tells me. When she first learned how to identify and process milkweed over a decade ago, she asked around in the Pokagon community for more teachings and recipes. But no one could help her. She explained to me that you have to boil milkweed three times to get rid of the poisons before consuming it. After that the plant is used to "clean out" your digestive system. We joked that this is the original Neshnabé detox diet. "They think they don't have stories, but they really do," Andy continues. After some years of reflection, it's unclear to me now whether she's referring to the milkweed's stories or to the humans who pick it.

After a grueling day of picking what Andy says was "waaaaay too much milkweed," zealously harvested without regard for the work that comes along with processing it, she spent an even longer night preparing it by boiling the leaves several times over. She didn't want to waste the gift she had already committed to harvesting, so she needed to finish the process and was obliged to finish preparing the amount she'd gathered before it spoiled. The next day, Andy shared her soup with some aunties and grannies in the community. "If you do things with elders and you make 'em smell, and see it, and taste it, they remember." Pretty soon after these aunties and grannies began eating Andy's soup, many of them who had previously claimed to have never heard of milkweed began sharing recipes they remembered their mothers preparing with the same plant. Similarly, on another occasion, an elder named Gerlad Wesaw, who had also claimed to have never eaten milkweed, accompanied Andy during her harvesting. He glimpsed her from a distance with her long silver hair and ribbon skirt whipping about in the wind as she collected milkweed into a plastic bag in the middle of a field. This scene emotionally moved him because it reminded him of his mother. In that moment he said he remembered his mother doing just what she was doing then. Memories blew over him as the wind did in that moment—memories of harvesting milkweed as a child, and he began sharing stories with Andy about it. The experiences Andy shared with elders around the harvest and preparation of milkweed exemplify the connection between landscape and practice; the land is an archive of experiences, stories, and knowledge.

Places and situations on the land can recall significant memories and stories for the individuals involved. The lands and waters humans occupy are emotive places in which communities co-create identities and kinships relations. Place-based identities and landscapes as repositories of knowledge are well-established approaches in the anthropology of space and place but were not always. The complex social relationships to land are exemplified in Basso's *Wisdom Sits in Places*, an ethnographic work ensconced in the theoretical tradition of Martin Heidegger and related meditations of space and place. Basso's well-known work with Western Apaches and their ways of dwelling in locales that catalyze the dissemination of moral and social lessons for individuals in their community lent to an emerging space-based methodology in ethnographic scholarship. As will be discussed, however, Basso's work and place-based ethnographies like his left considerable political discussions of land loss and access to natural resources unaddressed. Indeed, as Potawatomi historian John Low retorted in his legal exploration of Potawatomi rights to the land that the city of Chicago now occupies,

> What do Potawatomi peoples—who, according to their oral histories, are descendants of builders of great monuments, the mound builders—do

when the mounds and earthworks have been flattened and planted, when the landscape has been unrecognizably altered in their lifetimes? Where does this "wisdom sit" when the countryside is carved into small agrarian farms, the forest is clear-cut, and the wetlands drained?[2]

As we intellectualize cultural connections to land and at the same time histories and contemporary structures of dispossession, how are places experienced and internalized by Neshnabé peoples, and how are these experiences made meaningful in community? What issues exist in terms of access to traditional cultural properties or sacred landscapes? And what are the competing narratives of place that prohibit Neshnabé peoples from community actualization? The rest of this chapter teases apart the threads that bind ethnographies investigating social meaning with those that exposed unequal relationships of power to posit a more nuanced and critical anthropology of space and place from an Indigenous and, more specifically, Neshnabé perspective.

Spatialized Power

What is meaningful is not the identification or coordinates of space alone, but the experiences of those places. Experiences are then carried by devices we call stories. Narratives of place allow us to think of geography outside the limited notions of maps, plot points, property, and borders. The leading philosopher on space, Henri Lefebvre, asked the question, "Could space be nothing more than the passive locus of social relations, the milieu in which their combination takes on body, or the aggregate of the procedures employed in their removal?"[3] Is space simply a theater upon which history unfolds? If that is the case, is space of no anthropological importance? Lefebvre, of course, gives us a resounding "No," rejecting the Cartesian understanding of space. Used today in many disciplines such as geography and sociology, Cartesian mapping is a spatial logic in which everything is assumed to possess a codifiable, objective location in space. Eric Hirsch describes this Cartesian perspective of space as having the purpose to define an absolute position within physical space, and, therefore, a social space or social system. And that is because, he argues, as many theorists did after him, that space does not have a reality of its own; rather, space becomes place by way of the energy and social activity that constitute it.[4]

It is easy, however, to get lost in poetics of spatial meaning and lose sight of the very real histories of dispossession and violence that were experienced in those places that continue to have material effects on communities today. I return now to Low's provocative question, "Where does this 'wisdom sit'?" In what present-day Potawatomi tribal members colloquially understand as a history of Indian policy meant to "divide and conquer," more than 50 percent of Pokagon citizens live off reservation lands. This, they believe, has a negative effect on language and cultural revitalization, sense of identity, kinship ties, and political power. Space is a social product because it is affected by, as well as affects, the social realities of human beings. For example, policy informs how particular social geographies corporealize, influencing the arrangement of bodies, which is anthropologically important because humans do not arrange themselves randomly. Indeed, the processes by which socio-spatial arrangements are actualized is quite political. One example of this is apartheid. While it is often understood only in terms of its resulting social segregation, in *Seeking Spatial Justice* Edward Soja describes apartheid as "the system of spatial or territorial control . . . a symbolic reference to all forms of cultural domination and oppression arising from spatial strategies of segregation and boundary making."[5] Related to Potawatomi peoples, it is not an accident that, while they are indigenous to Michigan and Indiana (as well as parts of Wisconsin and Illinois), there were originally no Potawatomi lands in Indiana even after federal recognition was reaffirmed in 1994. Even today, there are no federally recognized tribes in Indiana at all.[6] Before European arrival there were hundreds of Indigenous villages in the region currently called Indiana such as the Myaamia, Potawatomi, and Shawnee, just to name a few. Marcus Winchester, director for the Pokagon Band Department of Language and Culture when we last spoke about this, explains that this is because Potawatomis and other tribes were driven out of Indiana early in American settler expansion into the area north. Indiana has many regions that are naturally flat and ideal for farming. Michigan, by contrast, was much more wooded, requiring copious amounts of labor in clear-cutting to make anything larger than modest gardens possible. In fact, while many tribes were being forced west of the Mississippi River during Removal era policies in the 1830s, Leopold Pokagon and his villagers were sent to live up north near present-day Traverse City, which was less desirable land to American settlers. Odawa communities already living in that area could not accommodate Pokagon's villagers, however, having just ceded much of their remaining land base. So, they had to find a place in southern Michigan to live.

When most of what would become the United States was "Unorganized Territory," still belonged to Spain, or was "Unclaimed" (by white American men, that is), Pokagon knew at least one thing was sacred to the young settler government—private property. With annuity payments received from ceded lands in the 1833 Treaty of Chicago, Pokagon returned to southern Michigan and bought private property in the township of Silver Creek, near present-day Dowagiac where the tribe's government center is today. Yes, immediately after being coerced into ceding their lands, the Potawatomis of southwest Michigan and northern Indiana bought it back.

Because of discriminatory removal policies and allocation of desirable land to white settlers, Neshnabék are unlike other tribes and their contemporary reservation-based relationships to place. Instead, some Pokagon lands—that were largely purchased by the tribe in recent years—today are put into "trust" and resemble discontinuous swaths whose borders checkerboard areas of southwest Michigan.[7] One could drive through several inconspicuous Native American jurisdictions throughout Michigan and never realize it. Policy informs how particular social geographies form and can lead to what Soja calls "distribution inequality."[8] This concept refers to the process of uneven diffusion of adverse effects such as pollution and the unequal access to beneficial resources such as hospitals and decent grocery stores. Soja directly identifies distributional inequality as contributing to all other forms of social inequality. Therefore, a critical spatial perspective is immensely important in any ethnography with a lens toward social justice. "Spatialized power" is simply the capacity of any individual to have desires and achieve their goals (agency), enabled or limited by elements in space and place. With this in mind, the next section presents current environmental issues in the Great Lakes region with specific attention to oil pipelines.

Place of Pipelines

A topical example in critical anthropology approaches to space and place, movements identifying and protesting environmental racism began to form in the late 1980s and early 1990s. Communities of color led this wave of environmentalism as they had been expected to deal with a disproportionate amount of pollution and other adverse environmental, health, and economic effects, giving the movement more sagacity than those that took root decades earlier. These earlier movements, emblematized by Rachel Carson's *Silent Spring* and new environmental policies both national and international, failed to identify how BIPOC communities bore the brunt of environmental issues. One of the interventions that emerged from this work is explained by Robert Bullard, who argues that, through processes of environmental racism, people of color are more likely than whites to suffer health risks associated with chemical toxins from a multiplicity of waste disposals released into their communities.[9] Nick Estes provides an operative example of this, showing that the Dakota Access Pipeline (DAPL) was rerouted from Bismarck, North Dakota (a town of over 90 percent white inhabitants), to its current route near the Standing Rock reservation without so much as a dissent letter from Bismarck residents.[10] The pipeline was rerouted from a mostly white residential area to one closer to the reservation before outreach to Bismarck was even conducted. None of this is to argue that rural or poor white families and occasionally entire communities have not been dispossessed of their property or adversely affected by federal policy, but as Bullard further explains it is just that whites of any class are more likely than communities of color to have their politics of dissent paid attention to and their concerns responded to. A critical spatial perspective reveals how adverse environmental and health effects follow these contours of race.

The critical spatial perspective of environmental racism, which unmasks the violent relations of production (resource colonization, pollution, etc.), is a particularly important arena in critical Indigenous studies. As Anishinaabé environmental activist and member of the Three Fires Midéwiwin Lodge Winona LaDuke pointedly explains, "We [Indigenous peoples] are central and essential to the North American industrial development plan—and we are at the end of it. We have the dubious honor of having had over one hundred separate proposals for toxic waste dumps forwarded to our reservations, a result of people in urban working-class communities organizing successfully to keep those dumps out of their communities."[11] LaDuke makes a very important point missed by mainstream environmental activism, even activism by other people of color—that reservations are still the most common U.S. "national sacrifice zones" via environmental inequality, whether it is uranium mining on Navajo lands,[12] clear-cutting and hydrofracking near Neshnabé lands, or pipelines in Sioux territory.

While the Great Lakes region is a landscape that has been subject to reckless "development" since soon after European arrival, only recently have proposals for major pipelines and hydrofracking raised the level of awareness and concern for residents. Pipelines are used to transport crude oil from places of extraction, such as the Alberta tar sands in Canada, to places of distribution for global markets. Controversial proposed projects like Keystone XL and DAPL have made the news headlines because of their large scope, but hundreds of pipelines already exist in the Great Lakes region and Midwest. Complex networks of inter- and intrastate pipelines pump hundreds of thousands of gallons of crude oil every year. They resemble cardiac veins implanted into the earth, supplying the lifeblood of oil for the capitalist accumulation of the rich (figure 4).

For the participants in my research, Line 5 has been the most contentious pipeline in recent years. It is a large oil pipeline that passes under the Straits of Mackinac between Lake Michigan and Lake Huron. In 2019, three Water Walkers, Nancy Gallardo, Sarah Jo Shomin, and Cody Bigjohn Jr., traveled from Mackinaw City to Lansing protesting Line 5, praying for the water along the over three-hundred-mile-long route. Indigenous activists and environmental groups fear that recent approvals of plans to intensify pumping through the nearly seventy-year-old pipeline by fifty thousand gallon a day will result in unprecedented oil spills in the largest freshwater system on Earth. What is more, activists claim that Enbridge, the energy company that owns Line 5, has not complied with consultation requirements outlined by the National Environmental Policy Act (NEPA)—a topic I cover more thoroughly in chapter 2.

But what makes environmental Indigenous political projects such an important topic for discussing space and place is the intertwined history of environmental politics and ethnicity. As Pramod Parajuli explains with

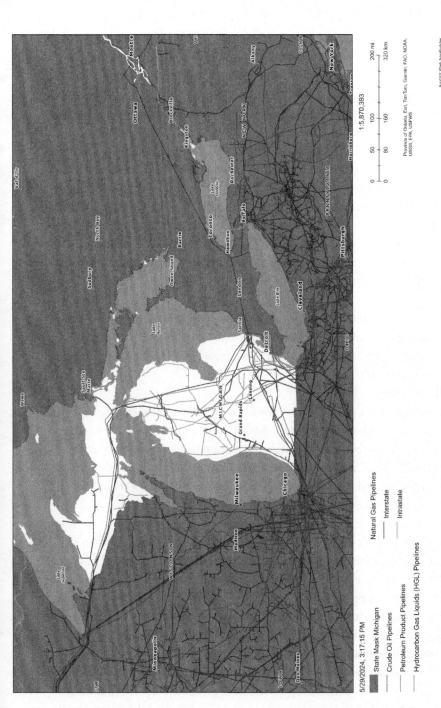

FIGURE 4 Map of crude oil and natural gas pipelines on the U.S. side of the Great Lakes region and in the Midwest and parts of New England. Courtesy of the U.S. Energy Information Administration (October 18, 2020, April 20, 2023), https://atlas.eia.gov/apps/all-energy-infrastructure-and-resources/explore.

his concept of "ecological ethnicity," "both ecology and ethnicity discursively contest the process of national integration by the developmentalist nation-state . . . if ecological subordination is the content, ethnicity is the form in which it is experienced and expressed."[13] Nature and the environment, especially pollution and other adverse factors, are experienced differently across racial lines.

Environmental issues in the Great Lakes region and climate change have made discussions and anxieties around how best to manage the environment more intense than in previous decades. As this exchange shows, Kyle Boone, environmental specialist for the Pokagon Band, struggled with how to generate community buy-in to more aggressively leverage the tribe's political voice against controversial development projects like Enbridge Line 5, and for the public to have less apathy towards global climate change.

> **Kyle**: . . . and I think everybody should know this stuff, but do they care enough to know it? You know what I mean? Like it takes a decent amount of work to understand these topics the way they should be understood.
> **Blaire**: Hmm.
> **Kyle**: And so at a certain point, I don't know if you've ever seen the movie *The Giver*, where like this dude has all the bad memories in his mind. At a certain point, like it's not a perfect analogy, but I think the analogy kind of fits sometimes because you're like, "Nobody knows this, but I know this and I . . . wanna give it out," but they don't care enough for you to give it out.

Kyle's frustrations are indicative of a larger decrease in American scientific literacy over the past several decades, as noted in social science literature.[14] But it is also because of a general apathy of non-Indigenous residents toward projects like Line 5 in Michigan. Neshnabé participants in my research felt this lack of interest was because of non-Indigenous failure to develop a sense of "rootedness" in place or act on provident responsibilities toward taking care of where they live.

Alternatively, the Indigenous participants in my research understand that this cycle of tourist development and pipeline construction on Indigenous sacred sites is part and parcel of U.S. empire building to meet the expansionary needs of capitalism at the expense of Indigenous land, resources, and lives. Resource colonization, pollution, and other adverse environmental effects are particularly pronounced issues for Indigenous communities, because: (1) Indigenous communities have a sense of "rootedness" in particular places, evidenced by our long histories in particular locales and the existence of sacred sites; (2) the political reality of reservation boundaries that are inextricably tied to our rights to sovereignty and territorial jurisdiction; (3) our geographical incarceration by established reservations that limits our abilities to move when something horrible happens to the environment or our resources near us; and (4) the importance of our traditional cultural properties with subsistence and cultural resources we use today, which are located in treaty-ceded areas that have continuous-use clauses.[15]

Anthropologists addressing these processes of resource colonization that affect Indigenous communities meaningfully advance space/place scholarship. This type of research attempts to frame how rights are understood in a particular place. It also traces the place-based histories of conflict regarding those rights. Al Gedicks's ethnographic work with Anishinaabé communities in Wisconsin demonstrates the very typical situation for tribes obligated to constantly fight for the right to access resources in many of their traditional properties even when their right to do so is clearly stipulated in treaties. What is more, even when tribes can afford to fight these legal battles, there is a lot of racist blowback, mostly by rural white communities that border the reservation. Those in Gedicks's research, which took place during the notorious "Walleye Wars" in Wisconsin, often intimidated Native fishermen with guns and held signs that read "Save a fish. Spear an Indian!" This is what Gedicks contextualizes in his research in the aftermath of the famous 1983 Voigt Decision that allowed tribes to fish in their traditional lands. He shows that rural white communities deploying anti-Indian rhetoric in these cases rarely see the situation for what it is, the legal confirmation of inherent rights agreed upon between two governments in treaty negotiations, but instead as minorities receiving "special privileges" at the expense of everyone else.[16]

This study is more than a case study about competing cultural politics or resource competition, however. Capitalism is at the root of these high-profile disputes. Corporate toxic waste disposal in nearby streams and other waterways in the area contaminated many marine resources. Gedicks argues that corporate interests instigated racial tensions and anti-treaty (read anti-Indian) sentiment, because they viewed treaty rights as a direct threat to their future exploitative ambitions. Despite everything, as Gedicks so adequately states, "[o]ne of the great ironies of the Chippewa spearfishing controversy is that the Chippewa and their white neighbors were fighting over the right to harvest contaminated fish."[17]

Contamination in waters of any kind is calamitous. But recent oil spills in the Great Lakes are particularly dangerous and unsettling since they are located in the largest freshwater resource on Earth. The Great Lakes hold 20 percent of the world's fresh water and supply 95 percent of the fresh water in the U.S. In tandem with westward expansion and American development, the Great Lakes became highly polluted with toxic metals and raw sewage, and experienced higher temperatures because of logging that depleted many of the Great Lakes fish and waterfowl species. Since the 1950s, Lake Erie has been so badly contaminated because of oil spills and legal and illegal dumping, resulting in beach closures and fish that are too dangerous to eat, that it is referred to as a "dead" lake. Despite some attempts to mitigate further damage to the Great Lakes via 1970s Environmental Protection Agency policies and international agreements with Canada, such as the Great Lakes Water Quality Agreement, oil spills continue to be an issue in the Great Lakes region. In July 2010, an Enbridge pipeline burst in a tributary near the Kalamazoo River in Michigan. It is known as one of the largest inland oil spills in U.S. history, and a significant portion of the contamination reached within several miles of Pokagon trust lands. The spill of over a million gallons of crude oil contaminated waterways for hundreds of miles and left heavy sediments submerged beneath the soil, resulting in a cleanup operation that took over five years. Despite the multiyear cleanup, even today there are areas that are restricted because of persistent diluted bitumen (dilbit) contamination in the soil. Dilbit is a substance mixed with lighter petroleum so that it is easier to transport, but it makes it extremely difficult to clean up after a major spill.

Neshnabé ke, Potawatomi homelands, have been sacrificed not only in the name of resource colonization and "development," but also to tourism. Madeline Island off the coast of Wisconsin in Lake Superior is a sacred landscape to Anishinaabé peoples and has been described as the mecca for Midéwiwin-practicing Neshnabék.[18] In Anishinaabé oral history, it is said that to find this island groups followed a migis shell—a shell described as the breath of life and used in Midéwiwin ceremonies. For hundreds of years, Anishinaabék gathered from all four directions to hold ceremony on that island. They called on *mnedowêk*[19] with bone whistles, sang ancient songs passed down through inscriptions on birch bark, conducted healing ceremonies, and carried instruments that, when played, echo the original sounds of creation. Today, Madeline Island has been dredged and developed for recreation, and properties have been divided up and sold to wealthy investors. It has sixty campsites, hiking and biking trails, yachts, golf courses, and vacation homes. The spiritual center of the Midéwiwin societies that still exist and practice ceremony in other locations from Canada to Kansas and from Michigan to Wisconsin can no longer access their sites of prayer on Madeline Island because of settler recreation industries.

This dispossession is partly because of the criminalization of Indigenous culture that can still be read on the landscape through place-names. Sheboygan, Wisconsin, is an anglicized corruption of the Potawatomi phrase *Zhabwagnak*, meaning "place of the sound of the drum coming through." It refers to clandestine meetings of Native peoples—not just Potawatomi, but Ojibwe, Odawa, Menominee, Meskwaki, and Ho-Chunk peoples—in the area to practice ceremony in secret. Dispossession is also partly because of extractive industries and development. At the same time that Madeline Island, the sacred place for Midéwiwin-practicing Neshnabék, is inaccessible to Native peoples and wealthy, mostly white tourists flock there in the summer months, artifacts of Neshnabé life and Midéwiwin ceremony are on display at the island's museum, as if the relationships to the land in that place were not inextricably entangled in the "artifacts" gazed upon by tourists. When tribes protest a pipeline or petition for access to sacred sites like Madeline Island, their narratives of place fall on deaf ears. Settler logics of place scream so loud that Indigenous stories cannot be heard.

Settler Futurity

White clouds swim across a watercolor sky of pink, blue, and violet hues. Pausing to consider the place in which we stand, a place somewhere between the southern shores of Lake Michigan and Lake Erie and on the settler borders of what is currently called the states of Indiana and Michigan, we see the sun stop in its tracks. Instead of setting on the western horizon to make room for twinkling stars against an inky sky, the sun returns to its eastern direction. It sets in the east. It emerges again in the west. We see this repeat again and again in the blink of an eye. Time is moving quickly now, in the opposite direction. Between these backward sunrises and sunsets, the night sky cools the warm hues of day, only for day to quickly return again. The days and nights pass in rapid succession to bring us to a time long ago and only experienced now through stories told by our elders. A Potawatomi woman whose name is Mishawaka calls this time and these lands home. As she is the daughter of a notable chief, her Romeo and Juliet love story with a French fur trapper would go down in history, especially after her Potawatomi betrothed retaliates in vicious jealousy against the Frenchman whom she loves.

The only issue with this story is that it is a bogus work of utter fiction. Mishawaka is the name of a suburb of South Bend in northern Indiana that gets its name from a Potawatomi word, *mshiwakwa*, meaning "place of big trees." What is the deal with this goofy story, then?

In July 2018, the city of Mishawaka, Indiana (a city whose seal depicts a Native woman with Caucasian features and nondescript feathers in her hair), sought input from the Pokagon Band on a project to authenticate representations of a fictional character. The city of Mishawaka's slogan is "The Princess City," referencing a myth about a Native woman who fell in love with a white fur trapper in the 1700s. As will be discussed in chapter 4, common myths about Native women falling in love with white men are a type of settler emplacement narrative. If settler colonialism were a genre of literature, Native women who fall in love with white colonizers would be their foundational epic. The story about the spurious Indian princess has been debunked as a fanciful myth made up by F. J. Littlejohn in his 1875 book entitled *Legends of Michigan and the Old North West*.

Despite years of sporadic dialogue with the Pokagon government about this issue and earlier explanations that Mishawaka was never a person who existed, city officials continue their settler romance of the "Princess City" through signs, public artwork, and tourist campaigns. In 2018, a city planner[20] was in communication with the then Director of the Pokagon Band Communications Department Paige Risser. One of those initial exchanges is below, edited for brevity.

As part of a large building project, we reserved a spot for a digital art display at the intersection of two streets. Our intent is to develop an image of Princess Mishawaka and have the graphics change with the weather and the season. The idea is to depict in a digital art form the area as it existed with the Princess before any English or French settlements occurred.

The city planner qualifies their request, stating that "[w]e are sensitive to the misrepresentations and degrading images of Native Americans that have occurred in this country in the past," even while the current misrepresentation of Potawatomi people with the mythical Princess Mishawaka is very much in the present. They see merit in perpetuating the myth, even after recognizing from a discussion with the mayor of Mishawaka that the princess was fictional:

> Chairman Warren identified that Princess Mishawaka never in fact existed. For our part, we are proud of having a strong Native American woman as the symbol for our City and still believe there is value in her image even if her story is only folklore. Real or not, we have also always maintained a respectful adulatory approach for Princess Mishawaka's image and intend nothing less as part of this display. That being said, not being Native American, we recognize what we don't know about the history and culture and do not want to unintentionally offend anyone. We are looking for help to review the conceptual artwork prepared and provide feedback, not in terms of the art or using the image of a Princess, but really to review it on a cultural level.

As the city planner explains, their proposal includes hiring an artist to design an image of an authentic precontact Indigenous woman to lend cultural and political weight to a settler fantasy. Their explicit claim is to acknowledge cultural misappropriation of Native Americans and strive not to unintentionally offend anyone. They also make very clear that they are *not asking for permission* to use Princess Mishawaka as a symbol; they have already decided that they are. Instead, they would like for the Pokagon Band to authenticate their predetermined decision and "review it on a cultural level." They also acknowledge the tribe's prior response—via the then chair—that Princess Mishawaka never existed. As city planner, they are not interested in historical fact or how the deployment of false narratives bastardizes Indigenous history, culture, and rights to place. Instead, what they want is an official Pokagon endorsement of their town's false settler genesis story and contemporary marketing campaign at the expense of Indigenous representational authority.

Paige responds:

> Tribal Council is reluctant to collaborate on this initiative because we have no evidence in Pokagon history of the tale of an Indian woman like the one in *Legends of Michigan and the Old North West* by Flavius J. Littlejohn, from which this myth likely came. Pokagon people have lived and still live in the area that is now Mishawaka. Ancestors called it Mshéwaké, which means land of the dead trees[21] in Potawatomi. Royal titles like princess didn't exist in our past. We would be happy to collaborate with the city of Mishawaka on an art installation that doesn't appropriate Potawatomi culture or history. But we can't support a story that isn't factual.

Settler fictionalizations of Indigenous place-names distort and erase Native presence while building up settler claims to the place they occupy. Settler stories like that of Princess Mishawaka erase Indigenous presence to make space to continue the settler colonial project of invasion while also damaging the self-actualization of Native youth.[22] Tuck and Yang also refer to this ubiquitous phenomenon as "frontier romance narratives" that function to move settlers to a position of innocence while they seek to manifest their own indigenous identity and sense of belonging to the land they occupy.[23] Settler expansion employs various technologies of Indigenous dispossession. The transfer of territory from Indigenous communities to settlers has been popularly understood in terms of plots of land, such as with the General Allotment Act of 1887. However, when settler colonialism is understood as a structure, the concept of territory extends beyond plots of land to access to natural resources, authority over visual representation, and many other arenas. Settler colonialism is a type of logic that seeks to disappear the Indigenous inhabitants, and this is done through many techniques that are structurally hegemonic.

To these ends, Ojibwe ethnohistorian Jean O'Brien surveys the large body of transcribed orations, pamphlets, and other historical material produced in New England from about 1820 to 1880 in *Firsting and Lasting*. Her rich analysis demonstrates how tropes about the vanishing

Indian that were developed in this time period and actualized in these materials were deployed in the rest of American historiography—even those not centered on studies of Native Americans. As a result, O'Brien explains, "[t]hese local stories were leashed to a larger narrative of the 'vanishing Indian' as a generalized trope and disseminated not just as the written word but also in a rich ceremonial cycle of pageants, commemorations, monument building, and lecture hall performance."[24] In what O'Brien calls "firsting" and "lasting" narratives, New Englanders convinced themselves that Indigenous peoples were extinct, even while Indigenous intellectuals and activists such as William Apess continued to fight very publicly for Indigenous rights throughout the rest of the nineteenth century.[25] O'Brien's intervention is that she points to one of the innumerable ways in which settler colonialism disappears Indians.

The dispossession of Indigenous lands combined with the discursive mechanisms of elimination are illuminating sites of analysis. Another ethnographically grounded example of settler colonial spatial techniques of dispossession is in Allaine Cerwonka's ethnography *Native to the Nation*. Through everyday spatial techniques such as gardening, contemporary non-Indigenous Australians use the land to fashion a conceptual break with British colonialism and in doing so "root" themselves in Australian landscapes and nationalist space.[26] As she explains:

> Reshaping the land by renaming places and by physically restructuring it into a picturesque landscape were ways of appropriating the land symbolically while imperial forces took possession of the land on a more literal level through wars, through forced removal of indigenous people, and by wiping out the indigenous population through the spread of diseases.[27]

These "spatial practices" legitimize the contemporary Australian multicultural state and constitute a conceptual rupture from the violent dispossessions of the British who colonized the continent. Yet, despite this conceptual break, settler Australians still benefit from colonization as they can own land and access resources on stolen Indigenous territory.[28]

Despite unfair land cessions under legally dubious circumstances, unacknowledged treaty obligations by the U.S., and legacies of removing Indigenous peoples from their original homelands, Indigenous peoples still maintain relationships with important cultural sites. Some well-known

Indigenous cultural sites that are in danger of or have already been damaged by development are Oak Flat in Arizona, Mauna Kea in Hawaii, and Bears Ears in Utah. These much-publicized controversies bring increased attention to tribes' grievances regarding important sites, many of which are national monuments or national parks. These parks buttress settlers' sense of national pride. Referring to Mount Rushmore, an illegally seized sacred landscape per the agreements in the Fort Laramie Treaty of 1868 between the U.S. federal government and Sioux peoples, Winona LaDuke addresses settler sense of place:

> Naming and claiming with a flag does not mean *relationship*; it means only naming and claiming. Americans have developed a sense of place related to empire, with no understanding that the Holy Land is also here. To name sacred mountain spirits after mortal men who blow through for just a few decades is to denude relationship.[29]

We come to know places by our experiences in them and the stories we hear about them. Indigenous spatial narratives are often purposefully distorted when they are not completely ignored. Despite the high-profile nature of some of these land-based controversies mentioned above, the legal intricacies and cultural understandings of these places remain not so well understood by the general public. However, what constitutes a meaningful place for Indigenous communities has been an increasing point of interest for scholars, for example as embodied social relationships,[30] networks of kin obligations,[31] narratives and stories,[32] and even sites of violence.[33] Settler colonialism is a structure of domination that seeks to continuously dispossess Indigenous subjects of their land and resources through strategies of genocide, assimilation, erasure, misrepresentation, and cultural appropriation.

This scholarship on spatial emplacement by settler colonists implicates nationalism as a form of what Gupta and Ferguson call "spatial commitment."[34] Because settler colonial nationalisms must subsume other competing forms of nationalism, Gupta and Ferguson explain that we must locate the "processes that are involved in the repartitioning and reterritorialization of space."[35] They reveal how the idea of "culture" or a multiplicity of "cultures" came to be spatialized in specific geographies by way of ethnographic writing. "The idea that 'a culture' is naturally the property of a spatially localized people and that the way to study such a culture is to 'go there' (among the so-and-so) has long been part of the unremarked common sense of anthropological practice." This presents a problem as differential identities are becoming less territorialized.[36]

When it comes to ethnographic approaches to embodied cartographies, anthropologists have a long tradition of conceptualizing particular places as repositories of social memory,[37] worldviews,[38] and nodes of social activity,[39] all of which are essentially forms of identity-making processes. Indeed, even early symbolic anthropological approaches drew meaning from local environments to interpret how these "cultural symbols" could help anthropologists better understand larger aspects of that society. More recent influential scholarship builds on this tradition. For instance, Setha M. Low and Denise Lawrence-Zúñiga's formative anthology, *The Anthropology of Space and Place: Locating Culture*, indexes in their title how deeply seated the common-sense anthropological understanding is that ethnographic approaches can identify place-based identities by spending a significant amount of time in particular locales. Similarly, Steven Feld and Keith Basso's influential anthology, *Senses of Place*, showcases the many ways in which place is constitutive of identity and social well-being.

Since anthropology can lend new perspectives in how "spaces"—arenas devoid of social activity—are made into to meaningful social "places," the study of narratives became an important methodological application in this tradition. Within this paradigm, because spaces encode meaning they become places that embody particular identities, and one way that landscapes are linked to and constitutive of identity is through narrative techniques. In this sense, narratives are forms of a spatialized identity-making process. For instance, George E. Bisharat contextualizes Palestinian refugee identity to explain how a phenomenological shift in the West Bank affects their identities and their nationalist position within the political landscape in that space specifically. This shift is informed by generational changes in the spatialized experiences of exile to one of a return.[40] Thus, Bisharat's work shows the relationship between space, place, and identity-making practices realized through everyday discursive practices and how these change over time.

Besides identities attached to place, there are other ways in which places encode meaning, and these more overt examples tie into processes of nationalism. For example, replacement narratives deputized white occupation in settler colonial contexts through various forms of dispossession. Banivanua Mar explains how in Australia the formation of national parks developed particular conceptions of wilderness. In doing so, these "untouched" landscapes established an Australian nationalist project that drew from place-based identities that erased any Indigenous presence in the area. As a result, these wildernesses became the settler colonial project of conservation for future generations to reflect upon their Australian nationalism and identity rooted in particular places and understandings of landscapes—ones that are free of competing Indigenous nationalisms or claims to place.[41]

From my field site, an example of disappearing Indigenous presence through the misappropriation of place-names is with the fictitious character Chief Doe-wah-jack. Named after the town in which the Pokagon Band is centralized, Dowagiac, Michigan, Chief Doe-wah-jack was a character developed in the late 1800s by the Round Oak Stove Company (figure 5). Besides print media and advertisements, Round Oak published children's books and commissioned sculptures of the mythological chief.

FIGURE 5 Round Oak's Chief Doe-wah-jack. Reproduced with permission from the Dowagiac Area History Museum.

The local history museum in Dowagiac has a permanent exhibit dedicated to explaining this history of misappropriation, because Round Oak was such a large company for many decades and was part of the reason Dowagiac used to be such a large town. Yet, local residents, even those who take an interest in local history such as the nearby Edwardsburg Historical Society, still believe that the town of Dowagiac was named after a chief. They are surprised to learn he never existed. Dowagiac comes from the Potawatomi phrase *Ndowathek*, meaning "place of harvesting." Somehow, settler narratives of place that include Indigenous words and imagined characters are more comfortable to them than knowing the real meanings of place, because acknowledging the accurate translation of a place-name such as "place of harvesting" or "place of large stand of trees" might mean acknowledging Indigenous deep-rooted connections to places settlers unethically and often illegally now occupy.

Bogus stories about Princess Mishawaka and Chief Doe-wah-jack not only erase Native articulations and relationships to place but ensure settler futurities. While pipelines dispossess Native peoples from traditional territories physically, stories about made-up Indians dispossess Neshnabé peoples symbolically and guarantee settler claims to place. Chief Doe-wah-jack's symbolic value was the marketing of stoves, while Princess Mishawaka's symbolic value is the marketing of the Indiana city—both result in significant material accumulations of wealth meant to ensure the prosperity of settler capitalist futurities.

CHAPTER 2

KENO'MAGÉWEN

Native Science and Ways of Knowing

Keno'magéwen—teaching, the earth demonstrates/shows us in the present[1]

On a gray September afternoon in 2018, an elder made an unexpected visit to the Department of Language and Culture. The bustling office came to a momentary halt as everyone stopped tapping on their computers and turned their attention to the unexpected visitor. The Department of Language and Culture is known for preserving and promoting Potawatomi heritage, but receiving spontaneous visits from community members is a treat—especially from one who is known for his skill in so many traditional practices. John Pigeon—a traditional teacher in the larger Potawatomi community of Michigan—brought a stalk with lime-shaped pods that looked dry and were slightly cracked open. I would say he instructed me and three of my co-workers to meet him in one of the conference rooms, but it was more like he invited himself down the hall to sit while we followed his gravitational pull. Without looking at any of us as we sat in a circle, he said, "Every breath you take matters. Milkweed is a good teacher that way." He used the stalk of milkweed to guide his instruction about doing work for our community—what he considered important work, though it is often criticized and underappreciated by tribal citizens. John took the stalk and swung it back and forth swiftly over his head, releasing dozens of feathered seed pods that slowly rained down on our heads and laps like snow. It was beautiful. I saw my co-worker, Rhonda, look up and smile while she lifted her palms to gently catch some of the descending puffs. "Most *ktthëkoman* (American person, literally meaning "long knife") think these are weeds . . ." His statement reminded me of a Ted Talk presented by Lakota chef Sean Sherman, in which he urged the audience to "[s]top calling everything a weed just because you don't know what it is."[2] My attention snapped back to John as he continued, "This part here is very nutritious." He ate one of the contents of the pods—a small fleshy bit left over after the feathered seeds were emptied out.

> But when I was little, my mom used to make us pick these tall stalks and swirl them in the air so that the little feathered seeds could blow around in the wind. This way, the milkweed grows back year after year and the monarch butterflies have something to munch on. Nowadays I take my grandkids out and we plant seeds. "*Mshomes* (Grandpa)," they ask me, "we plant these so we can harvest them next year, right?" "No, grandson, we plant them because it's the right thing to do."

John's milkweed teaching that day was about the importance of doing good work with integrity even if one does not have an audience or does not immediately reap the benefits of such work. In doing so, one learns to live *mno bmadzewen*, or the good life. What his teaching also exemplified is that land and nature are foundations to Anishinaabé "ways of knowing," also known as traditional knowledge.

Milkweed is an integral part of the ecology in Michigan. Dozens of beetles and other insects eat or lay their eggs on the plant. The Potawatomi word for milkweed is *nenwesh* or "male plant." Elders in the Pokagon community joke about the sexual nature of the name given the white sap that oozes from the stalk. The first time I heard that explanation during an interview with elder women back in 2015, I turned red from embarrassment while they all laughed. Bodwéwadmimwen is a very descriptive language, after all. Despite the lewd Potawatomi euphemism for milkweed, the Neshnabé practice of dispersing milkweed is a form of traditional knowledge that situates humans as agents in the well-being of the ecology. There is a balance of taking and giving in Neshnabé philosophies of mno bmadzewen. Milkweed is harvested in the spring, but humans aid in its dispersal in the fall. According to elders, Neshnabék have been doing this since time immemorial. This practice applies to specific ecologies and developed because of generations of observation, experimentation, and documentation. Traditional knowledge, such as milkweed dispersal and harvesting practices, is intergenerational, context specific, and rigorous. But how is traditional knowledge situated within anthropological scholarship, and what makes it different from other knowledge regimes?

Knowledge and the land are intricately connected in Neshnabé worldview. In this book I have used the phrase *Neshnabé ke*, which I translate as Potawatomi homeland. Ke refers to earth, dirt, or more recently territory in Potawatomi. The Potawatomi word for teaching is keno'magéwen, or learning and teaching through relationships to the earth. Rhonda Hopkins from Wikwemikong First Nation adds that the particle, ke, in keno'magéwen, meaning earth or dirt, indexes how instructors would draw information in the dirt to relay important information.[3] More than mere information transfer, traditional knowledge or Indigenous "ways of knowing" are developed by maintaining healthy relationships with the environment and the community in which one lives.[4] Articulating a basis of what is commonly referred to as Neshnabé traditional knowledge rather than what is understood as Western science is not to say that these forms of intellectual labor and protocols for teaching are any less rigorous than Western science. Indeed, there are many similarities in their methods. As Potawatomi biologist Robin Wall Kimmerer reflects in *Braiding Sweetgrass*, "[w]hen I stare too long at the world with science eyes, I see an afterimage of traditional knowledge."[5] As will be described in this chapter, traditional knowledge (TK for short) is important not only for understanding Potawatomi and wider Indigenous knowledge systems that often share similar ethical frameworks, but also for appreciating how these epistemologies advance more desirable futures.

Traditional Knowledge Systems

Is knowledge a material possession or a process? I encountered in my research an idea that one could "have" traditional knowledge or not. Most respected Pokagon elders, when asked, didn't feel like they had any traditional knowledge worth sharing. For the record, I did not ask anyone to share traditional knowledge with me or casually seek teachings for the sake of research. Rather, when talking about the *concept* of traditional knowledge, it seemed to be a pervading theme that community members understand TK as content rather than as a set of ethics, harvesting strategies, or skills. Marcus, interim director of Pokagon Language and Culture Department at the time of our conversation in 2015, explains:

> Yeah, the old ones are goofy like that. My mom's like that. The first time I ever had milkweed soup was—Goffy from Prairie Band Potawatomi was up here, and she made some for a feast and I ate it. I was like, "Oh my god, this is awesome. What is it?" She said, "Well, that's milkweed soup." I was like, "Oh, my God." I went home and, "Mom, I had this soup, it's called milkweed soup, it was so good." She said, "Oh, you know, that's nice." Talk about it every time. Every time I see Goffy, I ask for a bowl, always talk about it. Fast forward maybe five years, um, mom's talking, she's talking about a story, and she says something about, "Yeah that's when they used to have us go pick milkweed and we had to do it before a certain time of the year because then you can't pick it no more." And I was like, "Wait a minute, what?" She was like, "Yeah, Mom used to have to go pick the leaves all the time and then we make the soup." I'm like, "Mom, do you not remember me five years ago ranting and raving about milkweed soup and how awesome it was and this and that, and here this whole time you knew exactly how to make it, a recipe, you've been doing it your whole life since [you] were a girl and you've never once brought it up." She's like, "Oh, no. Guess I didn't." I was like, "Oh, man. Mom." So, I get that that type of stuff happens all the time.

In Marcus's story about milkweed soup and his mother's inability (unwillingness?) to recall how she also grew up eating the soup along with her important insights about when in the season is the appropriate time to harvest the leaves is an example of understanding traditional knowledge as content rather than process. Traditional knowledge is not just information shared and transferred within a community but a "process, a way of observing, discussing and making sense of new information."[6] Marcus continues:

> A friend of mine from Australia, I think he said it best because he's Indigenous from over there and they deal with a lot of like the exact same issues we do and so he was saying that like when you ask their old ones

about traditional knowledge, they're like, "We don't know anything about that." Because to them in their mind traditional knowledge, or culture, whatever, is like running around naked in the woods, you know, to them that's what they think of when you ask that. They don't realize that, um, when their mom used to tell them tadpoles got to freeze four times over and then after that, spring is finally here. They don't realize that is culture, you know?

It appeared Neshnabé elders simply didn't consider the knowledge they had or the practices they grew up with to be traditional, even when the youth would certainly consider it to be so. Why is this? It comes down to a label issue. Traditional knowledge, traditional cultural knowledge (TCK), and traditional ecological knowledge (TEK) are all extraneous terms developed in non-Indigenous contexts and meant for legislative purposes and have been marked by extractive, unequal relationships.

The World Intellectual Property Organization (WIPO)—having acknowledged decades' worth of intellectual property violations associated with Western individuals and institutions patenting discoveries and products developed from encounters with traditional knowledge holders—established a definition of traditional knowledge in 2010 as well as a set of protocols for researchers. WIPO defines traditional knowledge as "knowledge, know-how, skills and practices that are developed, sustained and passed on from generation to generation within a community, often forming part of its cultural or spiritual identity."[7] In comprehensive guidelines published as a result of several years of international consultation, negotiation, and collaboration with various nation states and with Indigenous communities around the world, WIPO explores a multiplicity of legal avenues traditional knowledge holders may take to protect the integrity of their intellectual labor and cultural expertise. Their databases, registries, and other resources identify alternative avenues for protecting traditional knowledge that extend beyond individualized copyright or patent licenses. Some examples include community ownership and establishing procedures for how shared traditional knowledge may be used by outside entities in the future. Among thousands of pages of notes, memorandums, and official publications, WIPO contextualizes the nuances of traditional knowledge from examples such as plant medicines, traditional foods, and art, just to name a few.

Traditional knowledge systems are often referred to as TCK and TEK—the latter when methods specifically address environmental and natural resource management. TEK can be thought of as a subcategory of TCK[8] as well as a "locally-derived way of interacting with the environment which often includes methods for managing a specific ecosystem."[9] TCK and TEK as I use the terms correspond to the definition provided by Vine Deloria Jr. in his influential book *Red Earth White Lies*, and that is "the distilled memories of thousands of years of living in North America."[10] This definition highlights the socially mediated, intergenerational nature of knowledge making that continues to be a principal means of making sense of the world and humanity's position in it. For example, in Great Lakes Native communities, one is often asked who one's teachers are. There are a lot of different teachings about how best to manage the environment, how to conduct oneself, when to pick the best medicines, how to prepare them, and more. That is not to say that one teaching is right and the others are wrong. But TCK is context-based instructions that may change depending on various circumstances—seasons, recipes, type of illness, personality of the student, etc. For example, all Neshnabé women interested in learning their traditional roles are taught about our responsibilities toward cedar. Cedar is one of our female medicines. At the Midéwiwin Lodge we harvest it, clean it, and use it for various purposes at ceremonies from sweat lodge to blocking off the moon lodge. When I was about six months pregnant with my son in summer 2017, I was helping to clean some cedar in preparation for ceremonies. A man told me I ought not to be doing that. I learned that cedar, like parsley, is sometimes used to terminate a pregnancy. So, while esteemed for its medical power in ceremony and everyday ailments, context of use matters greatly.

With TCK and medicines, context matters. Unfortunately, a lot of tribal members even within the Pokagon Band develop deep fracture lines between the students of different teachers. There are a lot of reasons for this, but it leads to arguments, conflicts, politics, and bad blood. However, the younger generation (thirty-five years of age and below) of Pokagon Band members with whom I spent the most time in professional, research, and familiar contexts, seem to believe that these hostilities are changing. Rhonda Purcell, Language Program manager for the Pokagon Band at the time of our conversation in 2018, calls the teachings passed down without proper consideration of context and purpose as "surface-level teachings." She is frustrated by strict protocols or declarations of rightness and wrongness with "nothing to back it up. Why? Tell me *why*," she demands in an interview with me as she reflects upon problematic assertions made by elders in the Pokagon community. If TCK is indeed socially mediated as Deloria Jr. states, Rhonda's desire to understand how an Indigenous methodology is appropriate for a contemporary context instead of uncritically inheriting meretricious rules speaks to the co-curatorial aspect of traditional knowledge.

Neshnabé traditional knowledge is entangled in networks of social relationships. A useful description of Neshnabé ethics embedded in traditional knowledge is offered by Potawatomi biologist Robin Wall Kimmerer in her text *Braiding Sweetgrass*. She describes traditional knowledge as both scientific and *affective* or felt attachments to place centered on kin relationships. Similarly, this is the way in which recent literature centrally concerned with knowledge making in local and Indigenous communities treats Indigenous knowledge systems. For example, in her ethnography *Blackfoot Ways of Knowing*, Betty Bastien explains how *Siksikaitsitapi*—a Blackfoot placed-based epistemology—is realized through everyday ontological responsibilities with kin relations past and present.[11] For her and the Blackfoot community members in her research, ways of knowing, whether utilizing Indigenous science for healing or ecological management, means seeking knowledge to maintain social relationships that situate oneself in the world physically, socially, and spiritually.[12] Thus, the socially mediated place-based epistemologies described in Bastien's ethnography demonstrate, similar to Neshnabé sensibilities, how identities become tied to places and our relationships built within them.

Keith Basso's exemplary scholarship on traditional knowledge *Wisdom Sits in Places* similarly enciphers how Western Apache places, specifically the stories attached to these places and their names, encode wisdom. Basso explains that "[p]laces and their meanings are continually woven into the fabric of social life, anchoring it to features of the landscape and blanketing it with layers of significance that few can fail to appreciate."[13] With this in mind, Western Apaches in Basso's research conjure teachings as well as "manipulate the significance of local places to comment on the moral shortcomings of wayward individuals."[14] For Western Apaches in Basso's research, wisdom constitutes a sophisticated mental aptitude that helps individuals evade potential harm, whether social or physical. The smoothness, resilience, and steadiness of mind that Basso describes are not endowed at birth but must instead be developed and nourished within each individual by knowing specific places and the stories/teachings associated with those places. In short, Basso's research demonstrates how Indigenous knowledge systems are locally derived, historically specific, and socially mediated—a process, not just content.[15]

Because many Indigenous communities have been living and interacting with a specific environment for hundreds or thousands of years, mainstream scientists have begun to appreciate ancestral lands as potential archives of environmental data and their Indigenous community stewards as co-producers of important knowledge and environmental management strategies. One example of how TEK is being taken up in anthropological literature is Steve J. Langdon's research on tidal pulse fishing. He explains that, by constructing crescent-shaped stone structures on the coastline, for thousands of years Tlingit communities in the northwest coast of the Americas have employed a method of salmon fishing that does not adversely affect salmon spawning.[16] Similarly, foraging practices of the Pokagon Band restrict members from picking certain plants at particular times of the year, lest they overharvest and adversely affect future yields. There are also instructions for determining whether an area is healthy or resilient enough to be harvested. Both methods demonstrate a deep understanding of locally specific habitats and an ecological ethic of allowing marine species and terrestrial flora to reproduce, ensuring their survival for generations to come. These newly formed partnerships between Indigenous intellectuals and those of mainstream science, however, are developed within matrices of unequal relationships of power that are connected to decades of extraction from, manipulation of, and damage to Native communities, causing great distrust of Western scientists.

Science and the Anthropology of Knowledge Production

Recent traditional Potawatomi methods for storing wood have been applied to combat modern problems, specifically an invasive species called the emerald ash borer. The East Asian beetle was accidentally introduced in the Great Lakes region in the early 2000s. Since then, the insect has killed millions of black ash trees throughout the Midwest. Neshnabé artists were some of the first to notice the destruction because of the black ash basket tradition that forms an essential pillar of Potawatomi identity. When one part of an ecology is damaged to that extent, it can have adverse effects on the ecological integrity of an entire region for hundreds of miles. Twenty years after the insect's arrival, scientists in the Great Lakes region and other parts of the Midwest are still researching and finding ways to mitigate emerald ash borer damage. Some of these research projects draw from Neshnabé knowledge systems to do so. Benedict and Frelich argue that, by drawing from local knowledge and negotiating with Indigenous communities about black ash tree harvesting, the spread of the invasive beetle is more holistically and effectively managed.[17] By submerging logs in a local lake for several months in 2015, the Pokagon Band DNR could kill off all the emerald ash borer eggs contained in the logs. Traditionally, Neshnabé communities might store spare wood in water, especially since black ash baskets can only be made by splitting the growth rings of wet trunks. Once they are too dry, they cannot be used. This traditional form of wood storage is now being used to combat the spread of the invasive species, lending to new opportunities for Indigenous intellectuals and scientists to collaborate on modern issues. As Berkes argues, if traditional knowledges were simply content or insights shared within a community from the past, they could not be adapted or change to fit new circumstances with black ash tree logs.[18]

At the time of this writing in 2019, the entire Pokagon DNR staff (except for their administrative assistant) is non-Native, which is a dynamic that matters in tribes with whom I work. Too much of what is colloquially referred to as "outside hires" damages the rapport a tribal government has with the community it serves. The lack of Indigenous representation is also problematic considering the existing issues between the appreciation and application of traditional knowledge and science. The Pokagon Band DNR is made up of specialists trained in standard scientific methods but must work to integrate Indigenous ways of knowing into the work that they do—whether that is controlled burns, landscaping, gardening, or invasive species management. Many of the citizens I spoke to about this are impressed with the work that Pokagon DNR does. Their expertise and respect for community members' voices have not gone unnoticed by tribal members. However, Pokagon Band DNR projects and their success in integrating knowledges are unusual compared to similar consultation efforts by agency officials in natural resource management projects because of the imbalance of representational authority in traditional knowledge versus science.

Persistent gatekeeping practices in science, technology, engineering, and mathematics (STEM) fields stifle diversity. The statistics from the 2017 National Science Foundation report on "Women, Minorities, and Persons with Disabilities in Science and Engineering" show that, while women (of all ethnicities) represent just under half of all employees in STEM, and representation of most non-white ethnicities are on the rise, Black and American Indian/Alaskan Native representation has decreased since 1995 (and it was already quite low back then).[19] Researchers have attributed these statistics to institutional and subconscious exclusionary practices intended to keep non-binary, non-whites out of coveted art and academic spaces.[20]

Lack of clear diversity, equity, and inclusion (DEI) progress is concerning because inclusion and diversity are not just ethical goals, they make disciplines such as science better by incorporating more perspectives, experiences, and wider considerations of solutions. "[A] more diverse group often yields more nuanced decisions. Fully deliberated decisions made from multiple perspectives and experiences result in deeper and wider considerations of ever-changing students, schools, and the world at large."[21] While it is true that heterogeneity in color does not necessarily yield heterogeneity in thought, by diversifying schools, workplaces, and other institutions, these places become more creative and effective in their missions. Yet, despite the societal benefits and industrial innovation that result from ethnic, religious, age, differently abled, and gender diversity, exclusionary practices, particularly in powerful and influential industries like the sciences, continue.[22] Worse yet, these exclusionary practices exist and are supported by the pervasive notion that science is an inherently white invention, which negatively affects science. The history of science as something uniquely developed by Europeans, however, is a grossly inaccurate idea. From algebra deriving from Persian mathematicians to independent astronomical observations of African and Indigenous American astronomers, science and its methods for observation and organizing information are not unique to Europe. Science, understood as deriving from Western or white thought, shares many methods and values with traditional knowledge, "Native science,"[23] and the other names given to Indigenous methods of engaging and understanding the physical and metaphysical world(s).

Notwithstanding the decades of research that proves this point, some of which is discussed in this chapter, Indigenous science and ingenuity are undervalued or, more commonly, completely ignored by media and the general public. As an archivist and educator in behalf of my tribe during the time of my dissertation research, I reflected on how I conveyed this point to different audiences. When presenting in front of nonacademic, usually non-Indigenous audiences, I draw from examples of Native ingenuity—such as Maya aqueducts similar to those found in Rome and Woodland-period earthen works or "mounds" comparable to Egyptian pyramids—to discredit the widespread notion that "Indians were *just* hunter gatherers." This is because I want to challenge lay audiences' prejudices of Native people rather than have anthropologically nuanced debates. By contrast, as an academic, I allocate a lot of intellectual labor to teasing apart the limiting notion that these examples of Indigenous engineering (which resemble developments from the Old World, aka Europe) are what make our knowledge systems worthy of respect. While these impressive feats exist, we do not need our ancestors' advanced metallurgy or trade routes that extended thousands of miles to prove we had and continue to practice legitimate science. That is because our ancestors developed governance systems and ecological management strategies that sustained our communities on this continent for thousands of years. As the 2017 Indigenous letter of support for the March for Science states:

> [L]ong before Western science came to these shores, there were Indigenous scientists here. Native astronomers, agronomists, geneticists, ecologists, engineers, botanists, zoologists, watershed hydrologists, pharmacologists, physicians and more—all engaged in the creation and application of knowledge which promoted the flourishing of both human societies and the beings with whom we share the planet . . . Western science is a powerful approach, but it is not the only one.[24]

While identifying the conclusive source of this unequal representation in the sciences is not the focus of this work, it does beg the question, what do these data tell us about the state of science and its relationship to Native peoples? Western-centric bias in science is exemplified in the famous "Draw-a-Scientist Test." Studies have shown that most children across cultures have been trained to envision scientists as white males.[25] In this experiment, young people are instructed to draw a scientist. These pictures often depict white males in lab coats, middle aged or older, working alone (highlighting individual instead of collaborative achievement) with Western symbols of knowledge production such as books and beakers. Repeated in different age groups across the world since the 1980s, children—even in places like rural China—often draw the same thing. This imagery affects the way even the youngest, most impressionable members of society consume knowledge and the development of their internalized potential lifetime success. Anyone who does not conform to the stereotypical image of scientist is not seen as possessing legitimate knowledge.

In 2018, the Pokagon Band Tribal Head Start school officially changed ownership from the state-regulated program to one owned, operated, and funded by the tribe itself. With this institutional sea change, the Head Start school hired new staff, changed its name to *Zagbëgon* or "little sprouts," and created new curricula based on Potawatomi traditional knowledge and its many applications to STEM. Children spend a lot of time outside as part of this new curricula such as at sugar bush camp (maple syrup harvesting) in the early spring, where they learn about the science of tree sap and how their ancestors developed tools and methods for harvesting this natural resource.

The tribally owned school for children between three and five years of age combines traditional knowledge through stories and practices with contemporary scientific discoveries. During one emotionally moving teaching session, Rhonda Purcell gathered the children in a room together and had them sit on the floor. Rhonda is a captivating and charismatic woman who is especially effective at keeping even the rowdiest kids' attention. She turned off the lights in the room so that the children's sense of sight was curtailed in favor of their sense of sound. Rhonda grabbed her *shishigwan* or rattle and rhythmically began to shake the instrument so that the pebbles inside produced a static type of sound that resembled rain. The pitch-black room was silent except for that sound.

Rhonda shared the story of the creation of everything—the birth of the Universe and the creation of the stars in the sky. It all began with that sound ... *Ktthémnedo* or the Great Spirit, the unknowable Creator, catalyzed all beings through the creation of sound waves. The frequencies of these primordial notes begat all life. This traditional story was then purposefully paralleled with the Big Bang theory and the cosmic microwave background radiation that astronomers discovered back in the 1960s. The cosmic background radiation is some of the first physical evidence for scientists' Big Bang theory for the creation of the Universe. Interestingly, the sound of the radiation resembles the static-like sound of Rhonda's shishigwan.

Because of teachings like Rhonda's, tribal children at Zagbëgon not only learn traditional stories, but also learn how these forms of traditional knowledge are applicable to STEM and their positions in the Universe. Thus, the curricula they are exposed to foreclose the gatekeeping practice of separating the rigor of traditional knowledge from arenas of "real science." The hope, according to the Department of Education director for the tribe, Sam Morseau, is that children know that becoming a scientist is possible for them without "losing their culture and sense of Potawatomi identity."[26]

Because science and traditional knowledge share similar methods but do not share the same respect or political weight, the philosophy of science, or more specifically the anthropology of knowledge production, is essential for understanding how knowledge is politically deployed. Anthropology has a long tradition of engagement with the problem of knowledge to create new knowledge about the world through research within academic institutions, as well as trying to understand other locally derived knowledges through employing ethnographic research methods. The body of literature that constitutes the anthropology of knowledge production or the philosophy of science posits that because knowledge systems are historically situated and politically deployed, the Western approach to scientific inquiry—while it continues to maintain power and political influence—is not superior to other ways and methods of knowing. Nevertheless, to discuss the anthropology of knowledge production presents a bit of a conundrum. This is because the anthropology of knowledge production, unlike many other bodies of literature, is not an easily codifiable anthropological tradition; instead, it encompasses a large breadth of literature with very different approaches. As Dominic Boyer reminds us in his "re-visit" to the anthropology of knowledge production, the discipline of anthropology has, in fact, always been centrally concerned with knowledge.[27] For this reason, in Malcom R. Crick's highly cited review of the anthropology of knowledge production, he is not apt to refer to a separate categorical anthropology of knowledge at all, even while there exists a "sociology of knowledge" and even an "archaeology of knowledge." So, while the anthropology of knowledge production is not a singular tradition or an emergent theme, per se, the topic of knowledge production within anthropological research envelops a multiplicity of important approaches and involves a number of significant interventions, especially into the topic of non-Western and Indigenous knowledge systems.[28]

By using ethnographic methods such as participant observation, anthropology is in the best position to approach differential knowledge systems—those divergent from Western pedagogies, developed through unique histories, and realized in distinct social contexts. Yet, this is not a call for a re-examination of the outdated and Eurocentric approaches of the early to mid-twentieth-century ethnographies that typically argued for the sophistication of "primitive" logic systems such as Radin's *Primitive Man as Philosopher* or Evans-Pritchard's *Theories of Primitive Religion*. These well-intentioned (or not?) texts were largely concerned with attempts to explain and sometimes validate the logic systems of non-Western peoples, while at the same time privileging Eurocentric pedagogies. "See! They're just like us if you look hard enough." Instead, even while anthropology has, for the most part, always been concerned with knowledge production, only in recent years have explicit discussions regarding the issues and politics of Indigenous knowledge systems intensified, most notably in research about environmental stewardship.

That knowledge and power are inextricably bound up with one another is not a new intervention. Indeed, how knowledge is realized through unequal relationships of power was a central topic of investigation for the eminent philosopher Michel Foucault in *Power and Knowledge*. Following this foundational awareness, Hans Weiler highlights the hierarchical aspect of knowledge production by drawing from nineteenth- and early twentieth-century theorists such as Friedrich Nietzsche and Max Weber to show how hierarchies in the production of knowledge are the expression of power par excellence. Power structures how knowledge is garnered, understood, and received at all levels. As Weiler states, "[w]herever [hierarchies] occur, they reflect structures of authority and power, and thus the essence of politics."[29] So, a true anthropology of knowledge production is indeed concerned with not only power, but also the larger political context of learning and knowledge dissemination.

One anthropological response to knowledge, power, and context is ethnography of science and science education. This type of research uses ethnographic methods to investigate science education and science learning in contexts that were previously only understood through detached quantitative methods (such as standardized test data). In Anna Traianou's research on science teaching she explains that in Western pedagogies and styles of teaching there are assumed milieus of knowledge that must be transmitted to learners. Often these lessons are in contradiction with students' already acquired frameworks and understandings. As a result, instructors in Traianou's research are faced with dilemmas about teaching. Traianou uses the term "dilemma" as a concept to explain the opposing forces of teachers' obligations to assert control over what students learn and to allow students to make sense of their own situated understandings. The instructors in Traianou's research identified an institutional disjuncture between what they were obligated to teach and in what order to meet the state-required standardized tests on the one hand, and children's intellectual enrichment, individual engagement, and development of critical thinking skills on the other. The lack of qualitative data—which are now being collected by this type of ethnographic research—highlighted the problem of underrepresentation of gender and ethnic minorities in science.[30]

By using qualitative research methods in arenas such as public schools, ethnographies of science education reveal how power operates within the classroom to determine who is a legitimate scientist, what scientific knowledge is, and how to engage with it "properly." What is more, early attempts at providing qualitative explanations for unequal gender and ethnic representation in the sciences tended to pathologize students of color. For instance, Heidi Carlone and Angela Johnson use ethnographic data they obtained by shadowing a specific group of middle school–aged children over the course of several years. Specifically, they use the data to survey several popular frameworks traditionally used to explain why from a young age some students are encouraged in the sciences over others. "Funds of knowledge" and "cultural difference" approaches, for example, locate the likely personal experiences that children (from nonwhite backgrounds in the latter model) bring with them to the classroom. Stemming from a pseudo-ethnographic understanding of culture, these models attempt to explain away inequality by foregrounding anecdotal evidence of cultural "difference" in place of revealing how structural forms of discrimination perpetuate inequality. As if you could more effectively teach Native kids fractions by dividing up a piece of frybread instead of a pie. These assumptions lead to formulaic teaching models to address how well particular students are likely to learn in different environments. However, Carlone and Johnson argue that these approaches misdirect attention away from the structural reasons, such as economics, why some schools are staffed with the best teachers and given new materials, as well as why some people are more readily considered scientists.[31]

With an eye toward future generations, using Neshnabé traditional knowledge, an outdoors curriculum, and lessons derived from everyday uses of the Potawatomi language, the Pokagon Band is deploying their ideas of Neshnabé futurisms. So, will the recent transfer of school ownership from the state to the tribe allow the Pokagon Band to increase the representation of tribal citizens in the STEM fields? That is impossible to answer for now, but the Pokagon Department of Education, teachers, parents, and advocates for building K–12 tribal schools believe that an increase in Indigenous representation in privileged fields like STEM, as well as a significantly higher retention of Bodwéwadmimwen, will be two of the many positive results.

Other projects within the literature of knowledge production attempt to understand learning and knowledge by looking to arenas outside the classroom, such as the internet. In Dariusz Jemielniak's topical ethnography *Common Knowledge?*, he explains how the popular online encyclopedia Wikipedia functions, who is part of this online community of contributors, and what some of the social issues are with producing open access, editable knowledge on the web within this platform. He describes his ethnography as "the first book on nonexpert open-collaboration communities that is based on longitudinal, participative ethnographic research."[32] Jemielniak's ethnography is particularly provocative because he reveals how, despite Wikipedia's egalitarian, democratic, and collaborative philosophy, this rhetoric does not prevent hierarchies and informal gatekeeping from emerging. Conflict is pervasive in the Wikipedia community of "nonexpert experts" tasked with sourcing articles that ostensibly disseminate particular understandings of the world. However, Wikipedia has many devices for creating consensus and mediating issues between community members. As Jemielniak explains, "[a] word enormously respected on Wikipedia is 'consensus' (CON) [and] requires all editors to seek a solution acceptable to the community [...] dedication to consensus may coerce an agreement and dilute minority views."[33] Thus, consensus is a regulatory tool within regimes of online knowledge making that actually contributes to the "perception" of democratic decision making while still privileging more popular or powerful perspectives.

The interventions developed within ethnographies such as Carlone and Johnson's and Traianou's ethnographies of science education, as well as Jemielniak's in coercing consensus in online spaces, show how inequality in knowledge production is not easily remedied by models of cultural difference or trying to force consensus to avoid debate or conflict. This is why, from a Neshnabé perspective, it is not enough to "accommodate" cultural differences for Native children in public-school settings. The tribe wants to be in charge of the school itself. As previously mentioned, the relationship between power and knowledge is self-reinforcing. Even while the specific processes are not always self-evident, there is a general anthropological understanding that some ideas and intellectual frameworks have been privileged over others. In *Envisioning Power*, Eric R. Wolf argues that "[i]deas or systems of ideas do not, of course, float about in incorporeal space; they acquire substance through communication in discourse and performance."[34] Therefore, structures of ideas and institutions that substantiate and deploy those ideas reproduce hegemony. For these reasons, the turns in anthropology toward democratizing the research process and privileging Native perspectives including traditional knowledge and cultural protocols is interesting.

Traditional knowledge systems and science as institutionalized sets of intellectual labor share similar methodologies and findings but are politically deployed and represented in radically different ways. One way anthropology has approached the topic of Indigenous knowledge systems is through deeply collaborative ethnographic methods and efforts to democratize the knowledge making process. Community-based participatory research (CBPR) falls under this tradition. This approach argues for viewing TCK as legitimate science. Because traditional knowledge systems are often intentionally separated from and contrasted with Western understandings of science in conventional forms of research, this trend in research emerged that took Indigenous knowledge systems, TEK in particular, as equally empirical and rigorous. This is because traditional knowledge systems rely on the same doctrines of science: observation, experimentation, and methodical reasoning. However, within this approach, researchers view TEK as more refined and nuanced, because it is more holistic and embedded in local context, with its methods resulting in less adverse effects on the environment.[35] For Chantelle Marlor, because TEK is learned and experienced in the everyday practices of communities, this is exactly what makes it so powerful and effective in managing natural resources more than any other pedagogy. Yet, power imbalances have resulted in conflicts in community-based scholarship.[36]

Consultation, Collaboration, or Co-option?

The anthropology of knowledge production has become increasingly concerned with democratizing the knowledge making process in recent years, and not just to give Indigenous pedagogies more voice, but to mitigate power imbalances in the research process itself.[37] While efforts to lift traditional knowledge systems into mainstream scientific ways of thinking are well intentioned, these projects have incited the question: Should TCK implementation into science be the aim of researchers in the first place? Is this appropriation, and does it do Indigenous communities any good? What many case studies in traditional knowledge systems and ecological management seem to promote is a less destructive alternative to extractive undertakings usually promoted by capitalism. In Caroline Butler's call to "historicize" Indigenous knowledge systems, she explains that TCK is promoted as an alternative to mainstream scientific engagements with the environment, and in some cases a potential space for the co-management of natural resources with Indigenous and local communities. However, Butler sees this as an issue of appropriation, because "[a]n uncomplicated and uncritical promotion of Indigenous knowledge as the solution to the global crisis in natural resource use is both practically and politically dangerous [...] And failing to recognize and highlight the impact of colonial domination on Indigenous systems of knowledge and management effaces the culpability of colonial states."[38]

Similar to looking to Neshnabé communities for managing emerald ash borer spread—an environmental issue discussed earlier in this chapter—multiple fields of research from academia to natural resource professionals are increasingly paying attention to Indigenous knowledge systems and methods for interacting with particular environments to restructure how the larger non-Native community manages natural resources. Inviting input and collaboration from Indigenous and local communities is not an inherently sinister endeavor. Seeking out alternative perspectives to mainstream understandings and assumptions about the environment and how to manage natural resources invites opportunity for better ecological management strategies and community-based partnership. Prior unfettered appropriation of traditional knowledge systems by intellectuals in positions of power, however, became problematic when it was "'distilled' into a product that is easily integrated into the Western resource management system."[39] As Charles Menzies succinctly explains, "[c]ommunity research priorities are not addressed, but community TEK is expected to be provided in order to benefit scientific research projects."[40] This presents a practical problem, as well, because TEK is understood to be effective for specific environments and contexts, not a codifiable, exportable regime of knowledge applicable to other parts of the world.[41]

Part of what makes the anthropology of knowledge production, and community-based participatory research projects in particular, difficult to qualify is in trying to ascertain the level of actual collaboration within the research process. This becomes even more difficult with the indiscriminate use of the buzzword "collaboration." As Anishinaabé archaeologist Sonya Atalay points out in her comprehensive text *Community-Based Archaeology*, there are several levels of community engagement that range from deeply collaborative CBPR frameworks to superficial levels of engagement such as legally mandated consultation.[42] Drawing from Stephen Silliman's *Collaborating at the Trowel's Edge*, Atalay explains that

> collaborative archaeology is not about the end point or what is produced, although conducting rigorous research and producing new knowledge is clearly important in [community-based participatory research]. Rather, what is important is the process involved in designing and implementing the research. Being committed to the ideology of producing knowledge in partnership is the first principle of practice. The second is acknowledging that community knowledge and involvement has value and contributes to scientific understanding.[43]

Addressing this, in my research I looked at natural resource management policy, specifically the two most important U.S. laws, the National Historic Preservation Act (NHPA) and the National Environmental Policy Act (NEPA), that outline legally mandated consultation requirements between agency officials of developmental undertakings and local stakeholders. Any developmental undertaking, from hydrofracking to constructing apartment buildings, must carry out a certain amount of community outreach. The purpose of this outreach is to inform residents of what is going on and invite community feedback for consultation to mitigate any unnecessary adverse effects from general inconvenience such as noise to more serious issues such as water contamination.

The specific purpose of inviting tribal entities for consultation and feedback is to ascertain whether there is a likely chance of disturbing human remains (which would invoke the Native American Graves Protection and Repatriation Act [NAGPRA]) or sacred sites. Consultation meetings are meant to be a space for deploying alternative points of view (which would include traditional knowledge), discussing alternative construction processes, and mediating the concerns of multiple "stakeholders." However, this platform of multivocality has had dubious benefits at best to Indigenous communities in my research. Tribal historic preservation officers and other tribal members have had their concerns dismissed, and traditional methods for engaging with the environment are almost nonexistent.

Current tribal historic preservation officer Matthew Bussler, with whom I shared an office for almost a year during my research, "consults" on nearly thirty project proposals a day. The thousands of pages contained within the copious amounts of mail he receives crowd his workspace. I asked him if he really offers meaningful consultation recommendations to all these proposed undertakings. "Psst. Of course not . . . Most of them are outside the Pokagon Band service area," he explained to me. "So, we don't consult on them at all. Some requests for tribal consultation," he says, "may be in our service area, but they don't really explain what it is they're doing very well."[44] He concluded that he sometimes feels that agency officials who are sending out these requests for consultation are just inundating him with bureaucratic time-wasting forms without the expectation that tribes will ever be able to sift through and identify important projects that we *should* be consulting on. Former tribal historic preservation officer for the Pokagon Band Marcus had similar views:

> **Marcus**: I know that for me . . . as far as the tribal historic preservation officer consultations, a lot of times environmental consultations will get sent my way, as well. And for a while I would get those and be like, "I don't even know how to respond to this because I don't know the first thing about water and whether or not you building this dock for your boat is going to ruin anything." So . . . if I get any of those letters in the mail, I just shoot them over to DNR and let them comment on them . . . I would say it was since the summertime, there's been a huge influx of federal agencies reaching out for tribal consultation, and I think that came from the top somewhere. Like I know Indiana Department of Transportation got an *F* on their tribal consultations—
> **Blaire**: I'm not surprised, but—[laughs]
> **Marcus**:—or following through with any of those federal regulations. And so now they're—Now they want to be our friends, where a year ago that was, you know, "You're just a bunch of Indians, we don't need to work with you," and since they got that *F*, now it's all smiles and handshakes.
> **Blaire**: Mm-hmm. So, do you see them just sending you more notifications about things going on or they're actually making an effort to build a relationship?
> **Marcus**: Hmm, I think it depends on the personality of who's ever in place. Uh, Army Corps of Engineers—actually, I just met them for lunch this past Monday, yeah four days ago, and, um, and so like their major thing

is if your project affects water in any way, they take authority over it to make sure that you do things within federal regulations. And they admitted that the Chicago district wasn't following through with tribal consultation because their previous staff archaeologist told them that there weren't any tribes that they should worry about in the Chicago district.

Blaire: No. Wow.

Marcus: And then they were working—how a lot of federal agencies determine which tribes they're going to work with and, um, consult with, is based on treaty sessions. So, for that piece of land, what treaty signed that land away and what were the tribes that signed that treaty. So that's how Chicago knew—they knew that they had to go in that direction, but their archaeologist told them there's no treaties in Chicago, so you don't got to worry about it.

Blaire: Except the 1821 and 1833 *Treaties . . . of . . . Chicago!* [laughs] (emphasis is original)

When tribes get a chance to consult on projects, their concerns are often not taken seriously. As Atalay explains, multivocality in these contexts is often a damaging enterprise because, when multiple interest groups are heard side by side, conventional science perspectives are privileged while traditional knowledge systems are dismissed as "quaint folk knowledge."[45] In fact, research by Stern et al. indicates that a hierarchical organization of priorities exists inherently within NEPA besides the hierarchy of stakeholder issues that Atalay points out. For instance, their findings from surveys with the Forest Service employees show that, depending on the duties associated with each position, employees worked to mitigate adverse environmental effects, accommodate multiple stakeholders, avoid legal ramifications, promote efficiency, or focus on full disclosure of the NEPA process and decisions exclusively. All priorities cannot be held simultaneously or with equal weight. This indicates that processes in natural and cultural resource management are even more complicated because of inherent hierarchies between multiple stakeholders. For example, if efficiency is promoted, the concerns of tribal members are quickly dismissed; if legal ramifications are avoided, agency officials will deploy full disclosure of long and complicated legal processes and decisions to legally comply with NEPA, but never fully address consultation with tribal governments in a meaningful way (since this is not exactly what is required by NHPA or NEPA nowadays, anyway).[46]

Additionally, the consultation process can be quite paternalistic and is often ineffective at meeting the needs and desires of tribal communities. For instance, even before this type of meeting takes place, there are other factors to consider if the effects that NEPA and NHPA have on Native communities are to be understood. The typical process begins when tribal governments, usually the tribal historic preservation officer,[47] receives a notification from a project manager or agency official that an undertaking may affect property historically or contemporarily significant to the tribe. The tribal historic preservation officer has thirty days to respond to this notice. Should the tribal historic preservation officer or the larger tribal community be interested or concerned about how the proposed project will adversely affect land that is important to them, the usual turn of events involves tribal members having to travel long distances (keeping in mind tribal communities that were removed far from their original homelands) on their own dime just to hear an agency official dismiss everything they have to say while they explain how the project will unfold as planned. This is because NEPA and NHPA require consultation, not negotiation. Distressed and dismayed, tribal members return home and perhaps issue a formal complaint under the Administrative Procedures Act (APA), only to have their concerns disregarded and branded as antiprogress or limiting "public" space and resources.[48] For Glen Coulthard, the form of multivocality used in consultation requirements of NRM is just subsumption. As he so succinctly explains, "[a]lthough the state no longer requires the formal 'extinguishment' of Indigenous rights as a precondition to reaching an agreement, the purpose of the process has remained the same: to facilitate the 'incorporation' of Indigenous peoples and territories into the capitalist mode of production and to ensure that alternative 'socioeconomic visions' do not threaten the desired functioning of the market economy."[49] In this sense, Coulthard sees consultation within NRM as a form of ideological state apparatus for nonviolent coercion.

The anthropology of knowledge production offers an important framework for understanding how Indigenous knowledge systems in the Great Lakes area are being dismissed by unequal relationships of power in multivocal platforms of NRM consultation and how they enact exploitative incorporation of Indigenous intellectual labor. As another form of co-option, Stuart Kirsch's research investigates corporations' tendency to co-opt the discourse of their adversaries in his ethnography about the Ok Tedi mine in Papua New Guinea and its adverse effects on Indigenous communities in *Mining Capitalism*. Similarly, in *Empire* Hardt and Negri identify a new global dimension of coercion and domination whereby "immaterial" labor such as knowledge production becomes the most important component into a biopolitical regime to reproduce empire.[50] This is an important insight, because while agency officials in developmental undertakings are often dismissive of tribes' concerns, they pay ever-increasing attention to the "importance" of consultation and knowledge gathering.

Admittedly, in my role as archivist I sometimes felt resentful of the amount of time I spent "consulting" on exhibits or research projects being done by nontribal organizations and non-Native individuals who sometimes seemed too lazy to do their own research. Emails, questions, and problematic assumptions that could easily be remedied by a decent (or even not so decent) Google search consumed a lot of my time and energy—time and energy that could be spent conducting oral history interviews with elders before they passed or working on new curriculum resources for our tribal Head Start school, as well as other activities that could be more beneficial to our community. As archivist for the Pokagon government in the Department of Language and Culture, one might assume my main job duties were conservation, digitization, and cataloguing to serve the Pokagon community. Instead, most of my time was spent explaining rudimentary history and culture about the tribe and Great Lakes Native tribes to organizations like museums—ironically, institutions that are often viewed by the general public as reliable sources of information and expertise on history, art, and science.

Futurity in Traditional Knowledge Bundles

So far, I have drawn from both Potawatomi-specific ways of knowing, how they can be held like archives on the land (chapter 1), and how many Indigenous knowledge systems share similar qualities of relationality and ethics of reciprocity. Indigenous traditional knowledges are locally derived and share similar principles of observation, experimentation, and organization of data with mainstream science. Peer review is not reserved for academics, but community-identified experts—usually elders. But traditional knowledge does not share the political respect of mainstream science. Efforts to democratize knowledge making processes and to develop holistic ways to manage the environment have been accomplished through deeply collaborative projects between traditional knowledge holders and scientists. When done poorly, consultation can turn into appropriation.

But if traditional knowledge is so rigorous and utilizes the same principles of observation and experimentation as science, why is it not just considered science? One answer is that traditional knowledge is set within cultural frameworks such that, when it is decontextualized, it loses most of its meaning. Traditional knowledge is wrapped in bundles of community-specific significance that enable full transmission of its content and methodologies. Without these contexts, metaphors cannot be decoded, talking animals seem ridiculous, the science is obscured, and the meaning of the story makes little to no sense.

Cultural protocol is also an important factor. Traditional knowledge holders and their respective communities have diverse conventions for sharing information. And traditional knowledge forms an integral part of identity for Indigenous communities. As a result, there is a resistance to allow traditional knowledge to be subsumed within the definition of mainstream science. Traditional knowledge is not intended to be part of the public domain and operates within a nexus of deep-time transmission from one generation to another.

Many of the traditional ways in which Neshnabé peoples transport tools and information are in bundles. The contents of bundles and their purposes can range from everyday utility, such as feast bundles that hold wood bowls and cutlery, to sacred items in ceremonial bundles. Like birch bark scrolls etched with pictographs that could be used as devices to recall long stories, Potawatomi peoples are finding new tools with which to keep our traditional knowledge alive and accessible to our community. Like the birch bark canoes discussed by Pokagon Potawatomi scholar John Low, a bundle is "a vessel [...] a tangible object, symbol, and a rich metaphor for carrying Great Lakes Indigenous peoples into their futures on their own terms."[51]

Similar to other forms of Potawatomi gathering and building, work is being done with the aid of innovative online platforms. The Pokagon Band is reclaiming some of their intellectual labor to serve their own needs and disseminate knowledge that is more in line with Neshnabé ethics of social relationships. *Wiwkwébthëgen* refers to a place where sacred items and knowledge are kept, or "bundle." It is the name for the Pokagon Band's online archives and dictionary. Wiwkwébthëgen is essentially a content management system called Mukurtu.[52] The site is maintained by the Pokagon Band's Tribal Historic Preservation Office within the Department of Language and Culture. As part of my primary job responsibilities as archivist and with the help of the folks at the Center for Digital Scholarship and Curation at Washington State University, I launched the site in 2018 along with the former director of the Department of Language and Culture, Marcus Winchester, and the former tribal historic preservation officer, Jason S. Wesaw.[53] Wiwkwébthëgen includes audio recordings of traditional stories, photographs of objects such as baskets and beadwork, digitized family photos from the turn of the twentieth century, and even a searchable dictionary with audio pronunciation and sentence samples. It also includes new work such as contemporary storytelling, painting, installation artwork, and oral history interviews, and is only available to tribal citizens or trusted researchers. Jennifer Wemigwans calls these spaces "digital bundles," and they serve as virtual spaces for nation-building, to create new articulations of Indigenous sovereignty—especially through the lens and creativity of youth who are engaged in what many would usually refer to as cultural and language "revitalization."[54]

What makes Wiwkwébthëgen unique from museums' and other archives' websites is the system's highly editable structure for cultural protocols and community management. For example, community members value hearing traditional stories, especially those told by notable storytellers who have since passed on. Concerns about the intellectual property of traditional stories that have been published in prior years without permission or proper citations from the communities who shared them with authors has been an issue for centuries. In literature about Indian "myths and legends," authors often problematically co-opted traditional stories without proper context for the significance of the layers of meaning provided by the storyteller or known cultural understandings from the original community. They also profited monetarily from the creative and intellectual labor of the original storytellers. Alternatively, Wiwkwébthëgen tags recorded stories with "traditional knowledge labels." Some tags acknowledge that stories may not be owned by one individual, but that the artistic measures the storyteller takes should be honored and protected. The story is not copyrighted, per se, but it is also not meant to be part of the public domain, with it perhaps being shared within a family, belonging to a specific clan, or society. One traditional knowledge label for a traditional story about a loon told by Keewaydinoquay (Margaret Peschel) reads:

> This label is being used to indicate that this material is traditionally and usually not publicly available. The label is correcting a misunderstanding about the circulation options for this material and letting any users know that this material has specific conditions for circulation within the community. It is not, and never was, free, public and available for everyone at anytime. This label asks you to think about how you are going to use this material and to respect different cultural values and expectations about circulation and use.

Users may listen and add comments to the "digital heritage item" (DHI) on Wiwkwébthëgen but are informed that, while traditional stories are not necessarily copyrighted by the orator, they belong to the community and are attached to a set of cultural protocols for their use. Additionally, Neshnabék traditionally only tell certain stories in wintertime so as to not offend spiritual entities. Therefore, stories on Wiwkwébthëgen are also tagged with the following warning:

> This item is identified as being culturally sensitive regarding seasonal use. Potawatomi stories are typically shared in the winter months when the snow covers the ground. Please be respectful in observing these protocols.

Other examples of traditional knowledge labels identify items such as appliqué regalia or beadwork designs as belonging to a specific family. While many traditional knowledge labels function as prohibitive transgressions against culturally inappropriate sharing, other traditional knowledge tags encourage community participation: "This item is part of our collective history as Pokagon Potawatomi people. We encourage you to add your knowledge to this item as a means to keep these stories vibrant for future generations."

The establishment of digital modes of engagement, developed from a framework of Neshnabé cultural protocols, was intended to actualize an alternative future. This futuristic imaginary is centered on meaningful sharing of traditional knowledge such as stories, harvesting protocols, and art—far beyond social contexts defined by narratives of revitalization or artificial transplantation of traditional ways into the contemporary. As argued by Eglash et al. in their discussion of Anishinaabé education, culture-based education needs to "[redirect] scientific knowledge production and technological innovation away from corporate and state goals and closer to the priorities of Indigenous and disenfranchised communities."[55] Neshnabék find the purpose behind their collective existence in the teachings and creative products of their ancestors. Their job, as they see it, is to maintain and build upon practices defined as traditional knowledge to pass relevant and useful cultural toolkits and ways of being on to future generations. While traditional knowledge is often understood with a lens to the past—ancestral knowledge and practices that have managed to survive into the present day—Neshnabék anticipate how their traditional knowledge will benefit their people for hundreds, perhaps even thousands, of years from now. Therefore, Neshnabé traditional knowledge is a form of Indigenous futurism—a concept I explore at length in the next two chapters.

CHAPTER 3

MÉNDOKASWEN
Ecology and Spiritual Doings

Méndokaswen—ceremonial or spiritual doing
Mnedo—spirit or entity that goes about causing change[1]

"But literally the ground beneath our feet is not the ground that your ancestors walked on. There are invasive species of worms that Europeans brought over that dramatically altered the soil, changed the soil chemistry, the soil health." Not mincing words, he continues, "The water's not the same anymore. The rivers have all been dredged, they've been channelized. Many of the farm fields that you see have got pipes running underneath of them to drain the water off them so they can be farmed and not be wetlands, which is probably what they *ought* to be."[2]

Vic Bogosian, natural resources manager for the Pokagon Band Department of Natural Resources (DNR), is a quiet man. He is nicknamed "the turtle guy" by tribal members because of his work catching and monitoring different species of turtles on tribal lands to study their behavior and ecosystem health, and to make recommendations for ecological changes both within and outside tribal property. The above statement was one of the rare occasions I observed him to have any sense of disquietude in his tone. I had asked him about invasive species; at the time of our interview in late 2015 I was specifically interested in the notorious emerald ash borer that has destroyed millions of black ash trees in the Great Lakes region. I was also interested in the work he and the rest of the Pokagon DNR team were doing to revitalize local ecosystems to combat invasive species and "fix" prior terraforming practices of the nineteenth and early twentieth centuries.³ I reread his statement about the insidiousness of ecological change on "the literal ground beneath my feet," and I realized how naive I was about the severity of environmental changes since my ancestors walked this ground before 1492.

What I discovered in my interviews, and what is encapsulated in Vic's statement, is that natural resource management (NRM) professionals do not make it a goal to restore any ecosystem to its pure or unaltered state. Re-meandering the channelized watersheds on and near tribal lands as well as mitigating invasive species in the Great Lakes are goals of the Pokagon Band DNR, as these projects help control dangerous soil erosion and return waterways to historic temperatures that indigenous marine species can actually live in, among many other results. That does not mean, however, that tribal DNR is attempting to be the lieutenants of some pristine landscape. Even with unlimited funding and expertise, it is not possible to identify a region and restore it to a version of itself that is untouched by humanity. One reason, explained to me by Grant Poole, water quality specialist for the Pokagon Band, is that the data for what an area might have been like simply do not exist. According to Grant, we have pieces of the puzzle to know how a certain river may have meandered in antiquity, but we do not know its optimal temperature or soil chemistry for the species that did or should live there. And even if some of these data exist, they are only from the 1970s when federal funding became more available for these kinds of inquiry and the general American consciousness about environmental issues emerged.

But, perhaps more importantly, the other reason NRM professionals are not interested in restoring an ecology to its "pure" state is because human activity—whether directly or indirectly—has always had effects on the natural world and vice versa. For better or for worse, all nature observable today and throughout human history is the product of cultural (read: human) activity. Take the huckleberry, for example. The Pokagon Band has an annual huckleberry powwow held every Labor Day weekend called Kee-boon-mein-kaa, which translates to "You have quit picking the huckleberries."⁴ Sweet fruits such as berries play an important part of Neshnabé traditional diet and cosmology. Neshnabék have many stories about the tiny, pinkish-red fruits that embed instructions about how to be a good human and how to conduct oneself. And berries and flowers are featured prominently in Native art from the Great Lakes region. But for this discussion, huckleberries are a great example of the dialectical relationship humans have with nature. For thousands of years Native Americans developed intricate agroforestry techniques. One of those was controlling forest fires. Without these fires, the huckleberry would never have evolved to grow in the places it does now.[5] In fact, the forests of precontact America would not have so much of the tangled understory that they do today without these efforts. Forests throughout most of this continent were intensely managed for the benefit of the Indigenous communities living during that time—beneficial in terms of food,[6] travel,[7] and overall environmental resilience.

Alternatively, poorly understood ecological management strategies such as conservation that unilaterally prohibits access to traditional foraging sites has alienated Native Americans from their traditional natural resources. Unsophisticated conservation and preservation strategies that strictly prohibit ecological activities that have been conducted for hundreds, if not thousands, of years can be detrimental to the resilience of the environment. For example, Jake Kosek's anthropological work in New Mexico showed how imperialist conservation regimes imposed on certain New Mexican landscapes stifled access to traditional foraging practices. These restrictions also caused some of the most deadly and violent wildfires in recorded history. Because traditional gathering activities were prohibited, communities suffered, and the New Mexican forests also became overgrown with dry underbrush that caused the fires. On the false supposition that pristine and untouched landscapes exist, the U.S. imperialist state imposed inadequate, though well-intentioned, conservationist ideologies most astutely seen in national parks that also are unceded Indian land.[8] All this is not to say that attempts to revitalize certain ecologies are fruitless. Instead of restoring ecosystems to an imagined pristine state, most NRM professionals attempt to mitigate damage to indigenous species and, when appropriate, maintain the "function" of an ecosystem.[9]

Reflecting further on the opening vignette of this chapter, the shock to the reality and extent of environmental change in *Neshnabé ke* (Neshnabé homeland) that struck me in this conversation would not be the last I experienced throughout the entirety of this research between the years 2015 and 2023. Several years after the interview with Vic, I learned about the traditional Neshnabé women's swan dance and saw firsthand how beautiful and elegant it is. It was demonstrated at the annual *Ggaténmamen Gdankobthegnanêk* (We Honor Our Ancestors) powwow hosted by the Pokagon Band and held on Memorial Day weekend in 2019. I observed how women were relearning and "bringing back" these old dances to our community. Anishinaabé women followed each other in dignified coordination with small steps and outstretched arms that fluttered to the beat of the drum.

As a performance that could be understood in terms of cultural revitalization, I was struck by the parallel synergies at play between ideas about ecological revitalization and what is colloquially understood as cultural. I was shocked to learn that, while these dancers in their finest powwow regalia were sharing their gift with spectators of a graceful dance inspired by swans, the Pokagon Band DNR was working to kill the swan population. How could the dancers be revitalizing a traditional swan dance while the tribal government was condoning the killing of swans? The answer, I discovered, was because the species of swans DNR is targeting is wreaking havoc on other indigenous fowl populations. Many of the swans observed in the Great Lakes today are not originally from the continent. They are not the same swans who inspired our ancestors to choreograph the women's swan dance, and they are destroying many parts of the marine ecosystem as they prey on other waterfowl. Similar to imagining pristine environments, this experience was a reminder not to fall into traps of romanticization.

To truly understand Indigenous conceptions of space and place and by extension appreciate what we aim to "reclaim" in the future, there is a need to de-mythologize ideas of revitalization. In chapter 1, I survey the literature of landscape, memory, spatial narratives, and histories of territorial dispossession. This chapter builds upon the ideas developed there and explains the agency of Neshnabé ecology as more than the mere environment that humans occupy. The Indigenous world in the Great Lakes is speckled with other-than-human, even "mythological," social relationships. These entanglements with the "unreal" can be found in Neshnabé storying about the past, the present, and the future. One can appreciate Neshnabé conceptions of other-than-human relatives through clan systems such as *mko* (bear) or *nimkibneshi* (thunderbird), and how these stories about them inform identity and action. Neshnabé peoples in my research value their relationship with and ceremonial responsibilities toward other-than-human relatives. At the same time, however, the severity of ecological change and species extinction over the last five hundred years has affected these relationships in important ways. The rest of this chapter takes seriously the affective social ties that Neshnabé communities have to other-than-human and "mythological" beings, but these relationships do not exist in an Indigenous ahistorical or apolitical vacuum. They exist and are constructed through centuries of ecological change and devastation. With this ecological past, how do Neshnabék envision the future via these relationships? Indigenous peoples are tasked with ecological revitalization, species management, and many other laborious and extensive undertakings if they want to live off, or interact with, their local ecologies in any meaningful or healthy way for generations to come.

Stories and Spirits

Like any significant intellectual exercise, this research project meandered and changed as it grew. Like the rivers and streams that my ancestors traveled on, the currents of ideas that flowed throughout my research experience made me think that ontology, or the study of being, was appropriate for theorizing my data. Then, as my understanding of science and traditional knowledge developed, I realized that epistemology, or the study of how we know what we know, was more suitable. As my participation in ceremony and environmental resistance movements of Water Walkers increased, I thought that ethics was more relevant than ontology or epistemology. Finally, as I lived, worked, researched, and wrote while dwelling in Neshnabé ke, I concluded that phenomenology—and by extension, the poetics of dwelling—was what fully articulated my participants' experiences. Phenomenology, or the study of experiences and consciousness, encapsulated the interviews, participant observation, and meditation that birthed this book. Like meandering rivers that carry and deposit particles on the point bar of a naturally meandering river, discarded philosophical frameworks like ontology, epistemology, and ethics were useful for carrying this research forward, but were ultimately deposited.

Insight is revealed not by objective truth but by the experiences we have on the quest for it. From a Neshnabé perspective, knowledge is a gift that does not belong to any one individual. These gifts are received in ceremony from the spirit world. Indeed, while many of us are lucky enough to learn from our elders, they too receive their teachings from their many years of living and experiencing the world and from their sacred proximity to the spirit world. Therefore, what role does the spiritual play in how we might better understand ecology and, by extension, futurity?

Anthropology has already addressed the concept of other-than-human beings in interesting ways. "How other kinds of beings see us matters. That other kinds of beings see us changes things."[10] In his ethnography, *How Forests Think*, Eduardo Kohn explains that, for the Indigenous Runa peoples of the Amazon with whom he lived and conducted anthropological research, sleeping facedown leaves you vulnerable to being attacked and eaten by a jaguar. This is because a facedown person cannot return the gaze of the jaguar, resulting in a perception of non-sentience. According to Runa understanding, jaguars respect and recognize those who sleep up and show their face as non-prey.

The words mnedo or *manitou* (the latter is the more common Ojibwe spelling) are often translated as "spirit." In fact, Manitou Beach located off Devil's Lake in southern Michigan is a popular tourist destination. Devil's Lake is the site of a Potawatomi village that existed until at least 1830. Clumsy visitor information about the tourist town near Devil's Lake incorrectly explains that the name derives from the Potawatomi word "Manitou" meaning evil spirit. Similar to the settler narratives of dubious origin about contemporary place-names discussed in chapter 1, tourist media at Devil's Lake go on to describe a story whereby a daughter of a Potawatomi chief drowned in the lake, resulting in the names Manitou (spirit) Beach and Devil's (aka evil spirit) Lake. Mnedo has never meant evil spirit; in fact, it barely means spirit at all. Mnedowêk have never lived as humans, and more accurately the word means "entity that goes about causing change." Because mnedowêk have never lived as humans, places where people have died are irrelevant to the use of mnedo as a place-name. Therefore, Manitou Beach being named after a tragic death is a specious story; it makes no actual sense. To discuss mnedowêk as ghosts is a gross misunderstanding.[11]

Unlike the tourist information explanation of how Devil's Lake got its name, Neshnabé writer Basil Johnston notes that some of the first wayfarers and missionaries translated manitou not as evil spirit, but as

God. Today Neshnabék still pray to *Gzémnedo* ("creating spirit") or *Gzé* meaning "creating" and mnedo, meaning "change-making entity." However, even God is a mistranslation that led to pedestrian understandings by Europeans. Given Johnston's literary candor, it is worth quoting him at length:

> Thereafter, whenever an aboriginal person uttered the word manitou, Western Europeans thought it meant spirit. When a medicine person uttered the term *manitouwun* to refer to some curative or healing property in a tree or plant, they took it to mean spirit. When a person said the word *manitouwut* to refer to the sacrosanct mood or atmosphere of a place, they assumed it meant spirit. And when a person spoke the word *manitouwih* to allude to a medicine person with miraculous powers, they construed it to mean spirit . . . Western Europeans took it for granted that aboriginal people, being of simple heart and mind, believed in the presence of little spirits in rocks, trees, groves, and waterfalls, much as the primitive peoples of Europe believed in goblins, trolls, and leprechauns. Men and women who addressed the manitous were believed to worship spirits, idols . . . But most aboriginal people understood their respective languages well enough to know from the context the precise sense and meaning intended by the word manitou or any of its other derivatives. Depending on the context, they knew that besides spirit, the term also meant property, essence, transcendental, mystical, muse, patron, and divine.[12]

Johnston explains that **Ktthémnedo** is an enigma that created the cosmos and all life. And to honor this gift, all humans could do was imitate Ktthémnedo's generosity. Therefore, the Midéwiwin Lodge is one of gratitude and thankfulness. Certain areas of Neshnabé ke—particular waterfalls, cliffs, or recesses in the forests—harbored greater presences of mnedowêk such that they became important sites for conducting ceremonies or, as translated by Jim Thunder in his coveted collection of stories, *mnedokazwek*.[13]

On my first trip to Midéwiwin ceremonies in June 2016, I walked along the skinny shores of Lake Superior at the bottom of a steep cliff. The shoreline is speckled with green, pink, and gray river rocks, driftwood, and coarse sand. Most famously, perfectly round river rocks, usually the size of marbles, can be found. They are possibly a kind of stone called

Omarolluk and form over thousands of years.[14] They look so peculiar because of their perfectly spherical shape. Stories shared with me from *Midés* of the Three Fires Lodge said that these rocks are what became of Neshnabék trying to escape malefic Indian agents and drowning in the rough currents of Lake Superior. They return to the shores and remind us to practice ceremony because they cannot.

The erosion in this part of the lakeshore is swift and can be dangerous. Where the forest meets the thin, rocky shores of Lake Superior can change yearly. Indeed, in 2017, the Three Fires Midéwiwin Lodge had to abandon the wooded cliff site as a place of ceremony that had been used for decades. Just one year after I participated in Midéwiwin ceremonies for the first time, I returned to the rocky cliff alone near dusk. It was a cold, gray late afternoon day and the space was eerie and desolate. Clouds had blocked the setting sun and diffused what would have been long shadows made by towering trees singing wind songs as leaves rustled hundreds of feet in the air. This rural area of Wisconsin near Michigan's Upper Peninsula has unique weather patterns, making even a summer day in July feel like a chilly mid-October evening. The durability and warmth of the space within the lodge where we would be nearly sitting on top of each other for lack of room had been replaced by a rickety, cold, and deserted frame. The ground looked the same, except that the cliff's edge was much closer, dangerous, and foreboding.

Midés lamented the loss of this ceremonial space because looking out toward the east near the cliff of an elevated plateau over the gleaming lake was so powerful for them, especially during a segment in ceremony where mnedowêk are called upon in all four cardinal directions. Any ceremony conducted by Neshnabék requires the aid of mnedowêk. They are summoned by whistling in all four directions in practices as ubiquitous as pipe ceremonies to those reserved for special times of the year. Being able to see for miles over Lake Superior provided a transcendental experience for participants in Midéwiwin ceremony. Cool breezes over the rough currents of the coldest, deepest Great Lake made it feel as though the mnedowêk were whistling back. Nestled a mile or two back in the woods, this cliff site is not dissimilar from sites Midéwiwin ceremonies were conducted on in secret until 1978 when the Indian Religious Freedom Act was passed, which provided protection for Indigenous communities in the U.S. to practice their traditional beliefs that were previously punishable by fine or imprisonment.

Neshnabé understandings of story and of mnedowêk complicate Western attempts to separate subjective and objective phenomena. In his review of phenomenology in anthropology, Throop explains that whether or not an ethnographer or an audience *believes* in "mythological beings" or stories of the supernatural from a particular context is irrelevant. It is worth quoting him at length:

> There is no strict line demarcating the subjective and objective because both are necessarily articulated by attitudes toward experience that may render certain aspects of experience as thoughts, images, feelings, sentiments, moods, sensations, perceptions, judgements, and forms of appreciation, on the one hand, and properties of physical objects, bodies, persons, animals, celestial phenomena, spirits, natural occurrences, etc., on the other.[15]

The binaries between the subjective and objective, the natural and supernatural, are not meaningful for understanding the expanse of our experiences as humans. Heidegger theorized existence and being as only possible in relationship to the supernatural. Heidegger's concept of the fourfold includes the earth, sky, divinities, and mortals. These component parts cannot exist independently. Humans occupy space and place in a physical sense—as I sit in a chair located on Earth while I write this book. By extension, humans exist under a sky while celestial bodies walk across the sky from east to west in relationship to our observations from below. And regarding divinities, mortals—while dwelling with each other on the land and under the sky—imbue divinities with existence, but also with meaning. Therefore, humanity is an existence of poetic dwelling.[16]

Social anthropologist Tim Ingold has written much on the topic of dwelling, principally in his extensive collection of essays in *The Perception of the Environment*. Most notable for this discussion, Ingold asks how people are to understand the different ways that humans understand caribou in the wild. "Wildlife biologists are liable to react to native stories about animals presenting themselves of their own accord with a mixture of cynicism and incredulity."[17] He goes on to ask:

> Are the folk who tell these stories mad, lost in a fog of irrational superstition, talking in allegories, or simply having us on? Whatever the answer may be, science insists that stories are stories, and as such have no purchase on what really goes on in the natural world.[18]

The issue that Ingold is reflecting on is the age-old duality between empirical versus conjectural, science versus art, objectivity versus subjectivity, and so on. Like nature and culture, which have a dialectic relationship because all life is in an interspecies relationship, Native stories and scientific explanation are both agents in human experience. We do not exist in an incorporeal space where reality is quantifiable and quaint folk tales are invented for our amusement. Instead of presuming the objective stance of the ethnographic observer, in his ethnography *Fictionalizing Anthropology*, Stuart McLean explains that "[mythical beings] appear less as human projections onto the blank screen of nature than as condensations out of the primordial matter from which everything in the universe is fashioned, including humans and (presumably) the stories that humans tell."[19]

Neshnabé stories have been recorded by anthropologists, folklorists, and hobbyists for centuries, but researchers have mostly failed to theorize how these stories evolve to articulate contemporary experiences, let alone imagine the future. As an alternative ethic and methodology of research, in *Routes: Travel and Translation in the Late 20th Century* James Clifford extends this discussion of *Bodwéwadmi* futurisms to other Indigenous communities in North America. He reflects on his consultation experience with the Portland, Oregon, Museum of Art, which was planning to reinstall an exhibit of Indigenous Northwest Coast artifacts. A group of Tlingit elders was invited to participate in the planning. Contrary to the museum's expectations that the Tlingit elders would explain the purpose and origins of the objects, instead they used these items as catalysts for memoir, politics, and moral discussions. Initiating songs and stories from a deeply felt appreciation for the works of their relatives and ancestors, these items were entangled in an Indigenous matrix of history, law, and "myths." What became clear, Clifford writes, is that "from the elders' viewpoint, the collected objects were not primarily 'art,' (but) 'records,' 'history' and 'law,' inseparable from myths and stories expressing ongoing moral lessons with current political force."[20] This exchange

Clifford calls a "contact zone" whereby items in a collection were used as texts to read and understand contemporary and perhaps future political relationships between museums, Indigenous communities, and beyond.

Other-than-human beings played a central role in one of the stories shared by elders in the basement of the Portland Art Museum. A headdress with representations of an octopus was brought out. The story that was shared by one of the Tlingit elders as a result recounts how a huge octopus with its appendages blocked the bay, keeping all the fish from reaching the shores. A Tlingit hero had to kill the octopus so that his community would not starve to death and the salmon could reach their spawning grounds. "And by the end of the story the octopus has metamorphosed into state and federal agencies currently restricting the rights of Tlingits to take salmon according to tradition."[21] The evidence for Indigenous storytelling, as seen in Clifford's accounts, is not new or rare. Indeed, it has been recorded in many works, but has been theorized in terms of traditional accounts "surviving" to the contemporary moment or Indigenous attempts to "revitalize" the stories of their ancestors. But rarely have these stories been viewed in light of their application to present-day issues, as Clifford's example shows. And more rarely still have these traditional stories been theorized to understand Indigenous conceptions of the future. Before embarking on a discussion of how these stories about other-than-human relatives and "mythical" beings imagine Neshnabé futures, I first situate scholarly theorizations of humanity's entanglements with other-than-human relatives.[22]

All Our Anthropocene Relations

All human societies have their own unique conceptions of creatures like monsters and ghosts. The stories we tell about them have powerful forces in our relationships with the natural world and with each other. They serve important functions for how society is structured or how some think it *ought* to be structured. Reflecting on the pageantry of "mythical" beings alongside mnedowêk or spirit beings, Ana Lowenhaupt Tsing argues that other creatures like ghosts "help us read life's enmeshment in landscapes," while monsters "ask us to consider the wonders and terrors of symbiotic entanglement in the Anthropocene [. . .] [they] point us toward life's symbiotic entanglement across bodies."[23] A new or perhaps more serious consideration of these entities in anthropology is part of the recent multispecies research turn in ethnographic inquiry, even while these investigations into human and other-than-human relationships have a long history in other disciplines. Kirksey and Helmreich offer a succinct review of multispecies anthropological scholarship. While their review tackles how multispecies work is addressed in all four subfields of anthropology, as well as biology, zoology, and even life sciences, their article is written for and made relevant to ethnographers. What has become popular to term "the species turn" in ethnology (similar to the anthropology of knowledge production written about in chapter 2) has had a phantom existence within cultural anthropology's over one-hundred-fifty-year existence in the U.S. Indeed, Kirksey and Helmreich point out that Lewis Henry Morgan's *The American Beaver and His Works* (1868) made an argument ahead of its time for the protection of rights of nonhumans.[24] Today's renewed interest in nonhumans' perspectives, agencies, and entanglements with humans has not only inspired new types of ethnographic research but also caused theorists to look at the discipline's roots and traditions in a different light.[25]

Biocultural evolution argues that changes in the human genome can be and often are caused by environmental factors. And because human populations do not all experience the same environmental factors in the same ways, the fractions by which humans are grouped in "races" or "cultures" will have higher likelihoods of passing down community-specific genetic mutations. Sickle cell anemia, for example, can be lethal to its carriers who are often from Central and North African countries, as well as some areas of the Mediterranean. However, when passed down from one parent, or when it is otherwise expressed heterogeneously as a sickle cell trait, this type of hemoglobin can actually be beneficial,[26] as the individual with this trait becomes resistant to malaria.[27] Therefore, sickle cell hemoglobin is an example of natural selection differentially experienced according to communities of people in a specific region.

Anna Tsing might argue, however, that all human nature is inevitably biocultural, and that "[h]uman nature is an interspecies relationship."[28] What is taught in nearly all undergraduate evolutionary anthropology classes as biocultural evolution is not actually all that unusual or special. Examples of biocultural evolution are everywhere: sickle cell trait, engorged fruits,[29] and the corn plant[30] are only the tip of the iceberg. These are just the most obvious examples of humanity's interconnectedness with all life. But this interconnectedness is sometimes violent, especially as climate change wreaks havoc on ecological methods and deeply rooted relationships that had been maintained for thousands of years. While multispecies ethnography is not new, just overlooked, today's scholarship is influenced by a much larger mechanism than that of nineteenth-century theorists like Lewis Henry Morgan and his beavers. That mechanism is climate change.

When atmospheric chemist Paul Crutzen officially introduced the idea of the Anthropocene in 2000, scientists and social theorists recognized that the world is changing in uncanny ways as the result of human activity. Some have acknowledged the need to consult with local and Indigenous communities to better manage natural resources in local contexts.[31] Others have critiqued these consultations when done poorly, as it leads to the consumption of intellectual property without giving anything back to the host communities who provided the knowledge and methods (see chapter 2).

Anthropologists have paid close attention to how climate change affects local communities and world systems in recent years, specifically in work on "the Anthropocene." The Anthropocene is an unofficial geologic category, but that humans have had a profound impact on Earth that has affected all observable life is a consensus in the scientific community. The Anthropocene is a concept that encapsulates an era when humans began to have a measurable effect on Earth's climate, starting after the industrial era of the global North. Anthropogenic climate change has affected how human populations interact with the environment, to say the very least. This may mean staying indoors more throughout the day because of high afternoon temperatures, being displaced from ancestral lands because of desertification, experiencing loss of marine resources because of warmer waters, etc. Unsurprisingly, anthropological research investigating how climate change is affecting communities has increased in recent years.

In her research on place-making trends in the tourism industry of the Caribbean, Amelia Moore calls this emergent tradition the "Anthropocene idea." She goes further to define it as "more than a 'mere' geologic category limited to the earth sciences. The Anthropocene idea is also a persuasive discourse that enables conceptual anxieties, productive contradictions, research opportunities, and entrepreneurial actions."[32] The Anthropocene as it relates to social science is both a context in which ethnographic research is conducted and an emergent tradition of anthropology that includes how anthropogenic climate change differently affects communities around the world. In this framework, research subjects are analyzed in light of their perceived lack of agency in the face of overwhelming climate change and the development of policies they may have felt they had no part in creating. However, Moore strongly urges anthropologists not to lose their fastidiousness by conducting research "in" an unreflexively and amorphous Anthropocene space:

> [E]ven in an era of rapid change, we still need critical analysis of the characterization of that change and responses to it . . . We need anthropological analysis that can examine the characterization of life and changes that are being made within authoritative fields of power and that can follow these ideas as they affect institutional policies with real consequences for the everyday lives of the people we work with around the world.[33]

Even in the dire circumstances that climate change creates for thousands of communities around the world, as theorists, our job is to make space to think and critique lest we cause more damage by problematic policies, privileging some voices over others, etc. Like the criticisms of Linda Tuhiwai Smith in *Decolonizing Methodologies* discussed in the introduction, crisis research empowers problematic outside institutions to describe what they perceive as Indigenous pathologies and offer patronizing solutions.[34] When it comes to something as ubiquitous as climate change, Neshnabék approach these issues having already survived what they view as the apocalypse. Potawatomi researcher Kyle Whyte has written extensively about the issues of well-meaning environmental projects centered on "crisis epistemology" whereby Indigenous peoples are asked to sacrifice their lands and access yet again for yet another emergency that they themselves do not feel they helped to create.[35]

By not considering the Indigenous stewards of the land in question, developers, environmentalists, policy makers, non-governmental organizations and others remain complicit in the same settler colonial project some of their ancestors began. National parks whose properties were seized from tribal nations—often treaty-based reservation lands—were once crises of national identity and settler nation-building; damming projects that displaced Indigenous peoples from their now-flooded land were once crises of energy and national infrastructure; bombing tests on Indigenous and Hispano communities in New Mexico resulting in radioactive fallout were once a crisis of national security between warring nations. There is an abundance of important anthropological research on how climate change disproportionately affects Indigenous peoples around the world. However, my challenge is not to repeat this brand of crisis research, since in doing so conclusions often arise about the inevitability of Indigenous demise—not unlike the salvage ethnographic projects at the turn of the twentieth century.

Anthropocene anthropology as crisis research forecloses Indigenous agency in the future. The participants I interviewed and with whom I worked already understand how changes in the environment have affected them. What they were interested in sharing with me were their articulations of agency within the Anthropocene and into the future. Unlike a human-centered cosmology in which humans cause and are future arbiters of the global atmospheric condition, Neshnabé communities see themselves as just a small link in the multispecies relationship, even in the crises of global climate change. In *Fictionalizing Anthropology*, Stuart McLean asks, "Could the capacity to imagine not only our connectedness to other kinds of beings but also the possibility of our radical absence from the scene be a prerequisite of thought and creativity, not least in our present and much discussed state of ecological emergency?"[36] To these ends, is there a way out of this spiraling crisis approach in what feels like a global climate disaster worthy of such anxiety? How do Neshnabé perspectives of the environment and our relationship to other-than-human beings help us see beyond crisis to imagine an approach that is ethical, that does not reproduce colonial violence, and that is agentive and empowering?

Settlers are especially anxious about climate change in this moment in time. This is understandable as we all reckon with species extinctions and endangerments, resource depletion, and social unrest in the Anthropocene. The uncanny processes of toxic waste, global temperature rises in the ocean and air, and extreme weather catastrophes are just a few examples that comprise anthropogenic and resulting feelings of anxiety and helplessness—made all the more dire given the blasé attitudes of many politicians and corporate boards that have the power to do something about climate change but obfuscate their responsibilities. Coupled with deep-time geological studies that show that global climate change is linked with multiple mass extinctions on Earth,[37] it is no wonder why anthropogenic climate change is anxiety-inducing. Anna Lowenhaupt Tsing's *Arts of Living on a Damaged Planet* is a book written in two parts: *Monsters* and *Ghosts*. The reader must physically turn the book upside down to read both. Like the physical awkwardness of the book, the collection is composed of multidisciplinary approaches to understanding climate change from authors in fields one would not normally interact with such as philosophers, environmental biologists, and medical doctors. In *Monsters*, researchers describe how humans are entangled with nonhumans, and how human actions have been damaging in a multiplicity of ways. *Ghosts* exposes the evidence of the less obvious forms of damage, principally the unnoticed presence(s) of "ghosts," such as the channelized waterways I describe later in this chapter, the lack of Native peoples in science fiction explained in chapter 4, and the swans mentioned in the beginning of this chapter. The editors explain that ghosts and monsters serve as analytical points from which cogent conversations emerge to challenge humanity as the primary agent to address climate change. They explain:

> In dialectical fashion, ghosts and monsters unsettle *anthropos*, the Greek term for "human," from its presumed center stage in the Anthropocene by highlighting the webs of histories and bodies from which all life, including human life, emerges. Rather than imagining phantasms outside of natural history, the monsters and ghosts of this book are observable parts of the world. We learn them through multiple practices of knowing, from vernacular to official science, and draw inspiration from both the arts and sciences to work across genres of observation and storytelling.[38]

In contrast to settler anxieties about climate change, Indigenous experiences of issues attributed to the Anthropocene are different: Indigenous communities have already undergone loss of place and access to resources, species extinction, and dire social unrest because of settler-colonialism. They continue to live with those consequences today. Potawatomi philosopher Kyle Whyte explains:

Different forms of colonialism, of course, whether through environmental destruction, land dispossession or forced relocation, have ended Indigenous peoples' local relationships to thousands of plants, animals, insects, and entire ecosystems. While these relationships often continue to be enacted through Indigenous peoples' living memories, heritage, "felt knowledges", social identities (e.g. clans), and philosophies, they have stopped as relationships involving direct ecological interaction.[39]

Indigenous peoples are ahead of the curve to process the emotional shock and trauma of cataclysmic environmental and social devastation. Indigenous communities are not exclusively engaging with psychologically working through this Anthropocene-induced anxiety the way mainstream ecologists are.

Stories about Neshnabé other-than-human relatives use traditional understandings of interspecies relationships to make sense of environmental trauma, humanity's requisite humility, and the role of human responsibility moving forward into the future. What has been written about interspecies relationships so far has focused strictly on very material organisms. I am adding to that conversation that interspecies relationships between humans and supernatural beings must also be considered. These different beings can teach us about interspecies relationships in ways that other kinds of living organisms do not.

Futurity in Ecological Revitalization

When Americans first settled in the Great Lakes area they spent a massive amount of time, energy, and resources in straightening out or "channelizing" the naturally meandering rivers and streams. In the late 1800s and early 1900s logging was a substantial industry in Michigan. Before trucks and railways could transport logs to mills and other processing areas, they had to be floated down rivers (figure 6). So, hundreds of wetland areas in Michigan were channelized for this form of log transportation to be possible. This was disastrous for water biodiversity, since these projects destroyed aquatic habitats and sent a lot of marine ecologies into environmental regime changes with adverse consequences that environmental ecologists still cannot fully account for. This straightening

FIGURE 6 Michigan logging practices in the early twentieth century. Photo courtesy of University of Michigan Bentley Historical Library / HS4687. https://quod.lib.umich.edu/b/bhl/x-hs4687/hs4687.

out of the waterways was beneficial for capitalism, because when logging was a more significant enterprise in the late 1800s until the 1930s, companies sent their products barreling down streams for easy transport. This commerce further disrupted marine life, and even destroyed the few remaining wild rice paddies that Indigenous communities relied on.

Now, tribes in my research are taking on projects to re-meander the rivers and streams. Starting in 2011, the Pokagon Band DNR began re-meandering the Dowagiac River on Pokagon Potawatomi tribal lands. During my preliminary fieldwork in October 2015, I remember finding the site where the Dowagiac River was being revitalized very unromantic. When one thinks of ecological *revitalization*, front loaders and backhoes posed next to new dredges and piles of dirt are not the first things to come to mind. This was one of the sites that the Pokagon Band was trying to re-meander to restore wetlands to their natural state. Jennifer Kanine, director for the Pokagon Band DNR, explains:

The thought was that re-meandering the river would provide a more intact ecological system, versus the currently straight and dredged Dowagiac River . . . Right now, the river is straightened, it's dredged, it's got deep banks, it's disconnected from its flood plain. It's a very flashy system when it rains, so by putting the river back into its meander bends, what you are doing is reconnecting it to its flood plains. You are slowing down that water, and you are helping filter that water that comes through that area.[40]

Re-meandering the Dowagiac River creates more niches for plant and animal species such as salmon, turtles, snakes, and even wild rice—a traditional food source for Neshnabé peoples. Overall, meandering rivers are more beneficial to flora and fauna and are significantly less prone to flash flooding. The temperatures of the water are more stable, and meandering rivers are more resistant to harmful invasive species.

As the physical scars of channelization are rerouted for more healthy meandering waterways, how capitalism and extractive industries are marked on the landscape is rewritten. Environmental historians similarly read the landscape in ways that tease apart the layers of human interactions that left their marks on the earth. Sandhya Ganapathy explains that "the work of environmental historians has illuminated how particular landscapes are formed through natural processes and complex historical events."[41] One ethnography that demonstrates this argument is Jake Kosek's *Understories*. In this ethnography, he reveals how histories of dispossession and cultural politics can be read on the landscape. One example he offers is the 2000 Los Alamos fire. What began as a prescribed forest burning on May 4, 2000, on Cerro Grande Peak became the most damaging fire in the history of the state of New Mexico[42] "consuming more than 47,000 acres of forest, destroying 239 homes, displacing 400 families, and sending 11,000 people from Los Alamos and 25,000 more from White Rock, Española, Santa Clara Pueblo, San Ildefonso Pueblo, and Chimayó from their homes."[43] Through a series of land-grant dispossessions by the U.S. government from Hispano farming communities, families lost their access to natural resources.

Another result of this dispossession was the ecological regime change of forests in the region. Dry undergrowth, which was managed and cleared away by Hispano farmers for generations, was allowed to grow after they were denied access to land by the U.S. settler colonial government. Instead of conserving a "pristine forest wilderness," what the negation of Indigenous and Hispano access to forest resources did was to create a "tinderbox effect" of dry undergrowth that would later fuel the most destructive fire in New Mexico's history. Like the tinderbox effect in Kosek's research, channelized waterways in the Great Lakes can be read as texts on the land and tell the stories of extractive industries.

My introduction to straightened rivers was via a discussion about wild rice with Roger LaBine (Lac Vieux Desert Band of Lake Superior Chippewa Indians) back in 2015. Roger is known as a Rice Chief in his community. When I first met him, he was facilitating a wild rice processing workshop with non-Native students at the Goodwillie Environmental School in Grand Rapids, Michigan, on behalf of the non-tribal Great Lakes Lifeways Institute. He explained to me that one of the species most affected by channelization was wild rice.

Wild rice was an important staple food source for Neshnabé peoples as it could be stored for long periods of time and grew in abundance, and is very nutritious. The Neshnabé word for wild rice is *mnomen* meaning the "good seed." Wild rice served either sweet with maple syrup and berries or savory with game meat is a dish used in Midéwiwin ceremonies as feast food. In fact, mnomen plays such a significant part in Neshnabé cosmology that it is part of our origin stories. One of those stories is the Neshnabé migration from the east coast of North America. It is said that at one time the Potawatomi, Odawa, and Ojibwe were all one people living in present-day Nova Scotia and Maine. They received instructions from prophets who told them that new people were coming to this land. These new people would bring disease and violence. Before this was to happen, Neshnabék were to migrate down the Saint Lawrence Seaway to "the place where food grows on water." That food was wild rice. And as these ancient Neshnabék "followed the migis shell" toward the Great Lakes, different communities broke off and became later identified as Odawa or Ojibwe. The story has been translated from traditional birch bark scrolls etched with pictographs and is still read in ceremony at Midéwiwin Lodges.

In tandem with re-meandering rivers, the Pokagon Band is also involved in wild rice revitalization. This is a laborious process that has been attempted using several different methods—some more successful than others. The most successful involved purchasing immature rice "transplants" from other Neshnabé communities with more established wild rice resources in Michigan. In summer 2017, while seven months pregnant, I helped transplant some of these "rice babies" in a lake on Pokagon tribal lands. Wild rice sprouts are gently laid on top of the water. Oars are used to shove the roots down into the mucky lake bottom just off the shores of the lake.

Summers in Michigan can be humid, unforgiving, and oppressive. The rubber muck boots and suffocating life vest on my thick pregnant body made the heat worse. But occasionally I and the two other women I worked with found respite in the gift of gentle breezes that tickled our sweat. My mother-in-law would later praise our efforts in rice transplanting. She exclaimed, "Aw, little Miksani's been ricing already!" Her comment motioned toward my future child's participation in ecological revitalization and the implication that he would continue to do so in the future. Two years later, as I write this, only some of the rice has taken root. It will likely take several years of intensive transplanting before sustainable growth occurs.

Despite some setbacks in transplanting wild rice in Pokagon tribal water, the tribe still hosts wild rice processing "camps" so that Potawatomi people do not forget these traditional ways of preparing heritage foods. By purchasing or receiving as gifts bags of unprocessed wild rice from other Neshnabé communities, the Pokagon Band shares with its citizens how it is done. Steps of the process include blanching the rice in large copper kettles over a fire, "dancing" the rice to shift the rice loose from its husks, winnowing the rice in birch trays so that the husks float into the air leaving behind the heavier rice contents in the tray, and finally manually de-husking the rest of the rice by hand.

Blanching is my favorite step. Stirring the rice with a wooden paddle is meditative, and the sweet smell of rice combined with the occasional "pop" sound of some kernels connects me to my ancestors. I can feel their labor through my clumsy efforts to process the rice myself. Blanching also offers another reward as an occasional snack. Blanching is meant to loosen the husks from the rice inside, but high heat results in a few popped kernels instead. Popped rice tastes a lot like popcorn. One can often catch the occasional rice thief helping themselves to some of the white puffs, tossing them in their mouth when they think no one was looking.

"Dancing" the rice is a bit more difficult. The dancer holds themselves up with two cedar poles on either side of their body while they gracefully use their clean rice moccasins to massage the warm oblong pebbles laid out on a leather mat on the ground. When done properly, dancing the rice results in de-husked rice and a few broken kernels. Maintaining a balance between leveraging the weight of one's body without snapping the rice in half is an exercise that puts any cross-fit workout to shame. Because dancers wear special moccasins for this process, they cannot leave the leather mat. Doing so would contaminate the rice. So, participants in the rice camp do their best to look after the dancer, checking in on them and offering them water.

After dancing comes winnowing—a process that challenges ricers' dexterity. This step is meant to fully de-husk the remaining kernels of rice by sifting the rice in midair. Using the momentum of the birch bark winnowing tray, the ricer must toss the rice into the air in a way that allows the light husks to float away, while quickly catching the remaining rice in the tray without dropping any. The sound of rice being sifted reminds me of gentle static sounds used in infants' white-noise machines to put them to sleep. I imagined this calming sound, combined with the fresh fall air when ricing camp traditionally takes place, lulling countless generations of Neshnabé infants to sleep in their cradleboards attached to low branches of trees, gently swinging back and forth.

Like embodied cartographies, the future is made meaningful and material because of the stories we tell about it. Ecological revitalization projects such as re-meandering rivers and transplanting wild rice are as agentive in actualizing Neshnabé futures as conducting ceremony or mnedokazwek, whereby mnedo are being called to conduct a specific purpose. The interplay of different forms of Neshnabé animate and inanimate storytelling advances Indigenous eco-politics in the Great Lakes region. These stories catalyze material change as re-meandering rivers and revitalizing wild rice. Like reclaiming space argued in chapter 1, traditional stories that contextualize present-day ecological issues combined with ecological revitalization projects are constitutive of Neshnabé futurisms.

CHAPTER 4

BKANATHMOWNEN

Indigenous Science Fiction and Neshnabé Futurity

Bkanathmownen—Stories that take an alternative perspective on things; science fiction

The title of this chapter combines two Potawatomi phrases, *bkan*, meaning different or speculative, and *yathmownen*, referring to stories, news, or doings. This neologism articulates a Neshnabé register of futurity that manifests in two ways: through storytelling, otherwise understood as "Indigenous science fiction," and activism or mobilizing Neshnabé futurity. Like Chippewa scholar Danika Medak-Saltzman, I contend that

> the emergence and proliferation of narrative and filmic imaginings of Indigenous futures [is] representing the creative arm of the Indigenous futurist movement, which joins the more overtly political arm of the movement evident in the protest, legal, and advocacy work, all of which are vital to seeing our way toward, fighting for, and calling forth better futures.[1]

Rather than just escapism, speculative storytelling plays an important role in society, especially for Indigenous communities. Everyone has a different frame of reference when it comes to science or speculative fiction. Therefore, I detail just what I mean by the term in the following section. The best way I found to do this is by braiding the co-constitutive histories of science fiction, the discipline of anthropology, and the colonial threads that inform the sort of representational work Indigenous peoples are engaged with today.

Anthropology and Science Fiction

Science fiction narratives have had a profound effect on society, with different communities affected in varying ways. Indeed, some theorists have argued that all interpretive portrayals are science fictional. In *Do Metaphors Dream of Literal Sleep?* Seo-Young Chu argues that all modes of representation exist on a spectrum of science fiction: "all representation is science-fictional because all reality is cognitively estranging."[2] Using Darko Suvin's concept of "cognitive estrangement," Chu argues that what differentiates nonfiction storytelling from creative works that are easily recognizable as science fiction—time travel, space explorations, extraterrestrials, and the like—has to do with whether the cognitive referents that are the focus of the narrative are considered mundane and possible by audiences or whether they are eccentric and impractical. According to Chu, while all representations are science fiction, nonfiction in literature or its equivalent in art—realism, for example—are modes that simply demand less intellectual and creative energy to achieve their referential goals. In this sense, we can understand science fiction as a "mimetic discourse whose objects of representation are nonimaginary yet cognitively estranging."[3] While some have focused their attention on the differences among genres similar to science fiction such as fantasy, surrealism, and magical realism, Chu argues that they all make up forms of science fiction. The differences between them are simply the cognitive referents that are featured. For example, in surrealism, the featured "cognitively estranging referent is the phenomenon of dreaming."[4] By extension, as this chapter will show, one feature of Indigenous science fiction is that it cognitively estranges colonialism as the normalized and naturalized referent.

Because science fiction, anthropology, and colonialism are braided together, this chapter cannot adequately address one without gesturing toward the other two. Anthropology is said to have been the "handmaiden of colonialism," and as John Rieder's excellent *Colonialism and the Emergence of Science Fiction* shows, the genre of science fiction as we know it today was manifested in the imperial centers of colonizing nations. Science fiction is a literary and aesthetic mode that emerges first in metropolitan centers such as Great Britain and the United States. Narratives of science fiction project versions of colonial anxieties onto imagined futures through stories told from the point of view of colonists.

As Rieder explains, "the period of the most fervid imperialist expansion in the late nineteenth century is also the crucial period for the emergence of the genre [...] Science fiction comes into visibility first in those countries most heavily involved in imperialist projects."[5]

Therefore, science fiction is distinctly colonial compared to other genres. In the same way the discipline of anthropology rode in the wake of European explorers to document different cultures around the world and pave the way for the exploitation and oppression of those communities, early science fiction imagined similar scenarios unfolding in speculative futures but with Europeans as the victims instead. As science fiction writers like H. G. Wells, author of the classic *War of the Worlds*, speculated about the violence of extraterrestrials upon making first contact with Earth, Wells made direct comparisons to European imperialism, thereby normalizing and naturalizing his country's specific brand of colonial violence by applying it to speculative alien societies throughout the Universe. Describing the invading Martians, Wells states:

> And before we judge of them too harshly, we must remember what ruthless and utter destruction our own species has wrought, not only upon animals, such as the vanished bison and the dodo, but upon its own inferior races. The Tasmanians, in spite of their human likeness were entirely swept out of existence in a war of extermination waged by European immigrants, in the space of fifty years. Are we such apostles of mercy as to complain if the Martians warred in the same spirit?[6]

Imagining a likeness between imagined alien races and those past (and concurrent) colonizer actions and predispositions is a "paranoid narcissism."[7] This inclination to naturalize imperial warfare is, as Rieder points out, a characteristic of social Darwinism of the times in which *War of the Worlds* and other major science fiction literary canons were written. Danika Medak-Saltzman has gone so far as to call mainstream science fiction depictions of "procolonial, prosupremacy of (certain) humans, proextractive, procapitalist, and promasculinist elements ... that present the natural world and (certain) peoples as needing to be tamed, exploited, civilized, removed, or vanquished."[8]

And as I have argued elsewhere, these procolonial representations include how Indigenous peoples are talked about in science fiction. Because, while there is ample evidence to suggest that Indigenous peoples would continue to be erased or made totally irrelevant in the future, ironically, the Indigene as a concept comes up surprisingly often in science fiction media—not just in classic texts like Wells's *War of the Worlds*, but in some of the most recent science fiction media. Following this paradoxical tradition of indexing the Indigene while absenting Indigenous peoples, in season three of *The Expanse*—a book and TV series that takes place in the year 2350—one of the main characters, Jim Holden, hovers over the shoulder of his comrade as they contemplate the existentially jarring reality of having discovered an extraterrestrial, perhaps even extra-universal, entity wreaking havoc on their solar system. He says, "When the European tall ships first arrived on the American continent, the natives couldn't see them." He goes on to explain that, because the sight was so shocking and the cultures so different, Native Americans faced an assured destruction. He concludes Native peoples were all wiped out, suggesting that they might face the same end.[9]

The Expanse is not a cherry-picked example to support my own musings, but a poignant one, because it is a futuristic science fiction series that takes social issues and class struggle as central plot points—a rather rare feature of science fiction until recently. This exciting focus on class and inequality in *The Expanse* series creates narrative depth, inspires critical reflection, and, frankly, makes for a better story than most science fiction that came before. That is why, despite the emphasis of social-political inequality, supported by the creative use of different pidgin languages by the oppressed populations as well as other ethnographically rich materials, the series is all the more disappointing from a Native person's perspective. Indigenous communities being discussed by the main characters as having been "wiped out" or altogether irrelevant is an especially tone-deaf choice since the book series was written during the rise of the Idle No More movement principally in Canada, and the TV series was launched during the NoDAPL movement in the United States, both of which drew international attention to the concerns of Indigenous peoples in North America. This specific on-screen conversation aside, it is also important to point out that, in a series that pays an incredible amount of attention to worldmaking such that the subaltern "Belters" who live in the asteroid belt and speak a variety of complex pidgin languages and whose cast is incredibly diverse in terms of ethnicity, there are no Native peoples whatsoever. *The Expanse* is no different from other science fiction in its lack of representation of Indigenous peoples; Native peoples are simply not there. Regardless of the social justice narratives and technological advancements of the series, the absence of Indigenous peoples produces a noticeable effect.[10]

Anthropologists deliberately depicted Native peoples as anachronistic since they considered them to be remnants of Europe's own past. Because of racist colonial-manufactured representations, Indigenous peoples have had to invest significant artistic and intellectual effort in correcting these misrepresentations as well as misappropriations of Native cultures. One such notable endeavor is Matika Wilbur's Project 562. As a photographer Wilbur set out on a journey to document and disseminate more accurate representations of Native peoples around the country, showcased in her recent publication of the same title.[11] Others have used empirical methods to demonstrate how stereotypes exemplified in inaccurate and two-dimensional representations of Native peoples in mascots and cartoons have measurable detrimental effects on Indigenous youth.[12]

Considering the deep connection between colonialism and science fiction, what could inspire an Indigenous artist to take an interest in this genre? Further, why are Indigenous-made science fiction media so popular with both Native and non-Native peoples? Observations have shown that science fiction alters societal perceptions of what is possible. As Chu states, "SF is distinguished by its capacity to perform the massively complex representational and epistemological work necessary to render cognitively estranging referents available both for representation and for understanding."[13] It can be so effective over time that "[a] work of SF can even help bring about its own obsolescence by causing its referent to grow more accessible to cognition and thereby less estranging."[14] This is precisely why earlier science fiction can seem so hackneyed or dated in just a few decades. Stanley Kubrick's base on the moon in *2001: A Space Odyssey* may not seem so science fictional to audiences today, while Octavia E. Butler's dystopian California plagued by wildfires and environmental destruction in *Parable of the Sower* may feel more realistic rather than speculative. While increased representations of Native people from lighthearted television series such as *Rutherford Falls* and *Reservation Dogs* to films with more serious human rights subject such as *Killers of the Flower Moon* normalize the richness and diversity of Indigenous lives in a society that thinks we are all irrelevant or dead, science fiction makes space to imagine worlds on our own terms. Indigenous science fictions are creative works that "cognitively estrange" observers from colonial representations of imagined futures. They create space outside colonial characterizations.

Indigenous Science Fiction

It is not at all surprising that Indigenous creators would employ the narrative arcs, aesthetics, or devices of speculation often found in the genre of science fiction. In fact, it ought to be expected to increase in frequency with time. The pantheon of science fiction created by Indigenous peoples signals the next phase toward visions of social equity. As Neal McLeod states in the introduction to his anthology of Indigenous science fiction, "speculative storytelling urge[s] us to move beyond our everyday parameters and experiences, in an effort to think of new possibilities."[15] Indeed, David Higgins has already identified Indigenous science fiction as an emerging genre of storytelling that advances Indigenous survivance.[16]

Anthropological discussions of science fiction are important for understanding a community's or a society's ideas about the future, but the mutually influential relationships between the discipline of anthropology and science fiction are also of significance. Samuel Collins argues that, outside speculating the desires of communities beyond the ethnographic present, anthropology has often been intertwined with science fiction itself.[17] American author Ursula K. Le Guin is one of the most accomplished and influential science fiction writers in the "New Wave" of the American science fiction genre (science fiction created during the 1960s and 1970s), and her literary work comprises dozens of award-winning novels and short stories. Le Guin was also the daughter of author Theodora Kroeber and anthropologist Alfred Louis Kroeber, lending to what Collins describes as her experimental style that pushes the "boundaries between science fiction and anthropology, interpolating the forms and conventions of ethnography into her fictions in a way, perhaps, ultimately transformative of both."[18] Thus, the discipline of anthropology has had a scholarly, methodological, and familial relationship with the science fiction genre in the U.S. for quite some time. Further, an ethical pillar of anthropology—even one that acknowledges and attempts to rectify its coloniality—is that, by gaining a better understanding of human difference and the diversity of historical experiences, we can co-produce a more just world. Likewise, science fiction imagines worlds alternative to the one currently experienced. Positive or utopian versions of these imagined landscapes are not prerequisites, however, because even dystopian representations project the undesired current realities of our world and what might occur if we leave them unchecked or underexamined—whether that is climate disasters, social issues, or artificial intelligence.

?E?ANX (The Cave) is a short film written and directed by Helen Haig-Brown, a Tsilhqot'in filmmaker from Canada. In the film, a lone Native man travels on horseback throughout the countryside in the Canadian plains, hunting a bear. After being waylaid in his pursuits by an uncanny and concussive phenomenon in a cave, he meets a group of naked and tattooed people milling about seemingly in the middle of nowhere. The unusual group gather and approach the man with mouths agape, opening and closing in strange unison. They communicate with him telepathically and instruct him to return from where he came. They explain he is not ready for "this place" yet. Involuntarily propelled backward by a wave of energy, he crawls back through the cave and comes across bones next to the tree where his horse was once tied. This film leaves the viewer with many questions about what really happened. Did the man travel through time or to the spirit world? And were the folks he met ancestors, or perhaps descendants? Is the realm he visited outside our everyday linear conceptions of time altogether?[19]

The experience shown in the film ?E?ANX (The Cave) resembles a concept originated by Mvskoke anthropologist Laura Harjo in Spiral to the Stars called a "kin-space-time constellation." This constellation, after unsettling fixed realms of social interactions in communal spaces, "operationalizes multiple dimensions—for instance, the spirit world, the practices of ancestors, cosmology, ceremony, and the everyday social reproduction of the community."[20] In addition, the film, narrated entirely in the Tsilhqot'in language, is an example of what Grace Dillon might call "slipstream" storytelling that collapses time or unsettles linear temporality. While making extraterrestrial contact or even meeting beings from another dimension are not new ideas in science fiction, ?E?ANX (The Cave) rejects the mainstream science fiction trope of violent alien invasion. In doing so, it cognitively estranges observers from colonial representations of meeting intelligent nonhumans for the first time and, as Lempert points out, assumptions of just who is in the best position to do so—a leader of a settler nation like the U.S. from an imperial city center like Washington, D.C., or New York, or a lone Tsilhqot'in hunter in the Canadian countryside?[21] The film helps create an imaginative space outside colonial characterizations of the invading, Armageddon-causing alien represented in science fiction canons like Wells's *War of the Worlds*, whose legacy continues in recent films like *Independence Day*.

Haig-Brown produced her film within a wave of Indigenous-made science fiction media that has multiplied in number and popularity in recent years, portraying new and thought-provoking visions of the future. This new wave of Indigenous-made media includes short films, novels, comic books, artwork, video games, and even podcasts. Some examples of short films include the lighthearted *Hoverboard*, which via its focus on the inventiveness of a young Native girl who makes advanced technology in her backyard exemplifies a form of what Dillon calls "reservation realism." Another is the space-travel setting of *The 6th World—An Origin Story* by Diné filmmaker Nanobah Becker, and the post-apocalyptic quasi-horror film *Wakening* by Cree filmmaker Danis Goulet. Besides short films, this wave includes literature such as the short stories in *Walking the Clouds* by Grace Dillon and the novel *Daughter of Dawn and Darkness* by Potawatomi author Carey F. Whitepigeon, video games like *Thunderbird Strike* developed by Métis artist Beth LaPensée, and podcasts like *Métis in Space* by Métis hosts Molly Swain and Chelsea Vowel. While there may be many reasons for the trend in Indigenous-made media created in the past decade, organizations and events like the 1998 founding of the imagineNATIVE Film and Media Arts Festival and the 2016 inaugural Indigenous Comic Con have certainly played a role.[22] Whatever the recent catalysts, Indigenous science fiction films are in some ways timeless as they blend traditional knowledge stewarded and shared through countless generations with a variety of Indigenous storytelling traditions and speculations about humanity's roles in the Universe.

While narratives that are categorically assigned science fiction either by the creator or externally by readers may blend elements of tribally specific Indigenous philosophies or include important figures like tricksters and spirit beings, we must be careful about collapsing traditional stories into the genre of science fiction altogether. This is because, by doing so, it implies to non-Native readers that these traditional stories are not real. Citing Cherokee scholar Adrienne Keene's critique of J. K. Rowling's *The History of Magic in North America*, Brown Spiers explains that "[t]he conflation of creation stories and tricksters with the genre of science fiction is bound to misrepresent the reality of Native spirituality and worldviews."[23] For example, one reading of *?E?ANX (The Cave)*— and indeed one that anthropologist William Lempert has made—is that it is "a species of speculative fiction within the sf realm [that] infuses stories with time travel, alternate realities and multiverses, and alternate histories [. . .] it views time as past presents, and futures that flow together in a navigable stream. It thus replicates nonlinear thinking about space-time."[24] Brown Spiers points out that Dillon argues that these nonlinear ways of conceptualizing space and time indicate actual lived experiences of Indigenous cultural frameworks and ways of understanding the world. Indigenous science fiction is not always fiction. Traditional storytelling is the medium through which these frameworks are shared by Indigenous communities. "If examples of the native slipstream 'model a cultural experience of reality,' then why categorize them as science fiction in the first place?"[25] I believe that Brown Spiers's question has merit, but that Dillon's definition of slipstream storytelling is still appropriate and constructive for theorizing and characterizing Indigenous science fiction.

Traditional stories can be both models of cultural realities *and* science fiction if they indeed meet Hans Robert Jauss's definition of science fiction: stories that expand the "horizons of our expectations."[26] By this definition, and with Chu's assertion cited previously that all experiences exist on a spectrum in some proximity to science fiction, then reality or belief is not material to the media's effect on viewers. As Brown Spiers later points out, "[w]here Indigenous knowledge intervenes in science fiction theory, it questions basic assumptions and expands the boundaries of the genre."[27] Similarly, in *This All Come Back Now: An Anthology of First Nations Speculative Fiction*, editor Mykaela Saunders explains that all collections of science fiction or, as she calls it, "spec fic," are indeed about Indigenous realities and experiences. They are "First Nations stories before they are spec fic stories; They centre and celebrate our communities, cultures, and countries while using spec fic tropes and techniques as literary devices."[28]

Indigenous science fiction indeed celebrates the communities that creators represent and come from; however, to fully understand Indigenous speculative fictions, the stories' axiologies, they need to be embedded in the everyday realities of Indigenous community contexts. In this way, we can better recognize these creative works as activating futurity. Indigenous futurism is how we "put into action that which our communities care about and desire."[29] Neshnabé communities in my research make space for themselves in the future. Kristina Baudemann defines Indigenous futurisms as "storytelling about the future," which is both linked to but differentiated from Western imperialism.[30] Traditional stories and prophecies, together with ecological revitalization and political demonstrations, which I define as Neshnabé futurity, guide Indigenous ecologists, theorists, and political activists in the Great Lakes region in mitigating and surviving ecological destruction of their homelands—destruction caused by climate change and controversial developmental undertakings such as oil pipelines and hydrofracking.

Prophecy and Neshnabé Conceptions of Time

Time travel is a keystone referent in science fiction from *The Time Machine*—the classic post-apocalyptic science fiction novella by H. G. Wells—to more recent film adaptations like *Interstellar*, *The Arrival*, and the popular TV series *Outlander*. While each takes place in unique social and political contexts, and, of course, time periods, they share common existentially disorienting specters of nonlinear experience and assumed passages of time. This subgenre of science fiction "cognitively estranges" audiences' perceptions of time, to borrow Chu's phrase. Conversely, however, while Indigenous science fiction has shown similar narrative motifs of nonlinear experience, unlike non-Indigenous perspectives, "time travel isn't such a big deal when you belong to a culture that experiences all-times simultaneously."[31] Like many Indigenous cultures that express a relation to the world via an understanding of and orientation to circular time, Neshnabék also consider time as cyclical. Specific to its use by

Indigenous creators in speculative fiction, Dillon calls this ubiquitous feature "spiraling time."

Similarly, some forms of Indigenous science fiction collapse time, often called slipstream narratives. Correspondingly, historians of social movements have also connected punctuated moments of demonstration and resistance as inextricably connected to one another despite what appears to be many years in between such movements, thus collapsing time as a historiographic device. In his text about the Standing Rock protectors against the Dakota Access Pipeline, Lakota historian Nick Estes reflects on the prophecy of the black snake and its relationships to the larger Indigenous-led social movements against dirty oil and settler colonialism: "prophets and prophecies do not predict the future, nor are they mystical, ahistorical occurrences. They are simply diagnoses of the times in which we live, and visions of what must be done to get free."[32]

Indigenous storytelling is often cyclical in nature. It connects pasts and futures in whirlpools and undertows, spiraling toward inherent truths. Like the "timeslip stories" often attributed to science fiction narratives, they describe nonlinear ways of telling a narrative, doing research, or making an argument. Timeslip interludes are literary devices that parallel the ethnographic data of this research, or the multiple temporalities of Neshnabé imaginaries. Popular in speculative fiction and espoused by creative and intellectual works by Neshnabék in this research, timeslips honor an Indigenous science fiction sensibility. Because Neshnabé futurisms make possible a multiplicity of potential futures, the use of timeslip passages reinforces the narratives of fluid temporality and sense of place investigated in this research.

One important aspect of Indigenous time and Neshnabék futurity not yet mentioned is prophecy. Women's Water Walkers and other activists associated with the Midéwiwin Lodge will often cite the Seven Fire Prophecy as an explanation for the environmental ethics they espouse. The Seven Fires Prophecy is a widely shared teaching throughout Indigenous North America. The prophecy has many iterations and is sometimes associated with the Seven Grandfather Teachings but overall it instructs how to live a good life—what Potawatomi peoples call *mno bmadzen*. As an oppositional feature of the prophecy, should humanity collectively choose the wrong path, individuals become greedy, violent, and wasteful, inevitably leading to the end of the world. In this prophecy, Neshnabék are encouraged to choose a path of spirituality, original languages, and the traditional values of their ancestors to avoid calamity. For Potawatomi people with whom I spoke about this, they define this path by speaking *Bodwéwadmimwen*, treating the land in a respectful and sustainable way, and practicing traditional ways within Wabeno, Midéwiwin, Big Drum, or some other spiritual lodge.

Seven epochs mark the prophecy. Starting in the Northeast, the Neshnabé migration story describes their journey ending in the place where food grows on water, or wild rice. The second epoch, or fire, describes a series of migrations and the loss of Midéwiwin ways. The third fire describes how Neshnabé peoples found the center of their spirituality—Manitoulin Island. Fires four through six detail the struggles of Indigenous peoples, including genocide and boarding schools meant to assimilate and shame Native children into living the way white Americans did, and describe these times as a waning fire. The seventh fire is the most highly cited aspect of this prophecy, because it explains how the rekindling of Neshnabé language, spirituality (in this case, Midéwiwin doings), and overall health will result from retracing the paths of our ancestors. Neshnabék can choose a path of overconsumption, environmental collapse, and conflict, or a path of spirituality and balance. The Seven Fires Prophecy, therefore, is multilinear as it makes space for Indigenous agency and choice.

This prophecy is paramount considering what other anthropological works show: what a community believes about the future informs their actions in the present. In his seminal text *The Future as Cultural Fact*, Arjun Appadurai explores the collective imaginings of the past and present and how disenfranchised groups ritualize and perform religion to reclaim space and voice. These are part of a larger strategy he calls a "politics of hope," defined as a refusal to be seen as hopeless or treated like victims with no future.[33] Women's Water Walks do something like what Appadurai describes. Departing from crisis research as described by Tuhiwai Smith, which situates Indigenous communities as the helpless victims of climate change and in need of protection from the state,[34] Water Walkers leverage the larger Neshnabé community to imagine a future in line with their values: sustainable stewardship of the land and water.

Midēwiwin, also referred to as The Grand Medicine Society, comprises a series of Lodges throughout the Great Lakes region in the U.S. and Canada. Walter James Hoffman published one of the first comprehensive ethnographic texts on the Midēwiwin Society in 1891 in *The Midēwiwin, or, "Grand medicine society" of the Ojibwa*. The Three Fires Lodge in Bad River, Wisconsin, from which Women's Water Walks began, is a more open Lodge. Much of the literature on Midēwiwin Society hyperbolizes it as a religion shrouded in secrecy. This is because many Indigenous practices went underground when anthropologists first studied them. Owing to assimilationist policies including government-run and mission-administered boarding schools and legalized human trafficking of Indian children who were placed into white homes by social services throughout the U.S. and Canada, Indigenous peoples learned quickly to either avoid non-Christian ceremonies or to do them in secret. In fact, some Big Drum societies still hold their "Warrior Dances" on Easter weekend. Some have theorized that Warrior Dances are held in honor of Easter in a merging of traditional Neshnabé ways with Catholicism.[35] Instead, participants with whom I spoke told me that this was to take advantage of the exodus of Indian agents during this time. Agents would return home from their work on and near Indian reservations for Easter, leaving Native participants to safely hold dances. During other times of year, traditional Anishinaabé practices associated with non-Christian religions were prohibited by the agents. Beyond the need to hold gatherings in secret as a matter of course, the element of secrecy associated with the Midēwiwin Lodge may also have to do with the privileged nature of ceremonial knowledge in Midēwiwin practices. There are successive levels of *Midés* with increasing degrees obtained through sacrifice, training, and learning new responsibilities as one "goes up through the Lodge." So, as one advances their "degree" in Midēwiwin ways and consistently takes part in seasonal ceremonies, Midés gain more ceremonial knowledge and teachings.

The Three Fires Lodge in Bad River, Wisconsin, has a reputation for being both open and less secretive, as well as being a "political" lodge. By open, what Neshnabé individuals whom I interviewed meant was that the Lodge is inclusive of "outsiders" or those not officially associated with Midēwiwin ways (yet). And the Three Fires Lodge initiates more members than any other Lodge. By political, what most of the people with whom I spoke meant was that Three Fires performed their politics outside Lodge contexts. This was unusual until about the early 2000s.

The long and intimate history between the group that became the Three Fires Lodge and the famous American Indian Movement (AIM) of the late 1960s and early 1970s made the performance of politics described in this chapter possible. Developed in concert with the sociopolitical momentum of the Civil Rights Movements, AIM began in 1968 in Minneapolis, Minnesota. The movement was multifocal in tackling issues including police brutality, treaty rights, misappropriation of Native cultures, and environmental issues. In concert with cultural revivals of Midéwiwin practices in Minnesota, Edward Benton-Banai-mba, the late Grand Chief of the Three Fires Midéwiwin Lodge, was active in the political actions throughout the 1970s.[36] As a result, there is a long history of political demonstrations with ceremonial doings in the Three Fire Lodge.

Women's Water Walks are a contemporary adaptation of traditional Midéwiwin ceremonies, specifically those ceremonies facilitated by Edward Benton-Banai-mba. They include a Women's Water Ceremony, which comprises one of many ceremonial elements that are conducted in the Lodge. Midés consider water to be the responsibility of women. Songs, prayer, cedar, and copper vessels are the primary tools in conducting this ceremony. At the end of the ceremony, the participants purify and share water to ingest, regardless of their gender. They also use the purified water for other elements of Midéwiwin doings, such as constructing the Little Boy Water Drum. Water Walks begin with a water ceremony and sometimes a Pipe Ceremony (the latter conducted by men). The purified water is then carried from one body of water to another to transfer prayers of Neshnabék into perpetuity and restore the original healthy conditions back to *Neshnabé ke* via its water ways. In this manner, people view water not only for its obvious utility in sustaining all known life but also for its ability to travel beyond their reach—to many parts of the world and to other dimensions of reality.

The transference of prayer from human minds to higher dimensions of existence is found in other forms of Neshnabé prayer. The laying down of *séma* (tobacco) at the base of a tree, as well as burning séma in sacred fires, also makes use of physical conduits found in this world to deploy powerful prayers from the hearts and minds of Neshnabé peoples to other dimensions. Prayer is an important part of being Neshnabé. In fact, one traditional story recounts that at one point Neshnabé peoples got lazy and stopped laying down tobacco in the mornings. The Creator initially considered destroying the earth because of humanity's laziness and lack of gratitude, but Eagle convinced them otherwise. Having faith in the integrity of humans, Eagle flew around the world for days and days trying to find evidence of Neshnabék who still conducted themselves in a good way by praying every morning and offering their tobacco to the Creator. Once he finally found some, he notified the Creator, and spared humans the end of the world. Eagle's ability to fly so high and communicate with Sky Beings makes him a sacred relative. And this is also why eagle feathers are worn in ceremony and used in prayer; they, like purified water and séma, are conduits of sacred messages to higher dimensions of being.

Women's Water Ceremonies, laying down séma, and praying with eagle feathers have been conducted by Neshnabék since time immemorial. So, what makes Women's Water Walks a contemporary adaptation, and why did they start? Women's Water Walks began in the early 2000s by Neshnabé elders from the Midéwiwin Lodge. More specifically, the first Water Walk began in 2003 and was part of a larger multiyear walk around each Great Lake in the U.S. and Canada and was led by Grandmother Josephine Mandamin-mba. Grandma Josephine, as she is commonly referred to, was a remarkably sweet and warm woman. Her presence was like kinnikinnick tea on a rainy day. Her joy was so big that I remember joy would squeeze her eyes shut when she laughed. Not only was she kind, she was incredibly strong. She walked the entirety of the Great Lakes in her old age—over four thousand five hundred miles of coastline. When the soles of her sneakers eroded, she bought new ones; when her knees gave out, she got new knees. She did all this to bring attention to the world's negligence and active harming of water.

As the popularity of the Women's Water Walks grew, the movement rose in numbers and in political focus. Going from a general call by Midé women to protect Mother Nature's waters, the Women's Water Walks included non-Midé folks and even non-Native folks protesting Nestlé's pollution of water in the Great Lakes in the early 2000s and inadequate governmental responses to the Flint Water Crisis in 2015. Where there were political issues involving water in the Great Lakes region, Women Water Walkers were there.

Some of the print media that circulated about the various Women's Water Walks throughout the Great Lakes region feature Grandmother Josephine Mandamin-mba and the copper vessel containing purified water. One image was taken during a water blessing ceremony at the Hudson River before the 2014 People's Climate March in New York. Grandmother Josephine-mba is wearing a Three Fires Midéwiwin Lodge T-shirt and is standing next to some of her medicine bundle items used in ceremony. I recognize some Midé women from the Three Fires Lodge marching behind her. Another image is a flyer advertising the 2015 Migration Walk. It reads, "Follow the path of our Anishinaabé ancestors as we retrace their journey to find the food that grows on the water." The food that grows on water refers to wild rice, which is discussed in chapter 3. The journey refers to the migration story also discussed in the same chapter and mentioned again at the beginning of this section. Together these images index the Midéwiwin Lodge as a point of origin, how women are leading these walks, and the elements of water ceremony that guide Water Walkers in their ecopolitics in a multiplicity of places—in New York, Canada, Michigan, and Wisconsin. Finally, they show how Neshnabé origin stories and traditional teachings inform Indigenous conceptions of the future.

Grandma Josephine-mba concluded the Women's Water Walk around every Great Lake on April 20, 2017, at the Saint Lawrence Seaway in Matane, Quebec. But that didn't stop the Women's Water Walk movement. Indeed, many tribes began smaller local Water Walks in their own communities. The Pokagon Band of Potawatomi Indians holds a Sunrise Ceremony, Pipe Ceremony, and Women's Water Ceremony before the annual Women's Water Walk on the Friday before Labor Day every year.[37]

Neshnabék actualize futurity in these spaces. To this point, Pokagon citizen Rebecca Williams sat down with me in summer 2023 to talk about what nation-building means to her. Her willingness to talk with me was particularly generous given her father walked on just weeks before. Ever the jokester, most of what she said made me laugh—even when talking about serious topics. Rebecca is the youth cultural coordinator, and I worked with her for several years in the Department of Language and Culture. From this experience, I knew that much of the work we did was shaped by community needs, government support, and allocated funding. We are used to working within limits, which, oddly enough, makes answering questions that have no limits a difficult task. She hesitated and asked clarifying questions about the nature of my prompt when I asked her to imagine a healthy Neshnabé community. Her response, surprising to me, was shaped in the context of Indigenous-led activism and resistance.

> **Blaire**: A lot of what we do every day has to do with what time we have, what resources we have, what money and support we have, but assuming you had unlimited time, unlimited funding, and personnel to do the work, what would it look like to you to have a healthy Neshnabé community?
>
> **Rebecca Williams**: Okay. So, for me, a healthy Neshnabé community would look something like, oddly, like, Standing Rock.
>
> **Blaire**: Mm-hmm.
>
> **Rebecca**: And I don't know if you've ever been there or not, but I can tell you what it was . . . my experience was like when I was there for the short time I was there and by no means was it perfect but it was close to what it felt like to being a child for myself. Um, within that experience I had there was seven days we were stuck there during a blizzard, um, pushing all those things . . . all the exterior things out- outward but understanding the function of the camp that we were at, y'know, people knew what their roles were.
>
> Children were allowed to play without any concerns for their safety, the women or other people who like to cook and clean, things like that, we were in the Michigan tent and we provided meals, three square meals a day if not more and that was our job. Really specific job, we knew we had to get up before sunrise before everybody else and make breakfast. We knew once we start breakfast that was it for the day, like, we're on a roll. Breakfast, lunch, dinner, snacks in between for all those vegan people. (Laughs)
>
> **Blaire**: (Laughs)
>
> **Rebecca**: Um . . . (Laughs) Um, and then, like, something as simple as just needing water, which is kinda ironic out there but something as simple as just needing water we said we needed water that meant the people who would go out and collect water went out and collected that water for the day.
>
> **Blaire**: Mm-hmm.

Rebecca: They were *wgetthdak*.[38] In my mind, they were the warriors of our community right? At least that little tiny community we were in 'cause, uh, Standing Rock had a lot of communities but if we focused just centrally on that Michigan tent there was like the guys that ran security or, y'know, the people I should say, it wasn't necessarily just men. The people who were security were in my mind the warriors of our community who looked out for us if we needed something. (Laughs) Like propane heaters, they went and got us propane heaters, they made sure that we were kept safe in this space.

So, it was like, in itself, a tiny little Neshnabé community. Again, like, we had our roles in the kitchen to cook all day, if we needed water there was water, if we needed firewood the people who collected firewood would get it, go out and get firewood, if we needed dishwashers there's dishwashers. The kids knew what they were doing and where they could be at, and where they were safe at.

Um, so in that way the very, very few days we were there, that's to me the epitome of what felt like a Neshnabé community. While we were in this, um, tense, intense situation with the government it, at the end of the day I was sad to leave even though it was so, um, trying that it had that, that feeling of cohesiveness. People knew what they're supposed to do and I've reflected a lot on that and I think it has a lot to do with us fulfilling those roles that we were supposed to be doing in our community, um, and truly functioning as if we were a Neshnabé community and that's the only time I've truly felt that outside of, like, ceremonies. Ceremonies would be second to that.

Activism as Futurity

If science fiction media imagines potential futures, activism catalyzes those creative and intellectual mappings. Bodwéwadmimwen, or the Potawatomi language, is a highly descriptive language, heavy with verbs, unlike English with its emphasis on nouns. The importance of movement and action in Neshnabé language and in thought cannot be overstated. For example, the sun, in Potawatomi *gizes*, is not simply *the* sun. Gizes translates to "he or she is rising"—an animate being in a constant state of movement. This holds true in naming conventions, as well. My son's name, inherited from his paternal great-grandfather, is often translated to "lightning walker." But a more accurate translation considers the particles of the word *Mekséni*, which includes the "sé" as in *bmosé*, or "he or she walks about." Thus, Mekséni (conventionally spelled Miksani and Miksanii) becomes a description of the sort of lightning that looks as if it is walking across the sky. Action, movement, and walking more specifically indexes an important axiom in Neshnabé frameworks of being. The highly cited concept of mno bmadzen, often seen in its Ojibwe spelling as *mino bimaadiziwin*, refers to walking the good path. This can mean many different things depending on context and is often talked about in relation to the seven Grandfather Teachings: Wisdom, Love, Respect, Truth, Honesty, Humility, and Bravery. To demonstrate all seven represents Neshnabé integrity. Between walking the good path known as mno bmadzen and looking seven generations into the future regarding one's actions, this Indigenous frame of reference activates Neshnabé futurity.

The term futurity generates a more accurate vocabulary for understanding Neshnabék nation-building projects than the value-laden terms revitalization or activism. This insight occurred to me while I attended Midéwiwin ceremonies in summer 2016. Sitting near a cliff on the coast of Lake Superior where the Three Fires Lodge used to hold their ceremonial doings,[39] I was startled by seeing famous activist, economist, and former Green Party vice presidential nominee Winona LaDuke. As she is someone whose work I reference and whose political advocacy I admire, I was a bit star-struck, especially since I did not know she attended that particular Lodge. I caught the attention of a couple women next to me when I blurted out,

"Is that Winona LaDuke?!"

"Who?" one of the women asked, annoyed.

"Winona LaDuke," I clarified.

"Who is that?"

"A famous author and environmental activist," I explained.

Without hesitation she said, "Activist? So? *All* of us here are."

Unphased by LaDuke's fame for both her academic and political work, ceremonial leaders from the Midéwiwin Lodge clarified that everyone's work at the Lodge was important. As Rebecca stated, everyone knows their roles.

By articulating the concerns and desires of multiple Neshnabé communities, the political activities of the Midéwiwin Lodge are forms of organic intellectualism. Women associated with the Midéwiwin Lodge enact a type of politics that privileges Neshnabé ways of knowing about the environment through ceremony and Water Walks to protest hydrofracking, pollution from tiles in upstream farms, and other environmental issues. These activists play an important role when they are viewed as organic intellectuals instead of as working in terms of cultural revitalization as they have been in the past.

Antonio Gramsci theorized that everyone is an intellectual because everyone thinks and possesses a conception of the world; what determines the productive nature of intellectual activity, however, is the role or the position that intellectuals play in society.[40] Intellectuals are specialists, and they occupy a specific place within the relations of production. Their intellectual "work," whether that is in science or filmmaking, must be understood within a specific relation to the state or the contemporaneous hegemonic forces in that society.[41] These theoretical foundations set up his argument that there are two types of intellectuals: traditional intellectuals and organic intellectuals.

Before I explain these two types of intellectuals, let us acknowledge that Gramsci employed the term "organic" to refer to a significant amount of analytical work he performed, particularly in the section of *The Modern Prince* that discusses the "Study of Philosophy and Historical Materialism." Organicism has to do with the theory-praxis nexus that Gramsci discusses in terms of the relationship between the intellectual arena of philosophy and the concrete expressions of politics. In speaking against this dichotomy, Gramsci argued that intellectual activity (i.e., philosophical activity) can be "organically" tied to real-world events, politics, circumstances, etc.,[42] just as creative work and literature in Indigenous futurity is tied to on-the-ground advocacy work. This development of the term "organic" can be easily overlooked, especially since Gramsci ultimately concludes that all philosophical activity is essentially political. But this explanation of organicism is material because it is what informs his conception of one of his most famous theoretical interventions: the concept of the organic intellectual. To emphasize this point, it is worth quoting Gramsci at length. He states:

[O]rganism of thought and cultural solidarity could only have been brought about if there had existed between the intellectuals and the simple people that unity which there should have been between theory and practice; if, the intellectuals had been organically the intellectuals of those masses, if they had elaborated and made coherent the principles and problems which those masses posed by their practical activity, in this way constituting a cultural and social bloc.[43]

This excerpt articulates several important things. The first is that organism or organicism results from the marriage of intellectual philosophical activity with the needs and concerns of a subaltern class (he was talking here about engagement with southern Italian peasants).[44] Next, this marriage of philosophy and subaltern concerns relates to the relationship between theory and practice. By making coherent the concerns of the subaltern class, intellectuals are the principal "organizers" of social activity. Finally, through this organization, intellectuals can develop and mobilize a new intellectual "bloc" as a counter-hegemonic force. Kate Crehan synthesizes this idea by stating, "A class which cannot produce its own intellectuals cannot transform itself into a hegemonic force."[45] Therefore, organic intellectuals speak to a subaltern class and work to effectively mobilize their class consciousness to institute a new, more desired hegemony.

Waskar Ari made a similar argument of organic intellectualism and Indigenous activism in his historical ethnography *Earth Politics*. The Bolivian Indigenous activists in his research effectively integrated traditional Aymara religious ideas with political claims in a larger effort to deploy "a project of decolonization."[46] Part of how the activists in Ari's research did this is through employing a "'politics of memory'" or "a system of ideas and strategies that used history and memory to influence the present."[47] To this point, Anishinaabé author Leanne Simpson argues in *Dancing on Our Turtle's Back* that:

One of the most crucial tasks presently facing Indigenous nations is the continued creation of individuals and assemblages of people who can think in culturally inherent ways [. . .] [W]e need intellectuals who can think within the conceptual meanings of the language, who are intrinsically connected to place and territory, who exist in the world as an embodiment of contemporary expressions of our ancient stories and traditions, and that illuminate *mino bimaadiziwin* in all aspects of their lives.[48]

By drawing from Midéwiwin ancestral teachings and ceremonial knowledge in tandem with political discussions at Water Walk events, these Neshnabé activists are organic intellectuals. Water Walks are intense physical challenges where participants rise before the sun and meet to conduct ceremony. Afterward, they walk all day, usually several days in a row, before taking any extended breaks. The logic behind such strenuous feats of endurance lies in pushing the limits of human capability and testing one's physical and mental resilience. In doing so, our prayers become more potent. We show not only our commitment to imagining an otherwise to the current capitalist status quo that is poisoning our world, but also an Indigenous belief that suffering brings us closer to the spirit world.

One's bed never feels more comfortable than when it is time to rise before the sun does. On August 30, 2014, at around 5 o'clock on a chilly Michigan morning, I joined other Neshnabé women, mostly from the Pokagon Band of Potawatomi Indians, in a rural part of an already small town in southwest Michigan, at the edge of Gage Lake on tribal lands in Dowagiac for the seventh annual Sunrise Ceremony and Women's Water Walk. While I have since participated in several Water Walks over the years, this was my first time. We stood close to each other while fatigue slowly evaporated from our bodies like the morning fog off the lake as the nascent sunrise greeted the water. The initial Pipe Ceremony lasted about three hours and was followed by a short feast before we began an approximately thirteen-mile walk around from Gage Lake to Rodgers Lake.[49] Both lakes are located on tribal lands, but most tribal properties in the town of Dowagiac are separated by non-reservation lands. The elders who conducted the ceremony showed a strong commitment to addressing contemporary environmental concerns. They focused on issues specifically related to hydrofracking in the region, using their public remarks during the ceremonies to educate and raise awareness. Not only did they incorporate discussions about politics, but they also seamlessly integrated these discussions with prayers, emphasizing the importance of spiritual guidance in addressing and resolving environmental challenges.

Facilitators of the various ceremonies that are conducted before Water Walks are involved in political activism. For instance, one elder active in the Women's Water Walk movement also leads the Domestic Violence Awareness Team in southwestern Michigan. Besides being on the Pokagon Band tribal council, she started the Purple Shawl Project. This project is a dance demonstration and a political mobilization. Women make their own shawls with traditional Potawatomi appliqué designs and coordinate a dance demonstration typically at powwows in the area to encourage discussions and action around women's issues. Most years, the Purple Shawl Project has specifically focused on passing the Violence Against Women Act (VAWA) in partnership with the National Congress of American Indians (NCAI).[50]

Women's Water Walks use ceremony to call attention to multiple political projects while deploying a register of Neshnabé spiritual and political ethics about how to be a good human. While the official aim of the walk is to honor the waters of the Pokagon Band homelands, it is embedded in a larger multifaceted political context. Women's Water Walks are not just Indigenous protest walks against one or two concrete issues (though they sometimes can be). The multiple activities and projects, which depart from but are conceptually oriented around the Women's Water Ceremony, incorporate politics of domestic violence and ecological issues. Our community's health is directly linked to the health of the water. This is a central understanding that is repeated in personal teachings, community events, workshops, and presentations by Neshnabé peoples. In fact, the sacredness of water became the predominant politics in the famous Standing Rock protests starting in April 2016 with their Lakota phrase *mni wiconi*, or "water is life."

"There is prayer in suffering," Pokagon Language Director Rhonda Purcell told me. In fall 2015, she reflected upon a Water Walk she took part in about a month earlier. "You get to mile six, seven, eight, and you're like 'Ok I'm good. I'm done. I'm exhausted, hungry, sore, and I want to stop.' But—" she says, "that's when you pray. That's when your prayers are the most powerful. You pray for those who have no clean water, who are fighting to keep toxic fracking off their lands and out of their children's blood." Rhonda, introduced in chapter 3 as a Pokagon Citizen and long-term leader in the Pokagon Band language program, is a member of the Three Fires Midéwiwin Lodge or *Midékwé*. Her work in revitalizing culture and language, along with her dedicated efforts to constantly increase her traditional knowledge through visits to other Neshnabé communities and various Midéwiwin and Big Drum Lodges, justifies her role as a spiritually knowledgeable person. Her remark that "there is prayer in suffering" is paralleled by other Neshnabé practices such as fasting.

In spring 2019, I took part in my first fast. Traditionally, a fast would last for four days and four nights. Individuals are instructed to make a modest camp in the forest and go without food, water, or sleep. "We're much weaker than our ancestors," Jason S. Wesaw, former Pokagon Band tribal historic preservation officer, explains to me. "So, we start off with one or two nights, and build up our stamina every year." I went out for one day and one night, but it was difficult. More than hunger, thirst, or exhaustion, the boredom eats away at one's resolve. "There is prayer in suffering," I repeated to myself. Fasting's purpose is to cleanse and spiritually mature a person. But it is also a practice meant to increase the potency of one's prayers. A person who participates in a fast is metaphorically and literally dying. Because of this flirtation with death, the faster is closer to the spirit world where prayers are mobilized by mnedowêk and ancestors. Fasting, then, is a way of giving back to one's community as one prays for the health and wellness of relatives.

In terms of the relationship between Women's Water Ceremony and larger ecological issues, hydrofracking initiatives in the state of Michigan have been central to recent Indigenous political mobilizations. While the state of Michigan has a long history of Indigenous dispossession, removal, violence, and ecological issues, the most salient topic of hydrofracking can be temporally located to 2010. This year marked a record for the state, which leased the most land in a year to oil and gas companies, mostly for hydrofracking.[51] This method of natural gas extraction from shale formations has numerous adverse effects on the environment, mostly relating to the water supply of large populated regions.

Hydrofracking, while it has existed since 1949, has significantly increased in frequency in recent years because of more efficient and cheaper drilling techniques.[52] This is potentially calamitous, because the risks associated with hydrofracking include chemical contamination of drinking water (not to mention water used in agriculture), spills (which are quite frequent), and infinite forms of aggregate chronic contamination over time. Additionally, tribal nations are reporting that chemicals used in hydrofracking are carcinogens, resulting in higher rates of tribal members with cancer and other health issues.[53] Also, because of the highly limited provisions for environmental protection through laws like NEPA and NHPA (which only apply to undertakings on public land or that require a federal permit), harmful effects from hydrofracking can extend for thousands of miles from the drill site to private and tribal lands.[54] This legal reality makes it impossible for tribes to refuse these undertakings or even have a voice in how these projects are implemented. For these reasons, environmental issues specifically revolving around hydrofracking have been taken up vehemently by Indigenous activists in the Great Lakes region through Women's Water Walks. But, as already stated, more than political demonstrations, Women's Water Walks embedded within them a web of ceremonial and ecological ethics that are meant to instruct and encourage Neshnabé peoples to be healthy and constructive humans in the future. Both speculative fictions and activist work imagine alternative futures. But they are only two parts of the three that I term Neshnabé futurity. The third concerns tribal data and, similar to traditional knowledge discussed in chapter 2, the failure of the information generated by tribes to be taken seriously by policy creators.

Grant Poole is the water quality specialist for the Pokagon Band of Potawatomi Indians Department of Natural Resources. He has been working there for nearly ten years. Before that he was employed by the Little River Band of Ottawa Indians as an Aquatic Researcher for almost eight years. I like his name because it is an apropos pun for his line of work. He spends a lot of his time managing statistical data at his computer or standing in waterways taking samples and measurements. His main responsibility, as he explains it, is using Environmental Protection Agency (EPA) Clean Water Act 106 funds and tribal funds to monitor lakes and streams on tribal property. He collects biological, physical, and chemical data on those water bodies and then compares them against water quality standards the tribe has adopted to see how healthy the waters are in terms of contact with humans or biological populations. As an intern for the Pokagon Band DNR in 2017, I assisted Grant in organizing his data tables that contained things like "turbidity" and "riparian" zones—data collected from subjective observations and standardized into numerable codes to track change over time.

Grant collects these data monthly by gearing up in tall heavy muck boots, water-resistant overalls, and a slew of measuring equipment that he packs in a government vehicle. When I accompanied him, it took us all day to measure five waterways (although I could have been slowing him down as I was seven months pregnant at the time). Some waterways were easy to get to. I remember one in particular that was located in a park and had an easy descent via shallow river rocks and wispy trees that hung overhead. Further areas, by contrast, could only be reached by trudging along barely discernible trails in the dense woods, with swarms of mosquitos buzzing incessantly around one's ears. The waterways in those parts were muddy and devoid of any picturesque charm. I sensed that researchers like Grant were the only ones who visited these inaccessible forgotten streams.

What I noticed in the meticulousness of Grant's work was that there are significant disconnects between the everyday work of natural resource management professionals and those of ceremonial leaders active in political movements like Women's Water Walks. Both groups care deeply about the health of the local water but had very different methods for expressing that care. Despite this difference, like Water Walkers, Grant, too, was concerned about the way water quality was being legislated.

> **Grant**: The tribe has adopted the state of Michigan's water quality standards and those—The state of Michigan water quality standards have to be equal to or greater protection than what the EPA's overall water quality standards are.
>
> **Blaire**: Oh, okay. In what ways do you feel like it's greater than or is it ever?
>
> **Grant**: Um, it's not too much greater than, I mean . . . They've adopted the Wetlands 404 Program and they've added some narratives for turbidity. So, I would say it's slightly greater than but it's not extremely greater. The EPA has told us they're actually out of compliance in some areas.
>
> **Blaire**: Oh really? What areas?
>
> **Grant**: Mainly because the state of Michigan has put a moratorium on passing water-related updates, rules and so until that moratorium is

removed the [Department of Environmental Quality] is kind of stuck with what the current laws are saying.

Blaire: Okay. I'm unfamiliar with that process. Like, what would a moratorium prevent you—Like, it puts a block on certain information or what's that exactly?

Grant: Yeah. Like, the officials in the state of Michigan put a block on any new changes to Michigan laws related to water issues . . . It's always been a question I had but, you know, we wear so many hats here it's like finding the time to to go chase that down. I haven't done that yet.

Grant explains that while information is being generated because of meticulous water quality measurements and tracking these data over time, there actually is not much that can be done with the data tribes produce. Because of the moratorium, which has been in place since at least 2015, any significant changes in water quality evaporate into a legislative void. And, to top it off, Grant explained that the state of Michigan is skeptical of data generated by tribes. So, despite copious amounts of empirical data collected and analyzed at the tribal level that are both valid and legible to the state, they cannot be mobilized to protect reservation lands or water.

Despite successes in terms of community cohesion around cultural doings and political mobilization, Women's Water Walks and the activists who lead them could be more effective in their mission by findings way to use empirical data about water generated by tribal governments. More research ought to be done with regard to data sovereignty and leveraging the research, political activism, and traditional knowledge that is all being generated by Indigenous communities. While Women's Water Walks rose from political activism in the 1960s and 1970s, they have been carried forward because activists and ceremonial leaders identified areas where Neshnabé voices were not being heard in extractive undertakings like hydrofracking. So, they leveraged their ceremonial knowledge to create cultural and political space for Neshnabé ethics. The result was a growing and ever evolving political movement grounded in Neshnabé traditional knowledge and values. If conventional ways of using environmental data are currently moot as Grant suggests, there are opportunities for Water Walkers to co-opt these data for their political projects. Some of these data are being produced by their own tribal governments, yet there is a disconnect between these two forms of intellectual activity— empirical data on the one hand, and traditional knowledge mobilized in Water Walks on the other. While there are areas of opportunity for the Midéwiwin Water Walks and tribal intervention in ecological management, both projects are catalyzed by the promise of how their actions positively affect the future.

CONCLUSION
Neshnabé Futurisms

Moonwatcher, in a depressed state of being, wedged between the threat of starvation and interspecies violence, dumps the carcass of his dead father into a ditch. He will never think about him again. He isn't cruel; rather, the faculties of his mind will not allow him to experience sadness or empathy for others. In what is supposed to be a setting in Pleistocene-era Africa before the rise of Australopithecines and other ancestors to Homo sapiens, science fiction writer Arthur C. Clark introduces readers to alternative realities of existence in the published novel version of his original 1968 screenplay of *2001: A Space Odyssey*. Moonwatcher is a distant ancestor to modern humans who lived millions of years before the present. He is different from his counterparts, however, because he can imagine the future. Quite contrary to his current state, he imagines lying around on a lazy afternoon with a protruding full belly and easy access to water—a potential future. Imagining a situation that departs from the lurid day-to-day realities his species experiences is a new intellectual ability made possible by the sudden arrival of an anachronistic alien device. The enigma of the towering monolith in Clark's novel and screenplay mysteriously appears in pivotal moments of humanity that "nudge" our ancestors and later Homo sapiens along toward an unknown destination. Rather than following a predetermined linear progression of evolution, in contexts where the monolith is discovered new creative and agentive framings are possible. *2001* tells a tale of the unimaginable becoming reality: Moonwatcher's theory of mind, Homo sapiens reaching the moon, and Dr. Dave Bowman's transcendence to a nonlinear and extracorporeal existence.

Neshnabé futurities are the multiplicity of potential futures imagined and enacted by Potawatomi traditional knowledge and prophecy as observed in Indigenous-made speculative media, ecopolitics leveraged by Women's Water Walks, and, finally, ecological revitalization projects on and near tribal lands in the Great Lakes region. These imagined landscapes of possibility depart from the versions of the future posited by mainstream settler society in which Indigenous communities are vulnerable, helpless, or completely irrelevant. Neshnabé futurity also creates space outside the colonial projections of settler nation states. Using new technologies, Neshnabék are doing more than just revitalizing traditional cultural knowledge, resisting controversial environmental issues, or revitalizing ecologies; these actions, when taken together, form unique versions of alternative futures that position Indigenous peoples at the center.

The deliberate focus on Indigeneity in opposition to persistent settler narratives serves as a vital means of highlighting and validating communities that are systematically erased. Settler myths about fake Indians like Princess Mishawaka and Chief Doe-wah-jack erase Neshnabé presence and attachments to land in Michigan and Indiana in favor of imagined settler tropes of—ironically—*their* belonging through self-indigenization to places they have colonized (or otherwise inherited from colonizers). These bogus narratives romanticize frontier violence and seek to manufacture an indigenous identity for settlers. Pipelines that puncture and tear through lands and waterways in the Great Lakes and other deleterious extractive industries further dispossess Neshnabé peoples from ceremonial spaces. Despite these circumstances, experiences like the ones Andy shared with elders around the harvest and preparation of milkweed exemplify the connection between landscape and experience as an archive of knowledge. Places and situations on the land can evoke cherished memories and captivating stories for Neshnabé communities. The sight of rolling hills of milkweed, the melodic sounds of chickadees, the comforting smell of sweetgrass and wildflowers, and the indescribable feeling of connection to the land our ancestors flourished on for thousands of years all serve as powerful triggers for imagining—no, conspiring for—our collective decolonial futures. The existence of these place-based "archives" persists despite the spatial and social separation experienced by Pokagon Band citizens because of land and resource loss, as well as the fragmented nature of their reservation caused by a checkerboard pattern of jurisdiction between the tribe, the state and federal governments, and more commonly, private property held by settlers.

Neshnabé peoples emphasize the importance of connecting with the land and nurturing relationships with other-than-human species. Invented binaries, such as the dichotomy between subjective and objective understandings, fail to capture the vastness of our human experiences. So, Potawatomi peoples utilize stories that combine the "mythical" and historical to address present-day environmental concerns. *Mnedowêk*, spirits or entities that bring about change, challenge anthropologists to move beyond traditional categorizations and embrace a more holistic understanding of reality, belief systems, ethics, and responsibility. Ecological revitalization projects such as re-meandering rivers and transplanting wild rice are as agentive in actualizing Neshnabé futurisms as conducting ceremony or *mnedokazwek*, whereby *mnedo* are being called to conduct a specific purpose. The interplay of different forms of Neshnabé animate and inanimate storytelling advances Indigenous ecopolitics in the Great Lakes region. These stories catalyze material change similar to re-meandering rivers and revitalizing wild rice. Like the efforts of reclaiming space argued in chapter 1, traditional stories that contextualize present-day ecological issues combined with ecological revitalization projects are constitutive of Neshnabé futurity.

With the devastating effects of climate change on communities globally, anthropology has shown a growing inclination towards crisis research. In doing so, this brand of investigation has ignored nuances of Indigenous agency and knowledge systems and has the potential to cause even more damage.[1] Indigenous communities in the Great Lakes region have already lived through ecological collapse over the past several hundred years of settler colonialism in the U.S. and Canada—species extinction, land loss, and the denial of access to natural resources. As a result, Neshnabé communities have been deploying their own narrative of Neshnabé futurity evidenced in Indigenous science fiction, Women's Water Walks, and ecological revitalization projects. Neshnabé futurity consists of traditional stories and prophecies, together with ecological revitalization and political demonstrations, that guide Native American ecologists, theorists, and activists in the Great Lakes region in mitigating and surviving ecological destruction of their homelands—destruction caused by climate change and controversial development undertakings like oil pipelines and hydrofracking.

Women's Water Walkers and other activists associated with the Midéwiwin Lodge will often use elements of prophecy to theorize and articulate their environmental ethics. Indigenous-made speculative film, art, video games, literature, and oral storytelling draw from autochthonous knowledge systems to envision and convey alternative futurisms and pasts to mainstream ones with Indigenous communities at the forefront of this imaginary landscape. Mainstream science fiction began as a modernist project projecting the hopes and dreams, as well as fears and anxieties, onto the pages of novels and into the imagined (singular) future—one often not inclusive of people of color. Departing from mainstream science fiction, which assumes a linear progress of humanity based on Western values of environmental domination and social Darwinism, Indigenous science fiction foregrounds Indigenous peoples and their knowledge systems. Indigenous science fiction makes space for Indigenous values and allows for a multiplicity of futures.

The primary motivation for Indigenous activists in my study to participate in politico-ceremonial practices, such as Water Walks, is the notable ineffectiveness of conventional legislative platforms. Indigenous traditional knowledge, science, or ways of knowing have been downplayed for their intellectual rigor, problematically co-opted, or completely ignored. And environmental consultation efforts at my research sites often problematically translate or stifle traditional knowledges and Anishinaabé peoples' experiences. Indigenous communities are staking claims for the future in the Great Lakes region outside these problematic state-mandated consultation requirements. Women associated with the Midéwiwin Lodge mobilize assemblages of people for ceremony and political demonstrations who would not normally protest on their own or as part of a non-Indigenous political group. Midéwiwin Water Walkers enact a type of politics that privileges Neshnabé ways of knowing about the environment and heals contaminated waters while constructing an alternative vision for the future. Thus, the process of Indigenizing the future may be healing as others have suggested in terms of repatriation and ceremony. When taken together, Indigenous-made speculative media, ecopolitics leveraged by Neshnabé Women's Water Walks, and ecological restoration projects on and near tribal lands in the Great Lakes region constitute a Neshnabé futurity—one defined by Indigenous notions of what a healthy community looks and acts like.

The argument I make in this work that defines Neshnabé futurity as speculative fiction, ecopolitics mobilized by prophecy, and ecological revitalization projects can and should alter theorists' ideas about Indigenous agency. More than just a definition or unique construct, futurisms refuse victimhood and erasure. Refusal, as Indigenous scholars like Tuck and Yang and Simpson have articulated, does not just resist settler incursions or violations of Indigenous space; rather it is active in constructing alternative modalities of Indigenous existence and freedom.[2] Therefore, Neshnabé futurity reclaims representational space and physical places, forging new, yet to be manifested, channels in the fabric of Indigenous space-time. These reclamation efforts by Anishinaabé communities go beyond mere inclusion. They not only reclaim space but also reshape the currents of Indigenous space-time. By charting new courses while allowing space for the natural meanders and flows, Neshnabé activists, artists, language specialists, and natural resource professionals open possibilities for decolonial futures. These futures are rooted in the intergeneration and interspecies confluence of our ancestors' ways of knowing, our stories, and our experiences shaped by *Neshnabé ke*—our homelands. The activities described throughout this book work together to "speak to futurity in registers of decolonization."[3]

Neshnabé futurity is not a type of reactionary politics or simply about advancing a certain set of grievance claims. Similar to how Mvskoke anthropologist Laura Harjo theorizes her community's actions, Indigenous futurities include "sites that allow community members to convene, visit, and build networks of relationality" in order to enact community desires and "imagin[e] unactivated dreams."[4] Because settler colonialism has dismantled tribal lands, peoples, and relationships to manifest settler desires in an invaded space, Indigenous attempts to reclaim our futures are often inaccurately described as protest or resistance. We need new language to describe the nation-building work that is being done on the land, in the skies, on the waters, and even in digital spaces. Futurity is one way I propose to rethink outside settler frames of reference.

Indigenous-made speculative fiction represents creative experiments of possibilities and makes space for alternative conceptions of the future. Explorations of cyclical time, slipstreams and whirling pools, revisit ideas about Indigenous traditional knowledge and social relationships to Indigenous lands and waters. Mark Rifkin's *Beyond Settler Time* teases apart how Indigenous cosmological references such as stories, land, and prophecies resist oppressive settler colonial conceptions of the future. As I explain elsewhere,

> The many ways in which Indigenous peoples accomplish the renegotiation of what the future holds includes dwelling in affective places, refusing settler normative constructs of family and lineal descent, and using prophecy to create emancipatory networked temporalities. To these ends, Rifkin (2017) introduces his concept of temporal sovereignty, defined as the refusal of settler-colonial recognition or inclusion in the goals, desires, and values of dominant society's ideas of the future. The term is useful for considering how U.S. settler-colonial temporality validates and normalizes itself while erasing Indigenous ones, limiting the actualization of alternative imaginaries for political and social change.[5]

Neshnabé futurity has an eye toward the ancestors and future generations. It accounts for the everyday practices of reclaiming narratives of space and place discussed in chapter 1, the application of traditional knowledge covered in chapter 2, the healthy maintenance of interspecies relationships explained in chapter 3, and, finally, the liberated spaces created by artists and activists to imagine the future in film, literature, and other works of art. The last section explores how Neshnabé futurity is utilized to reclaim and restore our connection to the land and skies.

Reclaiming Space

This monograph begins with an introduction to Neshnabé ke or Potawatomi homelands. And it is there that I wish to return. All Indigenous peoples with whom I am familiar have creation stories that embed them in specific places. Sometimes these places are bodies of water, regions on the land, or even places in the sky. For Potawatomi peoples specifically, we have stories of emergence from bodies of water in addition to stories about descending from a hole in the sky. Therefore, celestial and terrestrial currents are two parts of the same split atom. It is no wonder that the ways in which travel is spoken about in *Bodwéwadmimwen* are the same whether one is navigating through waters or in celestial canoes across the spirit path, also known as the Milky Way. I orient readers to Potawatomi homelands while at the same time critiquing the limitations of Western cartography in the introduction and to a greater extent in chapter 1. So, when considering the conventional sort of mapping that tribes, including the Pokagon Band, are engaged in, some readings of this activity may side with the "master's tools" argument.[6] I am not particularly interested in convincing anyone whether tribes' use of software like Esri Press ArcMap is colonial or not. I mention this because in the years I have worked on this project—over a decade now—this common knee-jerk reaction to tribes mapping their own lands is tiresome and not helpful. With that said, I wish to highlight the pragmatic work being done by Neshnabé peoples and how the products of this labor both mobilize Neshnabé futurity and, at the same time, inspire a renewed understanding of theories of space and place.

In *Mitêwâcimowina: Indigenous Science Fiction and Storytelling*, editor Neal McCleod describes space in relation to the future in the following way:

> Science fiction involves the idea of exploration of space—specifically the idea of outer space. However, space can also be thought of as the interior space—the space of the mind and the imagination. Space is not only the terrain of the physical world, but also the terrain of the soul which I think is the core of the âtayôhkêwina. The cartography of "space" does not only involve inner and outer aspects, but also the notion of ancestral space. Space is not only the stars in the sky—but the stars within us.[7]

To demonstrate Indigenous spiraling space and time as well as conclude with material acts of asserting sovereignty, I close with two projects that revolve around reclaiming space and place—on land and in the sky.

Poring over copies of historic maps that mark archaeological mound sites and old Potawatomi village locations, Kyle Malott and Matthew Bussler compare notes, look back at the Ersi ArcMap software open on the computer screen, and discuss cultural nuances of historical sites. Matthew is the Pokagon Band tribal historic preservation officer and Kyle is the Pokagon Band's advanced language specialist, also an unofficial tribal historian. His expertise is respected in the community, and so is that of Kyle's mentors. The two of them are creating geographic information data points on the best mapping software that exists. Some data are triangles with circles around them, others are *X*s, still others are dots, and so on. These symbols represent village sites, locations of trading posts, burial mounds, and several other categories of sites. There are complicated spatial deviations and inconsistencies in data, but they work through them. These spatial data are being turned into what Matthew calls "story maps" to create spatial archives of Potawatomi knowledge and history. More and more tribes are utilizing geographic information systems (GIS) to create these spatial archives to consolidate community cultural knowledge as well as to protect the physical locations of historic and culturally sensitive sites.

Amidst a rural landscape of gas stations, mini-marts, and parking lots that obscure Potawatomi presence, this form of counter-mapping stories the landscape with Potawatomi histories and perspectives, or, rather, *re-stories*. The maps show our deep-time relationship with these places and resist settler colonial attempts to erase Indigenous existence. However, non-Native residents in Michigan and Indiana hold tight to historical delusions in their caricatured bastardizations of Indigeneity. Cacophonic settler stories about manifest destiny, Indian princesses, and savage chiefs drown out non-Native relationships to place in the Great Lakes region.

Although Neshnabé peoples' histories are constructed through seasonal movements and mass migration, their histories are deeply rooted in the Great Lakes, their having been there for thousands of years. This is evident in the hundreds of place-names that still exist and are used by Neshnabé peoples as seen in figure 7. Despite the erasure of Indigenous presence in settler societies like the U.S. through renaming places or co-opting false narratives of Indigenous place-names, Anishinaabé communities are reclaiming spaces through counter-mapping projects. Pyne and Taylor use what they call a "critical cartography and participatory GIS" strategy to recalibrate taken-for-granted understandings of the Lake Huron Treaty relationships, which, at present, benefit the settler government of Canada at the expense of Aboriginal sovereignty. The terms

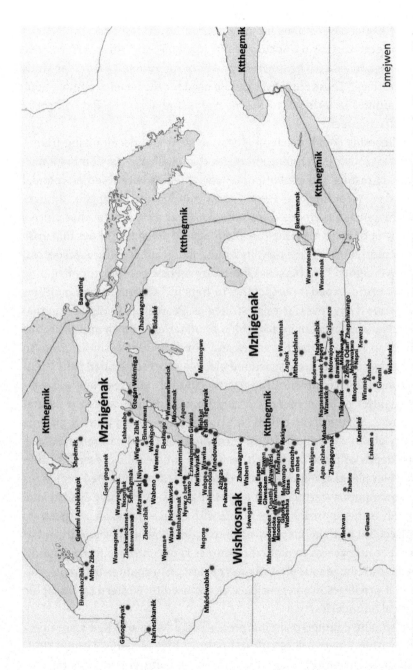

FIGURE 7 Map of known Potawatomi place-names in Michigan, Indiana, Illinois, and Wisconsin by Bmejwen Kyle Malott, redrawn by the author.

of land acquisition and the limiting of natural resources have detrimental consequences for Indigenous communities. In response, Indigenous mapping strategies such as storytelling, dancing, and other performative methods concede to the inherent power of maps to tell particular kinds of narratives.[8] These narratives can be used for the benefit of Indigenous communities in terms of territorial rights and access to and control of natural resources.

Indigenous counter-mapping is an exigent and decolonizing framework that employs mapping strategies that challenge the dominant narratives of history and contemporary social reality within settler-colonial contexts.[9] Accordingly, as Pearce and Louis succinctly explain, "Indigenous mapping has emerged since the 1970s as a movement that utilizes the power of maps for visually explaining and defending issues that arise from cultural use of territory, including land claims, natural resources, and sovereignty."[10] In this sense, literature on new participatory mapping takes a critical spatial perspective to benefit Indigenous communities even while it employs Cartesian strategies. Pearce and Louis explain that when Native Hawaiian cartographic boundaries—which are intricately bound up with natural resources and kin networks in similar ways to Neshnabé conceptions of space and place—were recalibrated to fit Western conceptions of private property, it negatively affected Native Hawaiian qualities of life centered on communal land and access to natural resources. So, they reinscribed Native Hawaiian conceptions of place as they relate to changing seasons, tidal variations, and natural resources. This "depth of place" approach resituates Indigenous presence within particular places as opposed to the depoliticized, unpopulated depictions of contemporary cartographic representations. As the authors explain, not only is this approach more in line with Native Hawaiian perspectives of place, but also the maps contribute to Indigenous sovereignty initiatives, because access to natural resources is of central concern. Sounds, smells, and Indigenous place-names coalesce in a counter-mapping project that privileges lived experience as opposed to Western cartographic political boundaries.[11]

Neshnabé counter-mapping projects like Matt and Kyle's are operating within a network of cultural politics that reclaims various kinds of space in the Great Lakes. The concept of cultural politics is important in contemporary anthropology inquiries, especially those revolving around spatial contestations. Arturo Escobar defines cultural politics as "the process enacted when social actors shaped by or embodying different cultural meanings and practices come into conflict with each other."[12] Often these conflicts arise in the attempts of subaltern groups to reclaim certain powers or representational space. Cultural politics can be further realized in competing claims to national space, competing nationalisms that are realized spatially. For example, in Rupel Oza's "The Geography of Hindu Right-Wing Violence in India," she reveals how violence is deployed to convert public spaces in India into "Hindu spaces." Through administrative spatial techniques of counting, census taking, and mapping, the Hindu Right deployed a series of attacks and systematic burnings of Muslim neighborhoods to "create a Hindu rashtra, a pure Hindu national space, one not contaminated by signs of the Muslim other."[13] This case shows the violent dimension to cultural politics, one that is inherently spatial in its attempts to claim space, both metaphorically and physically in what David Sibley calls "geographies of exclusion," or how unequal relationships of power monopolize space and resources to the detriment of some communities over others.[14]

As already alluded to, literature on "reclaiming space" combats processes of dispossession. Indigenous political actors reclaim space through a variety of discursive spatial techniques. For example, in her ethnography *Native Hubs*, Reyna Ramirez explains how in the Indigenous reclaiming of urban space, specifically in L.A. and other parts of California, Native Americans construct a productive arena in which to enact politics. Reclaimed urban spaces provide arenas in which agency can be enacted. This is especially important in a settler colonial society that finds the very existence of Indigenous peoples irrelevant to national policy and political vision.[15] This solidarity and social organization among Native Americans is so important because, as Ramirez explains, "[a] sense of unity in the Indian community cannot be taken for granted in an atmosphere of distrust, factionalism, and dislocation that government policy and academic discourses have encouraged. However, emotions, spirituality, and joking—important aspects of hub-making—can inform a gendered approach to belonging, ultimately breaking down a white masculine notion of 'politics' and who is a 'political actor.'"[16]

Anna F. Laing explores in her research how cultural politics is enveloped within natural resource management and how it informs Indigenous territoriality struggles. For Laing, sovereignty has come to mean resource repatriation, because "indigenous identities are not formed in a political vacuum but counteract government projects of extractive development that jeopardise the livelihoods of indigenous peoples within communally tied territories."[17] Like the concept of *mno bmadzewen* for Potawatomi people, for the Indigenous communities in her research, the concept of *vivir bien* constitutes a better, more just alternative to the violent realities of resource exploitation under capitalism.[18] Vivir bien is a tool developed within the space created through Indigenous cultural politics of resistance. Therefore, by (1) expanding the traditional one-sited method of participant observation through multi-sited analysis, (2) politically contextualizing affective attachments to place through competing Indigenous nationalisms, and (3) grounding these social processes in case studies of Indigenous resistance to natural resource exploitation, the anthropology of space and place is a productive arena for advancing an anthropological understanding of Indigenous social movements, conceptions of sovereignty, and social justice.

One of the most radical things an Indigenous person can be is visible. If settler colonialism seeks to disappear Native histories, rights, and futures, contemporary Neshnabé politics makes them visible and inevitably witnessed by mainstream society. Extending beyond Earth's surface, the Pokagon Band is also reclaiming place in the sky. Neshnabé means more than just the cultural designation of tribes in the Great Lakes region. Neshnabé refers to "the ones who were lowered down." Some Neshnabé creation stories explain our genesis from the stars. Specifically, there is an origin story that describes humans' descent from a celestial dimension in the Pleiades constellation known as *Mdodosenik* (Potawatomi meaning sweat lodge stones used in ceremony) or *Bagone'giizhig* (Ojibwe meaning hole in the sky). When one looks up at the night sky and is reminded of our vulnerable and insignificant place in the cosmos, it does not seem like a particularly politically contentious place. However, like counter-mapping on the ground, the revival of Potawatomi star knowledge through the identification of constellations has resulted in star maps circulating in the Pokagon community.

While Potawatomi and Ojibwe names for the Pleiades constellation differ—Mdodosenik or sweat lodge stones and Bagone'giizhig or hole in the sky, respectively—I contend that the significance is much the same.

All constellations rise in the east, where everything begins. The cardinal direction in the Neshnabé medicine wheel is yellow and represents the east and infancy and tobacco—one of the sacred medicines. It is the direction we face when communing with the Creator. The Ojibwe name, Bagone'giizhig/Hole in the Sky, indexes the creation story of Skywoman falling as the first woman, who helped create the world on the back of a turtle after a great flood. She fell from a hole in the sky between Earth and the Sky World. Assisted by swans and given a tiny paw-full of dirt retrieved after the sacrifice of muskrat who dove to the bottom of the water and drowned, she smoothed the dirt over the back of a great turtle. Dancing on the turtle's back and with seeds in hand from when she grasped a great tree before falling, she created the world we love today. For this reason, many Indigenous peoples in North America refer to this land as Turtle Island. The Potawatomi name for the Pleiades constellation, Mdodosenik/Sweat Stones, indexes the grandfather rocks or *nmeshomsêk*. Not only are Ojibwe folks known as elder brothers to the Potawatomi, but grandfather/sweat stones are the elders who have lived the longest on this planet. During sweat lodge ceremony, and like the eastern direction which represents renewal and rebirth, we are cleansed and reborn. Through the Indigenous frames of reference like renewal and beginnings, though "hole in the sky" and "sweat lodge stones" may seem to have nothing to do with one another, they are indeed very much related. One just needs to see things through a Neshnabé lens.

In March 2019, in my role as archivist for the Department of Language and Culture, I planned and coordinated a Potawatomi star knowledge event for the Pokagon community after learning about Ojibwe constellation and star-mapping projects occurring in the northern Great Lakes region. Michael Waasegiizhig Price, who was involved in the Ojibwe starmapping project outlined in Lee et al.'s *Ojibwe Sky Star Map Constellation Guide*, gave a presentation on the stories and traditional knowledge associated with Neshnabé constellations. As a result, many Pokagon citizens had a renewed interest in applying traditional Neshnabé knowledge to their STEM curriculum at the tribal Head Start school *Zagbëgon*, the name meaning "little sprouts."

Together with oral storytelling in the classroom, children at Zagbëgon and at the tribe's summer camp painted pictures of Potawatomi constellations. They used Kyle Malott's star map (figure 8) to engage in a

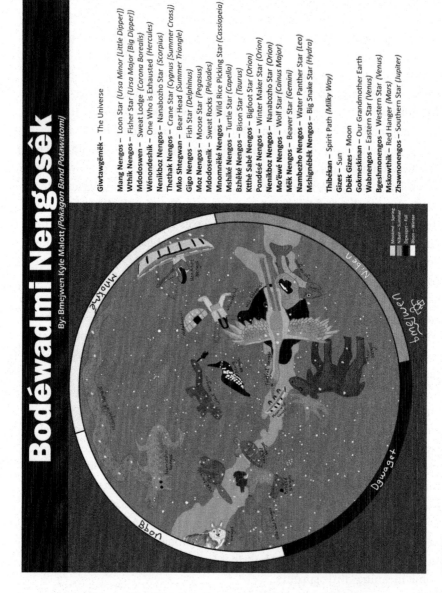

FIGURE 8 Map by Bmejwen Kyle Malott, 2023. Courtesy of the artist.

creative lesson designed to orient them to the cyclical seasons, associated harvesting practices, and stories from the sky. In doing so, children learned that their ancestors were indeed astronomers and that they paid attention to the movement of celestial bodies to make inferences about the environment and know when to harvest and grow certain crops, as well as to engage in complex constructions of self-identity.

Counter-mapping projects like those of Neshnabé constellations and reinscribing Great Lakes place-names with their original Indigenous ones are literal re-mappings. They are part of larger projects of "respatialization." Respatialization is an important emerging theme in the literature of space and place. It refers principally to the reclaiming of space that has been dispossessed and alienated from particular groups. In what Seneca scholar Mishuana Goeman calls "(Re)mapping," power is reassigned to Native ways of knowing, and this reconstitutes our destinies toward decolonial spatial justice.[19] One example of this is through the reclaiming of cultural space. Similarly, Crystal McKinnon identifies urban music performances by Aboriginal musicians in Australia as "critical sites of Indigenous resistance." In her research, the music group The Stray Blacks "shows an active pursuit and creation of Indigenous space by these people, who sought a way for the Indigenous community to gather in spite of the racism expressed by the Melbourne venues and the wider enduring forces of settler colonialism."[20] McKinnon concludes that the music performances reclaim space and, in doing so, contribute to the cultural survival of Indigenous peoples in other places. The activities of these musicians upset the normative settler forms of domination in which Indigenous peoples are forced to live. Arjun Appadurai explains in "Sovereignty Without Territoriality" in *The Geography of Identity* that any counterhistories such as those of Indigenous communities compromise the "territorial integrity" of the U.S. and are thus the unconscionable receptors of the settler state's violence.[21] Speaking to this point, Thomas Biolsi explains that Indian reservations are heterogeneous spaces of overlapping and often conflicting political geographies that stem from a long genealogy of federal court decisions. However, late-twentieth-century Indigenous resistances opened up pan-tribal space, in part to rectify the tribal nationalist factualism resulting from centuries of settler colonial oppression. In explaining the 1969–71 occupation of Alcatraz Island, Biolsi argues that "the space claimed by pan-Indians represents the social production of new political space: not a tribal homeland or even a mosaic of different homelands, but a generic Native space of U.S. national dimensions." This case study and similar trends construct Biolsi's concept of "indigenous cosmopolitanism" in which pan-tribal political mobilization creates a "national Indigenous space."[22]

Literature about contemporary tribal-based ceremonies and other culturally specific practices points to an increase in frequency and participation in these activities in recent years. These practices typically have been celebrated by social theorists while being cloaked in cultural revitalization rhetoric: "language revitalization," "Neshnabémwen Renaissance,"[23] and "cultural revivals" are some terms employed to describe these social phenomena. However, this rhetoric trivializes these practices because such language locates what is "vital" Indigenous activity or "culture" within a decontextualized and apolitical past whereby it can be brought back through cultural necromancy. This language and theoretical framing negate the important creative, intellectual, and political work Neshnabé peoples are doing to construct better futures. These "revitalizations" should instead be theorized using an Indigenous futurisms framework centered on reclaiming space and place. Social justice must not only incorporate but also be willing to be shaped by Indigenous experience and alternative conceptions of the future.

The counter-mapping projects and resistance to settler narratives of place discussed in this chapter, together with the Women's Water Walks, are a set of Indigenous cultural politics deployed as a form of competing nationalism against the U.S. settler colonial nation state. Additionally, these cultural politics are actualized by utilizing social networks in multiple sites across the U.S. and Canada with Water Walks and politically charged ceremonies in other Neshnabé communities throughout the Great Lakes region. Thus, I illustrate the multilocal affective attachments to place and how these attachments, when taken together, help construct a new landscape of conceptual space for social justice in the future. In light of pipelines that scar the landscape and settler narratives that erase Potawatomi presence in Indiana and Michigan, Potawatomi counter-mapping projects reclaim space and place in the Great Lakes region. Advanced mapping by Matthew and Kyle in programs like Esri ArcMap legitimize Potawatomi claims to place. These spatialized data are used to leverage Potawatomi deep histories in specific places that are currently under threat of pipeline construction. And the dissemination of ancestral knowledge via cartographic maps speckled with Bodwéwadmimwen and star charts of ancestral constellations ensures children in the tribe will bring this knowledge into the future. May they continue to imbue the sky, lands, and waters with their ancestral medicine and endure to navigate celestial currents of Neshnabék sovereignty through creative storytelling—speculative Neshnabék fictions that heal and are made real.

GLOSSARY

The following is a select list of words in Ojibwe and Potawatomi.

Ojibwe words (Anishinaabémowin):

Anishinaabé (Anishinaabék, plural). "the true humans" or "the original people"
Anishinaabémowin. Ojibwe and Odawa language
Jiibay Kona. "spirit path," the Milky Way
Midéwiwin. Medicine Lodge
nokomis. "grandmother"

Potawatomi words (Bodwéwadmimwen)

Bbon. winter
Bgeshmonengos. Western Star (Venus)
Bgwëtthnėnė. "he/she who lives naturally," a bigfoot-like being
bkanathmownen. stories that take an alternative perspective on things, science fiction
Bodéwadmi nengosêk. Potawatomi stars
Bodwéwadmimwen. Potawatomi language
Bzêké Nengos. Bison Star (Taurus)
Dbëk Gizes. Moon

Dgwaget. fall
Ggaténmamen Gdankobthegnanêk. "We Honor our Ancestors" Powwow
Gigo Nengos. Fish Star (Delphinus)
Giwtawgëmëk. The Universe
Gizes. Sun (or moon/month)
Gokmeskinan. "our Grandmother Earth"
Gzémnedo. "creating spirit," the Creator
ke. earth or dirt
keno'magéwen. learning and teaching
ktthe migwėtth. thank you very much
Ktthé Sabé Nengos. Bigfoot Star (Orion)
Mang Nengos. Loon Star (Ursa Minor [Little Dipper])
Mdodosenik. Sweat Rocks (Pleiades)
Mdodoswen. Sweat Lodge (Corona Borealis)
Mémégwésiwêk. "those whose face swings (referring to their long beard)," dwarf-like beings
méndokaswen. ceremonial or spiritual doing
mkedéwa. it is black
mko. bear
Mko Shtegwan. Bear Head (Summer Triangle)
mnedo (mnedowêk, plural). "entity that goes about causing change," spirit that has never lived as a human
mno bmadzewen. walking the good path
Mnokmé. spring
Mnomnëké Nengos. Wild Rice Picking Star (Cassiopeia)
Mo'ëwé Nengos. Beaver Star (Gemini)
Moz Nengos. Moose Star (Pegasus)
mshigmé. "big body of water," a big lake
Mshignébêk Nengos. Big Snake Star (Hydra)
Mshiké Nengos. Turtle Star (Capella)
Mshiwakwa. "place of big trees," Mishawaka, Indiana
Mskowthik. Red Hanger (Mars)
mskwa. it is red
Mzhigénak. "the place that has been clear-cut," Michigan
Nambezho. Underwater Lynx or Panther
Nambezho Nengos. Water Panther Star (Leo)

Nenikboz Nengos. Nanabozho Star (Orion)
Nenikboz Nengos. Nanabozho Star (Scorpius)
nenwesh. "male plant," milkweed
Neshnabé (Neshnabék, plural). "the true humans" or "the original people"
Neshnabé ke. Potawatomi homelands
Neshnabémwen. Potawatomi language
Niben. summer
Nimkibneshi. thunderbird
nokmis. "grandmother"
Pa'isêk. "little people," (known for stealing items and sometimes children)
Pekégen. "rib," name of Potawatomi leader later known as Leopold Pokagon
Pokégnék Bodwéwadmik. Pokagon Potawatomi, plural
Pondésé Nengos. Winter Maker Star (Orion)
Thethak Nengos. Crane Star (Cygnus [Summer Cross])
Thibékan. Spirit Path (Milky Way)
Wabnengos. Eastern Star (Venus)
wabshkya. It is white
Wénondeshik. One Who Is Exhausted (Hercules)
Windego. "one who is thought of as dirty," a giant cannibal-like being
Wthik Nengos. Fisher Star (Ursa Major [Big Dipper])
wzawa. it is yellow
Zhawnonengos. Southern Star (Jupiter)

NOTES

Preface

1. One could really keep going. Potawatomi has Sauk and Fox influences, Myaamia shares many of the same grammatical structures of other Algonquian languages, and so on. I recently heard a Penobscot friend and colleague give a prayer at a convening I attended, and I could recognize some of the words she uttered that we share in Potawatomi.
2. Saugatuck is spelled *Zagitëk* in the contemporary Potawatomi spelling system used by the Pokagon Band.
3. See the Appendix for a select list of words.
4. This monograph, however, is not a study on discourse analysis.
5. Malott and Morseau, "Introduction," 7–8.
6. Some have also interpreted particles in the word that reference a state of being low. They relate this to stories about the original Native peoples being lowered down from the Sky World, while others have said that the state of being "low" refers to the humble position of human beings as being the least important animal on earth.
7. Note here, too, the use of an English plural form for a Potawatomi word. What should be pluralized by the ending of "k" in the Potawatomi language is instead an "s"—"Neshnabés" instead of "Neshnabék."
8. I use "mythological" in quotes because of the negative connotation the term carries—that entities and stories in Neshnabé cosmology are not real. The use of quotation marks indexes the function of "for lack of a better phrase."
9. Michael Wassegijig Price, personal communication, March 20, 2019.

Introduction

1. Neshnabé (plural, Neshnabék) is the general Algonquian word for Indigenous peoples of the Great Lakes region—Miami, Potawatomi, Ojibwe, Odawa, and many others. Anishinaabé is the Ojibwe spelling, while Neshnabé is the Potawatomi spelling. I will use the Potawatomi spelling in most cases. Both words are often translated as "the true humans" or "original people," but are more accurately translated as "those who were lowered down," referring to the origin story of Great Lakes Native peoples being lowered down from the Sky World, or as "low beings" referring to the humble nature of humans.
2. Neshnabé is the Indigenous cultural group and identity for the lands and waters where the research for this book took place as well as the endonym with which I identify.
3. Owing to the opposing forces of power between the Sky World and the Underwater World, traditional medicine pouches will often feature a Thunderbird on one side with an Underwater Panther on the other—both protecting and adding potency to the medicine carried inside.
4. From the Potawatomi words *Pékégen*, which means "rib" and refers to Leopold Pokagon, and *Bodwé*, meaning "he/she builds the fire," as in the *Bodwéwadmik* or "those who build or keep the fire."
5. Many present-day tribal citizens of the Pokagon Band have relatives on tribal rolls of other Anishinaabé groups in Michigan and elsewhere. As an example, I have relatives on the Grand River Band of Odawa tribal rolls and my family name, Topash, is said to be of Miami origin. Even our tribe's namesake, Leopold Pokagon, was Ojibwe. It should also be noted that, in addition to the tribal groups already mentioned and like most Native North American communities, the Pokagon Band is ethnically diverse and includes citizens with heterogeneous ancestry from all over the world. I am of predominantly settler Scots-Irish background, for example, and was born with the surname Caldwell. Morseau is my spouse's last name. While blood quantum is certainly seen as real by some and as a colonial tool of erasure by others, this ethnic heterogeneity of Pokagon people does not adversely affect our nationhood or cultural identities as a whole.
6. Those familiar with any Indigenous language will know that there tends to be a frustrating number of different spellings for the same word—even within the same speech community. I've decided to use the version of Pokagon that I've seen the most of, but others include *bëgégen*, *pëgégen*, and *pokégen*.
7. These Potawatomi communities include the Match-E-Be-Nash-She-Wish Band of Pottawatomi Indians, formerly known as Gun Lake Band, the Nottawaseppi Huron Band of Potawatomi, the Hannahville Indian Community, and the Pokagon Band of Potawatomi, who are all located in Michigan. Forest County Potawatomi is located in Wisconsin, Prairie Band Potawatomi is located in Kansas, and Citizen Band Potawatomi is located in Oklahoma.
8. Wetzel, *Gathering the Potawatomi Nation*.

9. Though there are other communities in Canada and even on the U.S.–Mexico border (the Mexican Kickapoo) who have descendants of Potawatomi groups who fled during the 1800s. Communities in Canada include the Wasauksing First Nation, Walpole Island First Nation, Sault Ste. Marie Tribe of Chippewa Indians, the Anishanabeg of Kettle and Stony Point First Nation, Beausoleil First Nation, and Chippewas of Nawash First Nation.
10. For decent sources on Indigenous place-names in Michigan, see Vogel, *Indian Names in Michigan*, Walton, "Indian Place Names in Michigan," and Malott, "Cartographic Map with Potawatomi Place Names."
11. While context and the specific histories and languages of tribes and First Nations in North America are of cardinal importance, the political positioning of "Indigenous" as a global classification allows for some extrapolation to see how local contexts are indicative of larger processes of colonization and Indigenous resistance. Indigeneity is an international classification, one centered on a community's position in the context of settler colonialism and includes over three hundred million Indigenous peoples in at least seventy countries across the world. Therefore, while the diversity of Indigenous peoples, cultures, histories, and languages is indeed vast, the concept of Indigeneity as a political position allows for a global comparative opportunity to better understand Indigenous futurities or futurisms.
12. Heidegger, *Poetry, Language, Thought*.
13. Dillon, *Walking the Clouds*.
14. Baudemann, "Indigenous Futurisms in North American Indigenous Art," 117.
15. Medak-Saltzman, "Coming to You from the Indigenous Future," 144.
16. Secunda, "In the Shadow of Eagle's Wings."
17. Walton, "Indian Place Names in Michigan."
18. Walker and Salt, *Resilience Thinking*, 32. See also Frieswyk and Zedler, "Vegetation Change in Great Lakes Coastal Wetlands"; Nicholls, "Detection of Regime Shifts in Multi-Species Communities"; Sparhawk and Brush, *The Economic Aspects of Forest Destruction in Northern Michigan*.
19. For more on the unequal protection of Indigenous sacred sites, see Businge and Keim, "The Political Battlefield"; Gonzalez and Cook-Lynn, *The Politics of Hallowed Ground*. For issues of pollution and reservations as natural sacrifice zones, see Hall and Fenelon, *Indigenous Peoples and Globalization*; LaDuke, *All Our Relations*.
20. Sedell, Leone, and Duval, "Water Transportation and Storage of Logs"; Whitney, "An Ecological History of the Great Lakes Forest of Michigan."
21. Sparhawk and Brush, *The Economic Aspects of Forest Destruction in Northern Michigan*.
22. Sierra Club, "Hydraulic Fracturing in Michigan."
23. Manthos, "Cancer-Causing Chemicals Used in 34% of Reported Fracking Operations."
24. McGregor, "Indigenous Women, Water Justice and Zaagidowin (Love)."

25. Whyte, "Our Ancestors' Dystopia Now."
26. Contracted ethnographies specifically include that of James Clifton as expert witness during federal recognition application processes. See Clifton, *The Pokagons, 1683–1983*.
27. White, *The Middle Ground*; Secunda, "In the Shadow of Eagle's Wings."
28. Claspy, *The Dowagiac-Sister Lakes Resort Area*; Wetzel, *Gathering the Potawatomi Nation*.
29. Low, *Imprints*.
30. Miller, *Ogimaag*.
31. Landes, *The Prairie Potawatomi*. This ethnographic text includes the voices of some of my direct relatives including Tom W. Topash—my third great-grandfather.
32. Vennum Jr., *The Ojibwa Dance Drum*.
33. Whyte and Cuomo, "Ethics of Caring in Environmental Ethics"; McGregor, "Indigenous Women, Water Justice and Zaagidowin (Love)."
34. For an Anishinaabé perspective on climate change and the roles of traditional spirit beings, see Nelson, "The Hydromythology of the Anishinaabeg."
35. The particle *kwé* at the end of Neshnabé is for "woman."
36. Climate change causes anxieties at best. This does not take into account the experiences of people who are most directly affected now such as coastal communities, nations in the global South, and subsistence-based communities.
37. I envision a revisit to speculative fictions related to the latter in light of profound developments in artificial intelligence such as the recent proliferation of massive language and text-to-image models.
38. Whyte, "Indigenous Science (Fiction) for the Anthropocene."
39. However, as I argue in chapters 2 and 3, storywork is not fiction in the mainstream sense of the term, as in "not real."
40. Atalay, *Community-Based Archaeology*.
41. Hopkins, "Keno'magéwen."
42. Basso, *Wisdom Sits in Places*; for Potawatomi peoples in particular: Low, *Imprints*; Miller, *Ogimaag*; Willow, "Conceiving Kakipitatapitmok."
43. Bullard, *Confronting Environmental Racism*; Milton, *Environmentalism and Cultural Theory*; Parajuli, "Ecological Ethnicity in the Making"; Soja, *Seeking Spatial Justice*.
44. Hall and Fenelon, *Indigenous Peoples and Globalization*.
45. Appadurai, "Introduction: Place and Voice in Anthropological Theory."
46. Bourdieu, *Outline of a Theory of Practice*.
47. Low, *On the Plaza*.
48. Biolsi, "Imagined Geographies"; Scott, *Domination and the Arts of Resistance*.
49. McMahon, "Everything You Do Is Political, You're Anishinaabe."
50. Povinelli, *The Cunning of Recognition*.
51. Visual sovereignty: Raheja, *Reservation Reelism*; knowledge sovereignty: Norgaard, "Retaining Knowledge Sovereignty"; temporal sovereignty: Rifkin, *Beyond Settler Time*.

52. Wolfe, "Settler Colonialism and the Elimination of the Native"; Simpson, *Mohawk Interruptus*; Povinelli, *The Cunning of Recognition*.
53. I found out much later in this dissertation project (post research phase and halfway through writing) that rumor has it that Tom embezzled money from the Pokagon tribe in some way. I did not investigate this because it was much too late in this project to do so, and it didn't make any meaningful contributions to my research questions.
54. Vennum Jr., *The Ojibwa Dance Drum*, 18.
55. Elkins, *Stories of Art*, 54, quoted in Matthews, *Naamiwan's Drum*, 15. Also see Clifford, *The Predicament of Culture*.
56. The reader will hopefully forgive yet another anthropologist offering up a definition of culture.
57. Matthews, *Naamiwan's Drum*, 15; "an Ojibwe archipelago" references Comaroff and Comaroff, *Ethnography and the Historical Imagination*, 31.
58. Nelson, "The Ecology of Travel on the Great Lakes Frontier," 2–3. Indeed, chapter 1 includes a Potawatomi migration/origin story along the Saint Lawrence Seaway.
59. Marcus, "Ethnography in/of the World System."
60. Falzon, *Multi-Sited Ethnography*, 1–2.
61. This is a Potawatomi spelling of the more popular Anishinaabé spelling, Ashinaabékwé, used by First Nations and most Ojibwe peoples.
62. As evidenced by what my family had already told me, what is recorded in my official tribal enrollment papers, and what is reflected in what I found in the Bureau of Indian Affairs's administrative files in the collection of the Mount Pleasant Indian Boarding School student case files located at the National Archives in Chicago.
63. I present my family background not because I think I'm the main character here, but in response to the reckoning of dozens of recently exposed ethnic fraud cases (also referred to as "race shifters," "pretendians," and other terms)—academics in particular who claim and monetize an Indigenous identity on the basis of dubious family claims of a (usually distant, but often nonexistent) Indigenous ancestor. I also want to acknowledge that while I claim a Neshnabé community (and via my citizenship my community does indeed claim me), I benefit from a fair amount of privilege in multiple contexts, because owing to my phenotype I can pass as a white person.
64. What is more, some tribal members have recently (within the past ten years) switched their enrollment from the Pokagon Band to another tribe that they have descendancy from and vice versa. We socialize, work, and marry into other tribes all the time. So, inclusion criteria based on enrollment alone is restrictive and unnecessary.
65. Tuck and Yang, "R-Words: Refusing Research"; Simpson, *Mohawk Interruptus*.
66. Tuck and Yang, "R-Words: Refusing Research," 225.
67. Wilson, *Research Is Ceremony*, 135.
68. Geertz, *The Interpretation of Cultures*, 5.

69. I use the term "reservation" as an indirect substitute for the towns and tribal trust lands that make up the Pokagon community. The Band never had reservation land as they were not removed.
70. Kuwayama, "'Natives' as Dialogic Partners."
71. Kuwayama.
72. Smith, *Decolonizing Methodologies*, 175.
73. Smith, 111.
74. Mihesuah and Wilson, *Indigenizing the Academy*; "Indigenize the academy": Smith, *Decolonizing Methodologies*, 2.
75. James, "Corrupt State University," 53.
76. Mihesuah and Wilson, *Indigenizing the Academy*, 6.
77. Lea, Kowal, and Cowlishaw, *Moving Anthropology*.
78. Wilson, *Research Is Ceremony*, 22.
79. Wilson, 60.
80. Lea, Kowal, and Cowlishaw, *Moving Anthropology*, 6.
81. Wolfe, "Settler Colonialism and the Elimination of the Native."
82. Wolfe; Veracini, *Settler Colonialism*, 3.
83. Wolfe, "Settler Colonialism and the Elimination of the Native," 387.
84. Wolfe, 393.
85. LaPensée and Courchene, "The Skoden Podcast."
86. Lempert, "Decolonizing Encounters of the Third Kind," 166.
87. Bowler, "Politics as Art."
88. Eshel, *Futurity: Contemporary Literature and the Quest for the Past*, 4.
89. Fabian and Bunzl, *Time and the Other*.
90. Vizenor, *Survivance: Narratives of Native Presence*. A version of this passage has been previously published in a chapter I contributed to *The Routledge Handbook of Cofuturisms* to describe *Bodwéwadmi* futurisms. See Morseau, "Coding Potawatomi Cosmologies."
91. Lempert, "Decolonizing Encounters of the Third Kind," 173.
92. Wallace, "Revitalization Movements," 256.
93. Language: White, "Rethinking Native American Language Revitalization"; religion: Mooney and DeMallie, *The Ghost-Dance Religion*; ecology: Vayda, *Environment and Cultural Behavior*.
94. Low, "Vessels for Recollection."
95. Streeby, "#NoDAPL Native American and Indigenous Science, Fiction, and Futurisms," 41.
96. Baudemann, "Indigenous Futurisms in North American Indigenous Art," 117.
97. Hopkins, "Keno'magéwen."

Chapter 1
1. Harjo, *Spiral to the Stars*, 76.
2. Low, *Imprints*, 58.
3. Lefebvre, *The Production of Space*, 11.

4. Hirsch, "Landscape: Between Place and Space," 13–17.
5. Soja, *Seeking Spatial Justice*, 39.
6. The Pokagon Band of Potawatomi Indians' "service area" for citizens extends into a couple of counties in Indiana, but the tribal government is centrally located in Dowagiac, Michigan. There are no reservation lands in Indiana, though the tribe has acquired properties in the state that it has put into trust with the Department of the Interior.
7. All the land that the Pokagon Band now owns has been purchased by the tribe with revenue from the tribe's gaming ventures with the exception of one very small plot of land in Goshen, Indiana. In 2013, the elderly couple who owned the plot wished to repatriate human remains that were found there sometime in the 1950s as well as "donate" the property to the tribe. At this time, I was working for the tribe as an intern in the Department of Natural Resources under the tribal historic preservation officer and participated in a reburial ceremony of the ancestors found on that property.
8. Soja, *Seeking Spatial Justice*, 72.
9. Environmental racism takes a critical spatial perspective on issues such as pollution and access to natural resources. It takes as a point of departure that benefits and risks associated with resource extraction, pollution, and access to beneficial resources are not evenly distributed across all social groups. As Bullard poignantly explains, "social inequality and imbalances of social power are at the heart of environmental degradation, resource depletion, pollution, and even overpopulation. The environmental crisis can simply not be solved effectively without social justice" (Bullard, *Confronting Environmental Racism*, 261).
10. Estes, *Our History Is the Future*.
11. LaDuke, *All Our Relations*, 268.
12. Sleeper-Smith et al., "Powering Modern America."
13. Parajuli, "Ecological Ethnicity in the Making," 16.
14. Kahan et al., "The Polarizing Impact of Science Literacy and Numeracy."
15. Areas that are not part of the reservation per se, but which are, nonetheless, included in treaties that stipulate tribes' access to and use of natural resources found in those areas.
16. Gedicks, "Racism and Resource Colonialism."
17. Gedicks. 71.
18. LaDuke, *All Our Relations*, 7.
19. "Spirit," in Potawatomi, but one that has never lived as a human. A more accurate translation is "entity that goes about causing change."
20. The Mishawaka city official's name has been redacted here and their pronouns neutralized for privacy.
21. Mishawaka actually means "place of large stand of trees," not dead stand of trees. This may have been a typo, or a mistake on Paige's part since she is not Pokagon herself (or a member of any related tribe).
22. Fryberg et al., "Of Warrior Chiefs and Indian Princesses."

23. Tuck and Yang, "Decolonization Is Not a Metaphor."
24. O'Brien, *Firsting and Lasting*, xiii.
25. O'Brien, 178.
26. Cerwonka, *Native to The Nation*, 1–2.
27. Cerwonka, 66.
28. Cerwonka. 1.
29. LaDuke, *All Our Relations*, 66.
30. Goeman, *Mark My Words*.
31. Bastien, *Blackfoot Ways of Knowing*.
32. Basso, *Wisdom Sits in Places*.
33. Gonzalez and Cook-Lynn, *The Politics of Hallowed Ground*.
34. Gupta and Ferguson, *Culture, Power, Place*, 179.
35. Gupta and Ferguson, 181.
36. Gupta and Ferguson, 3.
37. Gonzalez and Cook-Lynn, *The Politics of Hallowed Ground*.
38. Basso, *Wisdom Sits in Places*.
39. Richardson and Jensen, "Linking Discourse and Space."
40. Bisharat, "Exile to Compatriot," 224.
41. Mar, "Carving Wilderness," 76.

Chapter 2

1. Hopkins, "Keno'magéwen."
2. Sherman, "The (R)Evolution of Indigenous Foods."
3. Hopkins, "Keno'magéwen." I have seen this demonstrated at Midéwiwin lodge as well as in more secular contexts. Recently, at the 2024 convening of the newly established Center for Braiding Indigenous Knowledges and Science (CBIKS) at the University of Massachusetts, Amherst, Shannon Martin (Match-E-Be-Nash-She-Wish Band of Pottawatomi Indians) led a sand scroll teaching about the hills—or what some refer to as seasons—of life. As a poignant display of braiding knowledges, this teaching was followed up by a Māori attendee who spoke about his community's traditional beliefs about the co-dependence of healthy communities.
4. Gross, *Anishinaabe Ways of Knowing and Being*.
5. Kimmerer, *Braiding Sweetgrass*, 46.
6. Berkes, "Indigenous Ways of Knowing," 153.
7. World Intellectual Property Organization, "Traditional Knowledge."
8. King, *Places That Count*.
9. Menzies, "Introduction: Understanding Ecological Knowledge," 2.
10. Deloria Jr., *Red Earth, White Lies*, xiv.
11. Bastien, *Blackfoot Ways of Knowing*, 2.
12. Bastien, 6.
13. Basso, *Wisdom Sits in Places*, 57.
14. Basso, 61.

15. Berkes, "Indigenous Ways of Knowing."
16. Langdon, "Tidal Pulse Fishing."
17. Benedict and Frelich, "Site Factors Affecting Black Ash Ring Growth in Northern Minnesota."
18. Berkes, "Indigenous Ways of Knowing."
19. This report was the most recent at the time of writing but has been superseded; at the time of publication, the newest report is from 2023 and reflects an increase—from 2011 to 2021—in Black and American Indian/Alaskan Native representation in STEM. National Center for Science and Engineering Statistics, "Diversity and STEM."
20. Mihesuah and Wilson, *Indigenizing the Academy*.
21. Surna, "Equitable Representation," 50.
22. Griffin, "Addressing STEM Culture and Climate."
23. Cajete, *Native Science*.
24. Kimmerer et al., "A Letter from Indigenous Scientists in Support of the March for Science."
25. Chambers, "Stereotypic Images of the Scientist."
26. Sam Morseau, personal communication, March 13, 2019.
27. Boyer, "Visiting Knowledge in Anthropology," 141.
28. Crick, "Anthropology of Knowledge," 287.
29. Weiler, "Whose Knowledge Matters?," 2.
30. Traianou, "Science Teaching."
31. Carlone and Johnson, "Unpacking 'Culture' in Cultural Studies of Science Education."
32. Jemielniak, *Common Knowledge?*, 1.
33. Jemielniak, 18.
34. Wolf, *Envisioning Power*, 6.
35. Menzies, *Traditional Ecological Knowledge and Natural Resource Management*, 9.
36. Marlor, "Bureaucracy, Democracy and Exclusion," 529.
37. Ascher, Steelman, and Healy, *Knowledge and Environmental Policy*.
38. Butler, "Historicizing Indigenous Knowledge," 107–8.
39. Menzies, *Traditional Ecological Knowledge and Natural Resource Management*, 11.
40. Menzies, 12.
41. Cepek, "Strange Powers."
42. Atalay, *Community-Based Archaeology*, 48.
43. Atalay, 129.
44. Matthew Bussler, personal communication, October 14, 2019.
45. Atalay, *Community-Based Archaeology*, 77.
46. Stern et al., "The Meaning of the National Environmental Policy Act."
47. Assuming the tribe has a grant or the economic infrastructure to support that THPO position. Not all tribes do.

48. Middleton, "'Just Another Hoop to Jump Through?,'" 1059.
49. Coulthard, *Red Skin, White Masks*, 66.
50. Hardt and Negri, *Empire*, 29.
51. Low, "Vessels for Recollection," 2.
52. Mukurtu is a Drupal content management system developed in close collaboration with Indigenous communities in Australia and is designed to be customized to meet the specific cultural protocols and community needs of Native peoples anywhere in the world. For more information about the system, see Thorpe et al., "Designing Archival Information Systems Through Partnerships with Indigenous Communities."
53. Both Winchester and Wesaw participated in the Tribal Digital Stewardship Cohort Program at The Center for Digital Scholarship and Curation at Washington State University in 2015. Their strategic planning for an archives program and future implementation of the Mukurtu platform allowed me to be able to launch the site several years later.
54. Wemigwans, *A Digital Bundle*.
55. Eglash et al., "Decolonizing Education with Anishinaabe Arcs," 1570.

Chapter 3

1. Morseau, "Coding Potawatomi Cosmologies."
2. Vic Bogosian, personal communication, October 2015.
3. I use "fix" in quotation marks because, as most natural resource professionals will explain, there is only so much that can be done to revitalize certain ecologies.
4. This is an old spelling that does not employ the official Potawatomi orthography of the Pokagon Band. We no longer use the double vowel system the way many Ojibwe speaking groups do. But the name of the powwow is still spelled like this.
5. Boyd, *Indians, Fire, and the Land in the Pacific Northwest*, 313.
6. Minnis, *People and Plants in Ancient Western North America*.
7. Howard, "Native American Routes."
8. Kosek, *Understories*.
9. Walker and Salt, *Resilience Thinking*.
10. Kohn, *How Forests Think*, 1.
11. The word for ghost in Potawatomi is *thibey*.
12. Johnston, *The Manitous*, 2.
13. Thunder and Thunder, *Wete Yathmownen, Real Stories*.
14. Despite research, questioning tribal community members, and consulting one geologist, no one has been able to identify their composition.
15. Throop, "Sacred Suffering," 89.
16. Heidegger, *Bremen and Freiburg Lectures*; Mitchell, *The Fourfold*.
17. Ingold, *The Perception of the Environment*, 13.
18. Ingold, 14.

19. McLean, *Fictionalizing Anthropology*, 9.
20. Clifford, *Routes*, 190.
21. Clifford, 190.
22. A version of this paragraph and the one above have been previously published in a chapter about Bodwéwadmi futurisms. See Morseau, "Coding Potawatomi Cosmologies."
23. Tsing et al., *Arts of Living on a Damaged Planet*, M2.
24. Kirksey and Helmreich, "The Emergence of Multispecies Ethnography." Some criticize the use of the term "nonhuman" because they consider it patronizing, inflating the superiority of homo sapiens. It has been compared to using the phrase "non-white" or "non-hetero." And, while I agree that referring to the millions of species and cosmological beings as "nonhuman" is demeaning, it is the most reliable shorthand I have that would not distract from my main arguments.
25. Kirksey and Helmreich, 549.
26. At least, beneficial when no vaccine is available for malaria.
27. See https://sickle-cell.com/clinical/malaria.
28. Tsing, "Unruly Edges," quoted in Kirksey and Helmreich, "The Emergence of Multispecies Ethnography," 551.
29. Pressured to grow larger and more fleshy as a result of humans and nonhumans picking the largest and ripest ones. The seeds of these fruit-bearing plants would be later deposited and dispersed through the feces of humans and nonhumans who ate the fruit.
30. Pressured to be larger, more fleshy, and sweeter than its wheat-like ancestor as a result of the agricultural methods developed by Native Americans.
31. Ascher, Steelman, and Healy, *Knowledge and Environmental Policy*; Menzies, *Traditional Ecological Knowledge and Natural Resource Management*.
32. Moore, "Islands of Difference," 515.
33. Moore, 528.
34. Smith, *Decolonizing Methodologies*.
35. Whyte, "Against Crisis Epistemology."
36. McLean, *Fictionalizing Anthropology*, ix.
37. The Ordovician-Silurian extinction, the Late Devonian extinction, the Permian-Triassic extinction, the Triassic-Jurassic extinction, and the Cretaceous-Paleogene extinction.
38. Tsing et al., *Arts of Living on a Damaged Planet*, M3.
39. Whyte, "Indigenous Science (Fiction) for the Anthropocene," 226. "Felt knowledges" references D. Million, *Therapeutic Nations: Healing in an Age of Indigenous Human Rights* (Tucson: Univ. of Arizona Press, 2013).
40. Culton, "Pokagon Band to Begin Work on River Restoration."
41. Ganapathy, "Imagining Alaska," 98.
42. It has since been surpassed by the Los Conchos fire and Whitewater-Baldy fire.
43. Kosek, *Understories*, 267–8.

Chapter 4

1. Medak-Saltzman, "Coming to You from the Indigenous Future," 144.
2. Chu, *Do Metaphors Dream of Literal Sleep?*, 7.
3. Chu, 2.
4. Chu, 9.
5. Rieder, *Colonialism and the Emergence of Science Fiction*, 2–3.
6. Wells, *War of the Worlds*, 4–5.
7. Rieder, *Colonialism and the Emergence of Science Fiction*, 131.
8. Medak-Saltzman, "Coming to You from the Indigenous Future," 140.
9. A version of this passage appears in a previous publication of mine describing Neshnabé futurisms as forms of sovereignty work. See Topash-Caldwell, "Sovereign Futures in Neshnabé Speculative Fiction."
10. Taylor, "Why I Write Indigenous Sci-Fi." Rieder, *Colonialism and the Emergence of Science Fiction*. While Native peoples are not represented by characters in the series, it should be noted, however, that one of the main characters, Camina Drummer, is played by actress Cara Gee, who is Ojibwe.
11. Wilbur, *Project 562*.
12. Fryberg et al., "Of Warrior Chiefs and Indian Princesses." Also see Black, *Picturing Indians*; Raheja, *Reservation Reelism*.
13. Chu, *Do Metaphors Dream of Literal Sleep?*, 7.
14. Chu, 8.
15. McLeod, *Mitêwâcimowina*, 5.
16. Higgins, "Survivance in Indigenous Science Fictions."
17. Collins, "Sail On! Sail On!" It is not necessary that a science fiction story takes place in the future, per se. Even imaginations of alternative existences in the present or past are still imaginations of non-existent or not-yet-existent potentials.
18. Collins, 184.
19. Portions of this section have been adapted from previously published material. See Topash-Caldwell, "Sovereign Futures in Neshnabé Speculative Fiction."
20. Harjo, *Spiral to the Stars*, 28.
21. Lempert, "Decolonizing Encounters of the Third Kind," 166. Lempert originally made this point in relation to another short film featured in his article called *The Visit* by Anishinaabé filmmaker Lisa Jackson.
22. Indigenous Comic Con is now called IndigiPop.
23. Spiers, *Encountering the Sovereign Other*, xvi; Keene, "'Magic in North America.'"
24. Lempert, "Decolonizing Encounters of the Third Kind," 167; Dillon, *Walking the Clouds*.
25. Spiers, *Encountering the Sovereign Other*, xv.
26. Jauss, *Toward an Aesthetic of Reception*, 15.
27. Spiers, xii.

28. Saunders, *This All Come Back Now*, 9.
29. Harjo, *Spiral to the Stars*, 11.
30. Baudemann, "Indigenous Futurisms in North American Indigenous Art," 117.
31. Saunders, *This All Come Back Now*, 8.
32. Estes, *Our History Is the Future*, 14.
33. Appadurai, *The Future as Cultural Fact*, 126.
34. Smith, *Decolonizing Methodologies*.
35. See Vennum Jr., *The Ojibwa Dance Drum*.
36. Matthews, *Naamiwan's Drum*. The suffix "mba" or "ben" is used when naming Neshnabé folks who have recently passed away. The use of mba at the end of a recently deceased person's name prevents "calling them back" from their journey into the spirit world.
37. With the development of a social movement initiated by Midéwiwin ceremonial leaders, however, there has been controversy in the Pokagon community particularly among those who do not view Midéwiwin as a religious identity held by Potawatomi peoples in the past. For some reason—one that I have not yet had the chance to explore—some Pokagon people who practice what they believe are traditional ways—fasting, sweat lodge, sugar bush, etc.—even some who already participate in Pokagon water ceremonies and Water Walks, do not have an interest in Midéwiwin ceremonies. Some Pokagon Midéwiwin members are confused by this, stating, "But what they're doing *is* Midéwiwin!" Disagreements and controversy surrounding Women's Water Walks in the Pokagon community stem from religious identity politics, some of which is discussed in the introduction to a collection I edited in 2023 (see Morseau, *As Sacred to Us*). While both Indigenous and non-Indigenous participants of the Women's Water Walks have a consensus on the sacredness and vital nature of water, still other Neshnabék have come to see the movement—specifically the Pokagon ceremonies and walks—as less of a legitimate ceremony or political demonstration and more of a collection of quasi-ceremonial theatrics. Some *Midés* do not value the Water Walks, specifically those organized by the Pokagon Band, in the same regard as those organized by the Three Fires Lodge. One informant once referred to Pokagon-based ceremonies (as opposed to Midéwiwin ceremonies in Wisconsin) as "glorified talking circles." Future research might look deeper into religious divides within the Pokagon community, but these questions go beyond the scope of the current work.
38. *Wgetthda* (*wgetthdak*, plural) means warrior(s) or, literally, "he or she has a big heart."
39. Near the beginning of this research the location by the cliff became geologically unstable and therefore too dangerous to hold ceremony.
40. Gramsci, *Modern Prince*, 121.
41. Gramsci, 118.
42. Gramsci, 61.

43. Gramsci, 64.
44. Translations of Gramsci's work typically use the term "organism," however I use organicism because organism is a biological term.
45. Crehan, *Gramsci, Culture and Anthropology*, 95.
46. Ari, *Earth Politics*, 2.
47. Ari, 36.
48. Simpson, *Mohawk Interruptus*, 31. The Anishinaabémowin phrase *mino bimaadiziwin* is often translated as "the good life" or the "good/healthy path/way of being."
49. I do not have permission to describe the specific ceremonial protocol, nor is it necessary to explain in detail the Pipe Ceremony or the Women's Water Ceremony for the purposes of this project. Instead, I focus on the political entanglements in which these practices are embedded.
50. The Pokagon Band has been extremely active in NCAI. The council funds tribal youth to go to all NCAI meetings, and as a result most of the NCAI youth office positions are held by Pokagons (about four officers) at the time of this writing.
51. Sierra Club, "Hydraulic fracturing in Michigan."
52. Rush, "The Threat from Hydrofracking," 27.
53. Manthos, "Cancer-Causing Chemicals Used in 34% of Reported Fracking Operations."
54. Rush, "The Threat from Hydrofracking," 28.

Conclusion

1. Whyte, "Against Crisis Epistemology."
2. Tuck and Yang, "R-Words: Refusing Research"; Simpson, *Mohawk Interruptus*.
3. Valentine and Hassoun, "Uncommon Futures," 245.
4. Harjo, *Spiral to the Stars*, 10, 33.
5. Topash-Caldwell, "Book Review."
6. The master's tools argument is a statement made by American author, Civil Rights activist, and radical feminist Audre Lorde in her 1984 essay "The Master's Tools Will Never Dismantle the Master's House." The quote, "For the master's tools will never dismantle the master's house," means that, while master's tools may temporarily allow someone to beat the oppressor at their own game, they will never enable true change. Lorde believed that this argument applied to underlying racism within feminism, which she described as an unrecognized dependence on the patriarchy. Lorde, *Master's Tools Will Never Dismantle the Master's House*.
7. McLeod, *Mitêwâcimowina*. 4.
8. Pyne and Taylor, "Mapping Indigenous Perspectives," 95.
9. Pyne and Taylor.
10. Pearce and Louis, "Mapping Indigenous Depth of Place," 108.
11. Pearce and Louis, 121.
12. Escobar, "Cultural Politics and Biological Diversity," 203.

13. Oza, "The Geography of Hindu Right-Wing Violence in India," 157.
14. Sibley, *Geographies of Exclusion*, ix.
15. Ramirez, *Native Hubs*, 58.
16. Ramirez, 83.
17. Laing, "Resource Sovereignties in Bolivia."
18. Laing, 157.
19. Goeman, *Mark My Words*, 4.
20. McKinnon, "Indigenous Music as a Space of Resistance," 256.
21. Appadurai, "Sovereignty Without Territoriality," 53.
22. Biolsi, "Imagined Geographies," 247.
23. Wetzel, *Gathering the Potawatomi Nation*.

BIBLIOGRAPHY

Appadurai, Arjun. *The Future as Cultural Fact*. London: Verso, 2013.
Appadurai, Arjun. "Introduction: Place and Voice in Anthropological Theory." *Cultural Anthropology* 3, no. 1 (1988): 16–20. https://doi.org/10.1525/can.1988.3.1.02a00020.
Appadurai, Arjun. "Sovereignty Without Territoriality: Notes for a Postnational Geography." In *The Geography of Identity*, edited by Patricia Yaeger, 40–58. Ann Arbor: Univ. of Michigan Press, 1996.
Ari, Waskar. *Earth Politics: Religion, Decolonization, and Bolivia's Indigenous Intellectuals*. Narrating Native Histories. Durham, NC: Duke Univ. Press, 2014.
Ascher, William, Toddi Steelman, and Robert Healy. *Knowledge and Environmental Policy: Re-Imagining the Boundaries of Science and Politics*. Cambridge, MA: MIT Press, 2010. https://doi.org/10.7551/mitpress/8398.001.0001.
Atalay, Sonya. *Community-Based Archaeology: Research with, by, and for Indigenous and Local Communities*. Oakland: Univ. of California Press, 2012.
Basso, Keith H. *Wisdom Sits in Places: Landscape and Language Among the Western Apache*. Albuquerque: Univ. of New Mexico Press, 1996.
Bastien, Betty. *Blackfoot Ways of Knowing: The Worldview of the Siksikaitsitapi*. Edited by Jurgen W. Kremer. Calgary: Univ. of Calgary Press, 2004.
Baudemann, Kristina. "Indigenous Futurisms in North American Indigenous Art: The Transforming Visions of Ryan Singer, Daniel McCoy, Topaz Jones, Marla Allison, and Debra Yepa-Pappan." *Extrapolation* 57 (January 1, 2016): 117–50. https://doi.org/10.3828/extr.2016.8.
Becker, Nanobah, dir. *The 6th World: An Origin Story*. ITVS International, 2012.
Benedict, Michael A., and Lee E. Frelich. "Site Factors Affecting Black Ash Ring Growth in Northern Minnesota." *Forest Ecology and Management* 255, no. 8 (May 15, 2008): 3489–93. https://doi.org/10.1016/j.foreco.2008.02.029.

Berkes, Fikret. "Indigenous Ways of Knowing and the Study of Environmental Change." *Journal of the Royal Society of New Zealand* 39, no. 4 (December 2009): 151–56. https://doi.org/10.1080/03014220909510568.

Biolsi, Thomas. "Imagined Geographies: Sovereignty, Indigenous Space, and American Indian Struggle." *American Ethnologist* 32, no. 2 (2005): 239–59. https://doi.org/10.1525/ae.2005.32.2.239.

Bisharat, George E. "Exile to Compatriot: Transformations in the Social Identity of Palestinian Refugees in the West Bank." In *Culture, Power, Place: Explorations in Critical Anthropology*, edited by Akhil Gupta and James Ferguson, 203–33. Durham, NC: Duke Univ. Press, 1997.

Black, Liza. *Picturing Indians: Native Americans in Film, 1941–1960*. Lincoln: Univ. of Nebraska Press, 2022.

Bourdieu, Pierre. *Outline of a Theory of Practice*. Translated by Richard Nice. Cambridge Studies in Social and Cultural Anthropology. Cambridge: Cambridge Univ. Press, 1977. https://doi.org/10.1017/CBO9780511812507.

Bowler, Anne. "Politics as Art: Italian Futurism and Fascism." *Theory and Society* 20, no. 6 (December 1991): 763–94. https://doi.org/10.1007/BF00678096.

Boyd, Robert, ed. *Indians, Fire, and the Land in the Pacific Northwest*. Corvallis: Oregon State Univ. Press, 1999, 313.

Boyer, Dominic. "Visiting Knowledge in Anthropology: An Introduction." *Ethnos* 70, no. 2 (June 2005): 141–48. https://doi.org/10.1080/00141840500141097.

Bullard, Robert D. *Confronting Environmental Racism: Voices from the Grassroots*. Boston, MA: South End Press, 1993.

Businge, Janice, and Wiebke Keim. "The Political Battlefield: Negotiating Space to Protect Indigenous and Traditional Knowledge Under Capitalism." *International Social Science Journal* 60, no. 195 (2009): 37–54. https://doi.org/10.1111/j.1468-2451.2009.01699.x.

Butler, Caroline. "Historicizing Indigenous Knowledge: Practical and Political Issues." In *Traditional Ecological Knowledge and Natural Resource Management*, edited by Charles R. Menzies, 107–26. Lincoln: Univ. of Nebraska Press, 2006.

Butler, Octavia E. *Parable of the Sower*. With an introduction by Gloria Steinam. New York: Seven Stories Press, 2017.

Cajete, Gregory. *Native Science: Natural Laws of Interdependence*. 1st ed. Santa Fe, NM: Clear Light Publishers, 2016.

Carlone, Heidi, and Angela Johnson. "Unpacking 'Culture' in Cultural Studies of Science Education: Cultural Difference Versus Cultural Production." *Ethnography and Education* 7, no. 2 (June 2012): 151–73. https://doi.org/10.1080/17457823.2012.693691.

Carson, Rachel. *Silent Spring*. Anniversary ed. Boston, MA: Mariner Books Classics, 2022.

Cepek, Michael L. "Strange Powers: Conservation, Science, and Transparency in an Indigenous Political Project," *Anthropology Today*, 28, no. 4 (2012): 14–17. https://doi.org/10.1111/j.1467-8322.2012.00885.x.

Cerwonka, Allaine. *Native to the Nation: Disciplining Landscapes and Bodies in Australia*. 1st ed. Minneapolis: Univ. of Minnesota Press, 2004.
Chambers, David Wade. "Stereotypic Images of the Scientist: The Draw-a-scientist Test." *Science Education* 67, no. 2 (April 1983): 255–65. https://doi.org/10.1002/sce.3730670213.
Chu, Seo-Young. *Do Metaphors Dream of Literal Sleep?* Cambridge, MA: Harvard Univ. Press, 2011.
Claspy, Everett. *The Dowagiac-Sister Lakes Resort Area and More About Its Potawatomi Indians*. Dowagiac, MI, 1970.
Clifford, James. *The Predicament of Culture: Twentieth-Century Ethnography, Literature, and Art*. Cambridge, MA: Harvard Univ. Press, 1988.
Clifford, James. *Routes: Travel and Translation in the Late Twentieth Century*. Illustrated ed. Cambridge, MA: Harvard Univ. Press, 1997.
Clifton, James A. *The Pokagons, 1683–1983*. Lanham, MD: Univ. Press of America, 1984.
Collins, Samuel Gerald. "Sail On! Sail On!: Anthropology, Science Fiction, and the Enticing Future." *Science Fiction Studies* 30 (2003): 180–98.
Comaroff, John and Jean Comaroff. *Ethnography and the Historical Imagination*. 1st ed. Boulder, CO: Westview Press, 1992.
Coulthard, Glen Sean. *Red Skin, White Masks: Rejecting the Colonial Politics of Recognition*. Minneapolis: Univ. of Minnesota Press, 2014.
Crehan, Kate. *Gramsci, Culture and Anthropology*. Oakland: Univ. of California Press, 2002.
Crick, M. R. "Anthropology of Knowledge." *Annual Review of Anthropology* 11, no. 1 (1982): 287–313. https://doi.org/10.1146/annurev.an.11.100182.001443.
Culton, Sarah. "Pokagon Band to Begin Work on River Restoration." Leader Publications, December 4, 2018. https://www.leaderpub.com/2018/12/04/pokagon-band-to-begin-work-on-river-restoration/.
Deloria, Vine, Jr. *Red Earth, White Lies: Native Americans and the Myth of Scientific Fact*. 1st ed. Golden, CO: Fulcrum Publishing, 1997.
Dillon, Grace L., ed. *Walking the Clouds: An Anthology of Indigenous Science Fiction*. Sun Tracks: An American Indian Literary Series, v. 69. Tucson: Univ. of Arizona Press, 2012.
Dimaline, Cherie. *The Marrow Thieves*. Toronto: DCB, 2017.
Eglash, Ron, Michael Lachney, William Babbitt, Audrey Bennett, Martin Reinhardt, and James Davis. "Decolonizing Education with Anishinaabe Arcs: Generative STEM as a Path to Indigenous Futurity." *Educational Technology Research and Development* 68, no. 3 (June 2020): 1569–93. https://doi.org/10.1007/s11423-019-09728-6.
Elkins, James. *Stories of Art*. 1st ed. New York: Routledge, 2002.
Emmerich, Roland, dir. *Independence Day*. 20th Century Fox, 1996.
Escobar, Arturo. "Cultural Politics and Biological Diversity: State, Capital and Social Movements in the Pacific Coast of Colombia." In *The Politics of Culture in the*

Shadow of Capital, edited by Lisa Lowe and David Lloyd, 201–26. Durham, NC: Duke Univ. Press Books, 1997.

Eshel, Amir. *Futurity: Contemporary Literature and the Quest for the Past*. Chicago: Univ. of Chicago Press, 2013. https://doi.org/10.7208/chicago/9780226924960.001.0001.

Estes, Nick. *Our History is the Future: Standing Rock Versus the Dakota Access Pipeline, and the Long Tradition of Indigenous Resistance*. New York: Verso Books, 2019.

Evans-Pritchard, Sir Edward E. *Theories of Primitive Religion*. Oxford: Oxford Univ. Press, 1968.

Fabian, Johannes, and Matti Bunzl. *Time and the Other: How Anthropology Makes Its Object*. New York: Columbia Univ. Press, 2002.

Falzon, Mark-Anthony. *Multi-Sited Ethnography: Theory, Praxis and Locality in Contemporary Research*. Farnham, UK: Ashgate, 2009. http://catdir.loc.gov/catdir/toc/fy0906/2008045374.html.

Feld, Steven, and Keith H. Basso, eds. *Senses of Place*. Santa Fe, NM, Seattle, WA: School for Advanced Research Press, 1996.

Fergus, Mark and Hawk Ostby, creators. *The Expanse*. Syfy, Amazon Prime Video, six seasons, 2015–2022.

Foucault, Michel. *Power/Knowledge: Selected Interviews and Other Writings, 1972–1977*. Edited by Colin Gordon. 1st ed. New York: Vintage, 1980.

Freeland, Sydney, dir. *Hoverboard*. Independently released, 2012.

Frieswyk, Christin B., and Joy B. Zedler. "Vegetation Change in Great Lakes Coastal Wetlands: Deviation from the Historical Cycle." *Journal of Great Lakes Research* 33, no. 2 (January 1, 2007): 366–80. https://doi.org/10.3394/0380-1330(2007)33[366:VCIGLC]2.0.CO;2.

Fryberg, Stephanie A., Hazel Rose Markus, Daphna Oyserman, and Joseph M. Stone. "Of Warrior Chiefs and Indian Princesses: The Psychological Consequences of American Indian Mascots." *Basic and Applied Social Psychology* 30, no. 3 (September 26, 2008): 208–18. https://doi.org/10.1080/01973530802375003.

Ganapathy, Sandhya. "Imagining Alaska: Local and Translocal Engagements with Place." *American Anthropologist* 115, no. 1 (2013): 96–111. https://doi.org/10.1111/j.1548-1433.2012.01538.x.

Gedicks, Al. "Racism and Resource Colonialism." *Race and Class* 33, no. 4 (April 1, 1992): 75–81. https://doi.org/10.1177/030639689203300406.

Geertz, Clifford. *The Interpretation of Cultures*. New York: Basic Books, 1973.

Goeman, Mishuana. *Mark My Words: Native Women Mapping Our Nations*. First Peoples: New Directions in Indigenous Studies. Minneapolis: Univ. of Minnesota Press, 2013.

Gonzalez, Mario, and Elizabeth Cook-Lynn. *The Politics of Hallowed Ground: Wounded Knee and the Struggle for Indian Sovereignty*. 1st ed. Urbana: Univ. of Illinois Press, 1998.

Goulet, Danis, dir. *Wakening*. Viddywell Films, 2013.

Gramsci, Antonio. *Modern Prince and Other Writings*. New York: International Publishers, 1959.
Griffin, Kimberly A. "Addressing STEM Culture and Climate to Increase Diversity in STEM Disciplines." *Higher Education Today*, April 23, 2018. https://www.higher edtoday.org/2018/04/23/addressing-stem-culture-climate-increase-diversity -stem-disciplines/.
Gross, Lawrence W. *Anishinaabe Ways of Knowing and Being*. 1st ed. London: Routledge, 2016.
Gupta, Akhil, and James Ferguson, eds. *Culture, Power, Place: Explorations in Critical Anthropology*. Durham, NC: Duke Univ. Press, 1997.
Haig-Brown, Helen, dir. *?E?ANX (The Cave)*. Rugged Media, 2009.
Hall, Thomas D., and James V. Fenelon. *Indigenous Peoples and Globalization: Resistance and Revitalization*. New York: Routledge, 2015.
Hardt, Michael, and Antonio Negri. *Empire*. Cambridge, MA.: Harvard Univ. Press, 2001.
Harjo, Laura. *Spiral to the Stars: Mvskoke Tools of Futurity*. Critical ed. Tucson: Univ. of Arizona Press, 2019.
Harjo, Sterlin and Taika Waititi, creators. *Reservation Dogs*. FX, three seasons, 2021–2023.
Heidegger, Martin. *Bremen and Freiburg Lectures: Insight into That Which Is and Basic Principles of Thinking*. Translated by Andrew J. Mitchell. Bloomington: Indiana Univ. Press, 1949.
Heidegger, Martin. *Poetry, Language, Thought*. New York: Harper Perennial Modern Classics, 2013.
Helms, Ed, Michael Schur and Sierra Teller Ornelas, creators. *Rutherford Falls*. Peacock, two seasons, 2021–2022.
Higgins, David M. "Survivance in Indigenous Science Fictions: Vizenor, Silko, Glancy, and the Rejection of Imperial Victimry." *Extrapolation* 57, no. 1–2 (January 2016): 51–72. https://doi.org/10.3828/extr.2016.5.
Hirsch, Eric. "Landscape: Between Place and Space." In *The Anthropology of Landscape: Perspectives on Place and Space*, edited by Eric Hirsch and Michael O'Hanlon, 1st ed., 1–30. Oxford, New York: Oxford Univ. Press, 1995.
Hopkins, Rhonda. "Keno'magéwen." In *Potawatomi Dictionary*. Accessed November 19, 2023. https://www.potawatomidictionary.com/Dictionary/Word/3283.
Howard, Tanner. "Native American Routes: The Ancient Trails Hidden in Chicago's Grid System." *The Guardian*, January 17, 2019, sec. Cities. https://www.the guardian.com/cities/2019/jan/17/native-american-routes-the-ancient-trails -hidden-in-chicagos-grid-system.
Ingold, Tim. *The Perception of the Environment: Essays on Livelihood, Dwelling and Skill*. 1st ed. London: Routledge, 2021.
Jackson, Lisa, creator. *The Visit*. National Film Board of Canada, 2009.
James, Keith. "Corrupt State University: The Organizational Psychology of Native Experience in Higher Education." In *Indigenizing the Academy: Transforming*

Scholarship and Empowering Communities, edited by Devon Abbott Mihesuah and Angela Cavender Wilson, 48–68. Lincoln: Univ. of Nebraska Press, 2004.

Jauss, Hans Robert. *Toward an Aesthetic of Reception*. Minneapolis: Univ. of Minnesota Press, 1982.

Jemielniak, Dariusz. *Common Knowledge?: An Ethnography of Wikipedia*. 1st ed. Stanford, CA: Stanford Univ. Press, 2014.

Johnston, Basil. *The Manitous: The Spiritual World of the Ojibway*. St. Paul: Minnesota Historical Society Press, 2001.

Kahan, Dan M., Ellen Peters, Maggie Wittlin, Paul Slovic, Lisa Larrimore Ouellette, Donald Braman, and Gregory Mandel. "The Polarizing Impact of Science Literacy and Numeracy on Perceived Climate Change Risks." *Nature Climate Change* 2, no. 10 (October 2012): 732–35. https://doi.org/10.1038/nclimate1547.

Keene, Adrienne. "'Magic in North America': The Harry Potter Franchise Veers Too Close to Home." *Native Appropriations* (blog), March 7, 2016. https://nativeappropriations.com/2016/03/magic-in-north-america-the-harry-potter-franchise-veers-too-close-to-home.html.

Kimmerer, Robin Wall. *Braiding Sweetgrass: Indigenous Wisdom, Scientific Knowledge and the Teachings of Plants*. 1st paperback ed. Minneapolis, MN: Milkweed Editions, 2015.

Kimmerer, Robin Wall, Rosalyn Lapier, Melissa K. Nelson, Kyle P. Whyte, Neil Patterson Jr., Patty Loew, Patricia Cochran, et al. "A Letter from Indigenous Scientists in Support of the March for Science." *Milkweed* (blog), April 21, 2017. https://milkweed.org/blog/a-letter-from-indigenous-scientists-in-support-of-the-march-for-science.

King, Thomas F. *Places That Count: Traditional Cultural Properties in Cultural Resource Management*. Walnut Creek, CA: AltaMira Press, 2003.

Kirksey, S. Eben, and Stefan Helmreich. "The Emergence of Multispecies Ethnography." *Cultural Anthropology* 25, no. 4 (November 2010): 545–76. https://doi.org/10.1111/j.1548-1360.2010.01069.x.

Kirsch, Stuart. *Mining Capitalism: The Relationship Between Corporations and Their Critics*. 1st ed. Oakland: Univ. of California Press, 2014.

Kohn, Eduardo. *How Forests Think: Toward an Anthropology Beyond the Human*. 1st ed. Berkeley: Univ. of California Press, 2013.

Kosek, Jake. *Understories: The Political Life of Forests in Northern New Mexico*. Illustrated ed. Durham, NC: Duke Univ. Press Books, 2006.

Kubrick, Stanley, dir. *2001: A Space Odyssey*. Metro-Goldwyn-Mayer, 1968.

Kuwayama, Takami. "'Natives' as Dialogic Partners: Some Thoughts on Native Anthropology." *Anthropology Today* 19, no. 1 (February 1, 2003): 8–13.

LaDuke, Winona. *All Our Relations: Native Struggles for Land and Life*. Cambridge, MA, Minneapolis, MN: South End Press, 1999.

Laing, Anna F. "Resource Sovereignties in Bolivia: Re-Conceptualising the Relationship Between Indigenous Identities and the Environment during the TIPNIS Conflict." *Bulletin of Latin American Research* 34, no. 2 (2015): 149–66. https://doi.org/10.1111/blar.12211.

Landes, Ruth. *The Prairie Potawatomi: Tradition and Ritual in the Twentieth Century*. Madison: Univ. of Wisconsin Press, 1970.

Langdon, Steve J. "Tidal Pulse Fishing: Selective Traditional Tlingit Salmon Fishing Techniques on the West Coast of the Prince of Wales Archipelago, Southeast Alaska." In *Traditional Ecological Knowledge and Natural Resource Management*, edited by Charles R. Menzies, 21–46. Lincoln: Univ. of Nebraska Press, 2006.

LaPensée, Elizabeth. *Thunderbird Strike*. 2017. Microsoft Windows, iOS, Android.

LaPensée, Elizabeth, and Ashley Courchene. "The Skoden Podcast." Indigenous Futurisms and the Politics of Video Games. Accessed December 27, 2023. Patreon.com/skodenpodcast.

Lea, Tess, Emma Kowal, and Gillian Cowlishaw, eds. *Moving Anthropology: Critical Indigenous Studies*. Darwin, N.T.: Charles Darwin Univ. Press, 2006.

Lee, Annette Sharon, William Peter Wilson, and Carl Gawboy. *Ojibwe Sky Star Map—Constellation Guidebook: An Introduction to Ojibwe Star Knowledge*. Illustrated ed. St. Cloud, MN: Native Skywatchers, 2014.

Lefebvre, Henri. *The Production of Space*. Translated by Donald Nicholson-Smith. 1st ed. Malden, MA: Wiley-Blackwell, 1992.

Lempert, William. "Decolonizing Encounters of the Third Kind: Alternative Futuring in Native Science Fiction Film." *Visual Anthropology Review* 30, no. 2 (November 2014): 164–76. https://doi.org/10.1111/var.12046.

Littlejohn, F. J. *Legends of Michigan and the Old North West: Or, a Cluster of Unpublished Waifs, Gleaned Along the Uncertain, Misty Line, Dividing Traditional From Historic Times*. Forgotten Books, 1874.

Lorde, Audre. *Master's Tools Will Never Dismantle the Master's House*. London: Penguin, 1984.

Low, John N. *Imprints: The Pokagon Band of Potawatomi Indians and the City of Chicago*. 1st ed. East Lansing: Michigan State Univ. Press, 2016.

Low, John N. "Vessels for Recollection—The Canoe Building Renaissance in the Great Lakes." *Material Culture* 47, no. 1 (2015).

Low, Setha M. *On the Plaza: The Politics of Public Space and Culture*. 1st ed. Austin: Univ. of Texas Press, 2000.

Low, Setha M. and Denise Lawrence-Zúñiga, eds. *The Anthropology of Space and Place: Locating Culture*. 1st ed. Malden, MA: Wiley-Blackwell, 2003.

Malott, Bmejwen Kyle. "Cartographic Map with Potawatomi Place Names by Kyle Malott | Wiwkwébthëgen," 2018. https://wiwkwebthegen.com/digital-heritage/cartographic-map-potawatomi-place-names-kyle-malott.

Malott, Bmejwen Kyle and Blaire Morseau. "Introduction." In *As Sacred to Us: Simon Pokagon's Birch Bark Stories in Their Contexts*, edited by Blaire Morseau, 1–20. East Lansing: Michigan State Univ. Press, 2023.

Manthos, David. "Cancer-causing Chemicals Used in 34% of Reported Fracking Operations." *SkyTruth*, January 22, 2013. https://skytruth.org/2013/01/carcinogens-fracking/.

Mar, Tracey Banivanua. "Carving Wilderness: Queensland's National Parks and the Unsettling of Emptied Lands, 1890–1910." In *Making Settler Colonial Space: Perspectives on Race, Place and Identity*, edited by Tracey Banivanua Mar and Penelope Edmonds, 73–94. Houndmills, UK; New York: Palgrave Macmillon, 2010.

Marcus, George E. "Ethnography in/of the World System: The Emergence of Multi-Sited Ethnography." *Annual Review of Anthropology* 24, no. 1 (1995): 95–117. https://doi.org/10.1146/annurev.an.24.100195.000523.

Marlor, Chantelle. "Bureaucracy, Democracy and Exclusion: Why Indigenous Knowledge Holders Have a Hard Time Being Taken Seriously." *Qualitative Sociology* 33, no. 4 (December 1, 2010): 513–31. https://doi.org/10.1007/s11133-010-9168-7.

Matthews, Maureen. *Naamiwan's Drum: The Story of a Contested Repatriation of Anishinaabe Artefacts*. 1st ed. Toronto, Buffalo, London: Univ. of Toronto Press, Scholarly Publishing Division, 2016.

McGregor, Deborah. "Indigenous Women, Water Justice and Zaagidowin (Love)." *Canadian Woman Studies* 30, no. 2/3 (2015): 71–78.

McKinnon, Crystal. "Indigenous Music as a Space of Resistance." In *Making Settler Colonial Space: Perspectives on Race, Place and Identity*, edited by Tracey Banivanua Mar and P. Edmonds, 255–72. Houndmills, UK; New York: Palgrave Macmillan, 2010.

McLean, Stuart J. *Fictionalizing Anthropology: Encounters and Fabulations at the Edges of the Human*. 1st ed. Minneapolis: Univ. of Minnesota Press, 2017.

McLeod, Neal. *Mitêwâcimowina: Indigenous Science Fiction and Speculative Storytelling*. Penticton, B.C.: Theytus Books, 2016.

McMahon, Ryan. "Everything You Do Is Political, You're Anishinaabe. Or, What Idle No More Is To Me." In *The Winter We Danced*, edited by The Kino-nda-niimi Collective, 138–41. Winnipeg: Arbeiter Ring Publishing, 2014.

Medak-Saltzman, Danika. "Coming to You from the Indigenous Future: Native Women, Speculative Film Shorts, and the Art of the Possible." *Studies in American Indian Literatures* 29, no. 1 (2017): 139–71.

Menzies, Charles R. "Introduction: Understanding Ecological Knowledge," in *Traditional Ecological Knowledge and Natural Resource Management* edited by Charles R. Menzies, 1–17. Lincoln: Univ. of Nebraska Press, 2006.

Menzies, Charles R., ed. *Traditional Ecological Knowledge and Natural Resource Management*. Lincoln: Univ. of Nebraska Press, 2006.

Middleton, Beth Rose. "'Just Another Hoop to Jump Through?' Using Environmental Laws and Processes to Protect Indigenous Rights." *Environmental Management* 52, no. 5 (November 1, 2013): 1057–70. https://doi.org/10.1007/s00267-012-9984-5.

Mihesuah, Devon A., and Angela Cavender Wilson, eds. *Indigenizing the Academy: Transforming Scholarship and Empowering Communities*. Lincoln, NE: Bison Books, 2004.

Miller, Cary. *Ogimaag: Anishinaabeg Leadership, 1760–1845.* Illustrated ed. Lincoln: Univ. of Nebraska Press, 2016.

Milton, Kay. *Environmentalism and Cultural Theory: Exploring the Role of Anthropology in Environmental Discourse.* London, New York: Routledge, 1996.

Minnis, Paul E., ed. *People and Plants in Ancient Western North America.* Illustrated ed. Tucson: Univ. of Arizona Press, 2010.

Mitchell, Andrew J. *The Fourfold: Reading the Late Heidegger.* Edited by Anthony J. Steinbock. Evanston, IL: Northwestern Univ. Press, 2015.

Mooney, James, and Raymond J. DeMallie. *The Ghost-Dance Religion and the Sioux Outbreak of 1890.* Lincoln, NE: Bison Books, 1991.

Moore, Amelia. "Islands of Difference: Design, Urbanism, and Sustainable Tourism in the Anthropocene Caribbean." *The Journal of Latin American and Caribbean Anthropology* 20, no. 3 (November 2015): 513–32. https://doi.org/10.1111/jlca.12170.

Moore, Ronald D., creator. *Outlander.* Starz, seven seasons, 2014–2023.

Morgan, Lewis Henry. *Ancient Society.* Chicago: Charles R. Kerr, 1877.

Morseau, Blaire, ed. *As Sacred to Us: Simon Pokagon's Birch Bark Stories in Their Contexts.* East Lansing: Michigan State Univ. Press, 2023.

Morseau, Blaire. "Coding Potawatomi Cosmologies: Elements of Bodwéwadmi Futurisms." In *The Routledge Handbook of Cofuturisms*, edited by Bodhisattva Chattopadhyay, Grace L. Dillon, Isiah Lavender, and Taryne Jade Taylor, 153–61. Routledge Literature Handbooks. New York: Routledge, 2023.

National Center for Science and Engineering Statistics (NCSES). *Diversity and STEM: Women, Minorities, and Persons with Disabilities 2023.* Special Report NSF 23-315. Alexandria, VA: National Science Foundation. Accessed December 28, 2023. https://ncses.nsf.gov/pubs/nsf23315/report.

Nelson, John William. "The Ecology of Travel on the Great Lakes Frontier: Native Knowledge, European Dependence, and the Environmental Specifics of Contact." *Michigan Historical Review* 45, no. 1 (spring 2019): 1–26. https://doi.org/10.5342/michhistrevi.45.1.0001.

Nelson, Melissa K. "The Hydromythology of the Anishinaabeg: Will Mishipizhu Survive Climate Change, or Is He Creating It?" In *Centering Anishinaabeg Studies: Understanding the World Through Stories*, edited by Jill Doerfler, Niigaanwewidam James Sinclair, and Heidi Kiiwetinepinesiik Star, 213–33. East Lansing: Michigan State Univ. Press, 2013.

Nicholls, Kenneth H. "Detection of Regime Shifts in Multi-Species Communities: The Bay of Quinte Phytoplankton Example." *Methods in Ecology and Evolution* 2, no. 4 (2011): 416–26. https://doi.org/10.1111/j.2041-210X.2011.00093.x.

Nolan, Christopher, dir. *Interstellar.* Warner Bros, 2014.

Norgaard, Kari Marie. *Retaining Knowledge Sovereignty: Expanding the Application of Tribal Traditional Knowledge on Forest Lands in the Face of Climate Change.* Happy Camp, CA: Karuk Tribe, 2014. https://pages.uoregon.edu/norgaard/pdf/Retaining-Knowledge-Sovereignty-Norgaard-2014.pdf.

O'Brien, Jean M. *Firsting and Lasting: Writing Indians out of Existence in New England.* 1st ed. Minneapolis: Univ. of Minnesota Press, 2010.

Oza, Rupal. "The Geography of Hindu Right-Wing Violence in India." In *Violent Geographies: Fear, Terror, and Political Violence,* edited by Derek Gregory and Allan Pred, 153–74. New York: Routledge, 2006.

Parajuli, Pramod. "Ecological Ethnicity in the Making: Developmentalist Hegemonies and Emergent Identities in India." *Identities* 3, no. 1–2 (October 1, 1996): 14–59. https://doi.org/10.1080/1070289X.1996.9962551.

Pearce, Margaret, and Renee Louis. "Mapping Indigenous Depth of Place." *American Indian Culture and Research Journal* 32, no. 3 (January 1, 2008): 107–26. https://doi.org/10.17953/aicr.32.3.n7g22w816486567j.

Povinelli, Elizabeth A. *The Cunning of Recognition: Indigenous Alterities and the Making of Australian Multiculturalism.* Politics, History, and Culture. Durham, NC: Duke Univ. Press, 2002.

Pyne, Stephanie, and D. R. Fraser Taylor. "Mapping Indigenous Perspectives in the Making of the Cybercartographic Atlas of the Lake Huron Treaty Relationship Process: A Performative Approach in a Reconciliation Context." *Cartographica: The International Journal for Geographic Information and Geovisualization* 47, no. 2 (summer, 2012): 92–104. https://doi.org/10.3138/carto.47.2.92.

Radin, Paul, Neni Panourgiá, and John Dewey. *Primitive Man as Philosopher.* Main ed. New York: NYRB Classics, 2017.

Raheja, Michelle H. *Reservation Reelism: Redfacing, Visual Sovereignty, and Representations of Native Americans in Film.* Illustrated ed. Lincoln: Univ. of Nebraska Press, 2013.

Ramirez, Renya K. *Native Hubs: Culture, Community, and Belonging in Silicon Valley and Beyond.* Durham, NC: Duke Univ. Press Books, 2007.

Richardson, Tim, and Ole Jensen. "Linking Discourse and Space: Towards a Cultural Sociology of Space in Analysing Spatial Policy Discourses." *Urban Studies* 40 (January 1, 2003): 7–22. https://doi.org/10.1080/00420980220080131.

Rieder, John. *Colonialism and the Emergence of Science Fiction.* Illustrated ed. Middletown, CT: Wesleyan Univ. Press, 2008.

Rifkin, Mark. *Beyond Settler Time: Temporal Sovereignty and Indigenous Self-Determination.* Durham, NC: Duke Univ. Press, 2017.

Rush, Paul V. "The Threat from Hydrofracking." *Journal AWWA* 102, no. 9 (2010): 26–30. https://doi.org/10.1002/j.1551-8833.2010.tb10185.x.

Saunders, Mykaela. *This All Come Back Now: An Anthology of First Nations Speculative Fiction.* St. Lucia, Australia: Univ. of Queensland Press, 2022.

Scorsese, Martin, dir. *Killers of the Flower Moon.* Paramount Pictures, 2023.

Scott, James C. *Domination and the Arts of Resistance: Hidden Transcripts.* Revised ed. New Haven, CT, London: Yale Univ. Press, 1992.

Secunda, Benjamin. "In the Shadow of Eagle's Wings: The Effects of Removal on the Unremoved Potawatomi." PhD diss., Univ. of Notre Dame, 2008. https://www.librarything.com/work/14044896.

Sedell, J. R., F. N. Leone, and W. S. Duval. "Water Transportation and Storage of Logs." In *Influences of Forest and Rangeland Management on Salmonid Fishes and Their Habitats*, edited by William R. Meehan, 325–368. American Fisheries Society Special Publication 19. Bethesda, MD: American Fisheries Society, 1991.

Shelley, Mary. *Frankenstein*. London: Lackington, Hughes, Harding, Mavor and Jones, 1818.

Sherman, Sean. "The (R)Evolution of Indigenous Foods." Filmed August 2020 in Sioux Falls, SD. TEDx video, 18:27. https://www.ted.com/talks/sean_sherman_the_r_evolution_of_indigenous_foods.

Sibley, David. *Geographies of Exclusion: Society and Difference in the West*. London: Routledge, 1995.

Sierra Club. "Hydraulic Fracturing in Michigan." Accessed October 2, 2023. https://www.sierraclub.org/michigan/huron-valley/hydraulic-fracturing-michigan.

Silliman, Stephen W. *Collaborating at the Trowel's Edge: Teaching and Learning in Indigenous Archaeology*. Tucson: Univ. of Arizona Press, 2008.

Simpson, Audra. *Mohawk Interruptus: Political Life Across the Borders of Settler States*. Illustrated ed. Durham, NC: Duke Univ. Press Books, 2014.

Sleeper-Smith, Susan, Juliana Barr, Jean M. O'Brien, Nancy Shoemaker, Scott Manning Stevens, and Andrew Needham, eds. "Powering Modern America: Indian Energy and Postwar Consumption." In *Why You Can't Teach United States History Without American Indians*, 240–58. Chapel Hill, NC: Univ. of North Carolina Press, 2015.

Smith, Linda Tuhiwai. *Decolonizing Methodologies: Research and Indigenous Peoples*. 2nd ed. London: Zed Books, 2012.

Soja, Edward W. *Seeking Spatial Justice*. 1st ed. Minneapolis: Univ. of Minnesota Press, 2010.

Sparhawk, William N., and Warren David Brush. *The Economic Aspects of Forest Destruction in Northern Michigan*. Technical Bulletin / United States Department of Agriculture, no. 92. Washington, D.C.: U.S. Department of Agriculture, 1929.

Spiers, Miriam C. Brown. *Encountering the Sovereign Other: Indigenous Science Fiction*. American Indian Studies Series. East Lansing: Michigan State Univ. Press, 2021.

Stern, Marc J., S. Andrew Predmore, Michael J. Mortimer, and David N. Seesholtz. "The Meaning of the National Environmental Policy Act Within the U.S. Forest Service." *Journal of Environmental Management* 91, no. 6 (June 1, 2010): 1371–79. https://doi.org/10.1016/j.jenvman.2010.02.019.

Streeby, Shelley. "#NoDAPL Native American and Indigenous Science, Fiction, and Futurisms." In *Stories Through Theories/Theories Through Stories: North American Indian Writing, Storytelling, and Critique*, edited by Gordon Henry, Nieves Pascual Soler, and Silvia Martínez-Falquina, 34–68. American Indian Studies Series. East Lansing: Michigan State Univ. Press, 2009.

Surna, Alex. "Equitable Representation Among People of Color and Women in Higher Ed." *The Journal of College Admission* Summer (2018): 48–53.

Swain, Molly and Chelsea Vowell. *Métis in Space*. Podcast, six seasons, 2014–2021.
Taylor, Drew Hayden. "Why I Write Indigenous Sci-Fi," *Canadian Art*, December 6, 2016. https://canadianart.ca/essays/why-i-write-indigenous-sci-fi/.
Thorpe, Kirsten, Kimberly Christen, Lauren Booker, and Monica Galassi. "Designing Archival Information Systems Through Partnerships with Indigenous Communities: Developing the Mukurtu Hubs and Spokes Model in Australia." *Australasian Journal of Information Systems* 25 (2021).
Throop, C. Jason. "Sacred Suffering: A Phenomenological Anthropological Perspective." In *Phenomenology in Anthropology: A Sense of Perspective*, edited by Kalpana Ram and Christopher Houston. Bloomington: Indiana Univ. Press, 2015.
Thunder, Jim, Sr. and Mary Jane Thunder. *Wete Yathmownen, Real Stories: Potawatomi Oral History*, 2018. https://shop.fcpotawatomi.com/products/wete-yathmownen-real-stories-potawatomi-oral-history/.
Topash-Caldwell, Blaire. "Sovereign Futures in Neshnabé Speculative Fiction." *Borderlands Journal* 19, no. 2 (October 1, 2020): 29–62. https://doi.org/10.21307/borderlands-2020-009.
Topash-Caldwell, Blaire Kristine. "Book Review: Mark Rifkin, *Beyond Settler Time: Temporal Sovereignty and Indigenous Self-Determination*." *AlterNative: An International Journal of Indigenous Peoples* 13, no. 4 (December 2017): 267–68. https://doi.org/10.1177/1177180117730229.
Traianou, Anna. "Science Teaching: A Dilemmatic Approach." *Ethnography and Education* 7, no. 2: 213–26. doi:10.1080/17457823.2012.693694.
Tsing, Anna Lowenhaupt. "Unruly Edges: Mushrooms as Companion Species." Unpublished MS, Department of Anthropology, Univ. of California, Santa Cruz.
Tsing, Anna Lowenhaupt, Nils Bubandt, Elaine Gan, and Heather Anne Swanson, eds. *Arts of Living on a Damaged Planet: Ghosts and Monsters of the Anthropocene*. 3rd ed. Minneapolis: Univ. of Minnesota Press, 2017.
Tuck, Eve, and K. Wayne Yang. "Decolonization Is Not a Metaphor." *Decolonization: Indigeneity, Education and Society* 1, no. 1 (2012): 1–40.
Tuck, Eve, and K. Wayne Yang. "R-Words: Refusing Research." In *Humanizing Research: Decolonizing Qualitative Inquiry with Youth and Communities*, edited by Django Paris and Maisha T. Winn, 223–47. 1 London: Sage Publications, Inc., 2014. https://doi.org/10.4135/9781544329611.
Valentine, David, and Amelia Hassoun. "Uncommon Futures." *Annual Review of Anthropology* 48 (2019): 243–260.
Vayda, Andrew P., ed. *Environment and Cultural Behavior: Ecological Studies in Cultural Anthropology*. 1st ed. Garden City, NY: Natural History Press, 1969.
Vennum, Thomas, Jr. *The Ojibwa Dance Drum: Its History and Construction*. St. Paul: Minnesota Historical Society Press, 2009.
Veracini, Lorenzo. *Settler Colonialism: A Theoretical Overview*. Houndmills, UK, New York: Palgrave Macmillan, 2010.
Villeneuve, Denis, dir. *The Arrival*. Paramount Pictures, 2016.

Vizenor, Gerald, ed. *Survivance: Narratives of Native Presence*. Lincoln: Univ. of Nebraska Press, 2008.
Vogel, Virgil J. *Indian Names in Michigan*. Ann Arbor: Univ. of Michigan Press, 1986.
Walker, Brian, and David Salt. *Resilience Thinking: Sustaining Ecosystems and People in a Changing World*. Illustrated ed. Washington, D.C.: Island Press, 2006.
Wallace, Anthony F. C. "Revitalization Movements." *American Anthropologist* 58, no. 2 (1956): 264–81. https://doi.org/10.1525/aa.1956.58.2.02a00040.
Walton, Ivan. "Indian Place Names in Michigan." *Midwest Folklore* 5 (2023): 23–34.
Weiler, Hans N. "Whose Knowledge Matters? Development and the Politics of Knowledge." In *Entwicklung Als Beruf*, edited by Theodor Hanf, Hans N. Weiler, and Helga Dickow, 485–96. Baden-Baden: Nomos, 2009. https://doi.org/10.5771/9783845219424-485. This work cites his English translation available at https://web.stanford.edu/~weiler/Texts09/Weiler_Molt_09.pdf.
Wells, Herbert George (H. G.). *The Time Machine*. 1st ed. London: William Heinemann, 1895.
Wells, Herbert George (H. G.). *War of the Worlds*. 1st ed. London: William Heinemann, 1898. https://ia804706.us.archive.org/15/items/warofworlds00welluoft/warofworlds00welluoft.pdf.
Wemigwans, Jennifer. *A Digital Bundle: Protecting and Promoting Indigenous Knowledge Online*. 1st ed. Regina, SK: Univ. of Regina Press, 2018.
Wetzel, Christopher. *Gathering the Potawatomi Nation: Revitalization and Identity*. 1st ed. Norman: Univ. of Oklahoma Press, 2016.
White, Frederick. "Rethinking Native American Language Revitalization." *American Indian Quarterly* 30 (2006): 91–109.
White, Richard. *The Middle Ground: Indians, Empires, and Republics in the Great Lakes Region, 1650–1815*. Cambridge: Cambridge Univ. Press, 1991.
Whitepigeon, Carey F. *Daughter of Dawn and Darkness: Book 1: Spark Aflight*. Independently published, 2017.
Whitney, Gordon G. "An Ecological History of the Great Lakes Forest of Michigan." *Journal of Ecology* 75, no. 3 (1987): 667–84. https://doi.org/10.2307/2260198.
Whyte, Kyle. "Against Crisis Epistemology." In *Routledge Handbook of Critical Indigenous Studies*, edited by Brendan Hokowhitu, Aileen Moreton-Robinson, Linda Tuhiwai-Smith, Chris Andersen, and Steve Larkin, 52–64. 1st ed. London: Routledge, 2020. https://doi.org/10.4324/9780429440229-6.
Whyte, Kyle P. "Indigenous Science (Fiction) for the Anthropocene: Ancestral Dystopias and Fantasies of Climate Change Crises." *Environment and Planning E: Nature and Space* 1, no. 1–2 (March 2018): 224–42. https://doi.org/10.1177/2514848618777621.
Whyte, Kyle Powys. "Our Ancestors' Dystopia Now: Indigenous Conservation and the Anthropocene." In *Routledge Companion to the Environmental Humanities*, edited by Ursula Heise, Jon Christensen, and Michelle Niemann. London: Routledge, 2017.

Whyte, Kyle, and Chris Cuomo. "Ethics of Caring in Environmental Ethics: Indigenous and Feminist Philosophies." In *The Oxford Handbook of Environmental Ethics*, edited by Stephen M. Gardiner and Allen Thompson. Oxford: Oxford Univ. Press, 2015. https://doi.org/10.1093/oxfordhb/9780199941339.013.22.

Wilbur, Matika. *Project 562: Changing the Way We See Native America*. 1st ed. Emeryville, CA: Ten Speed Press, 2023.

Willow, Anna J. "Conceiving Kakipitatapitmok: The Political Landscape of Anishinaabe Anticlearcutting Activism." *American Anthropologist* 113, no. 2 (2011): 262–76.

Wilson, Shawn. *Research Is Ceremony: Indigenous Research Methods*. 1st ed. Black Point, N.S.: Fernwood Publishing, 2008.

Wolf, Eric R. *Envisioning Power*. 1st ed. Berkeley: Univ. of California Press, 1999.

Wolfe, Patrick. "Settler Colonialism and the Elimination of the Native." *Journal of Genocide Research* 8, no. 4 (December 2006): 387–409. https://doi.org/10.1080/14623520601056240.

World Intellectual Property Organization. "Traditional Knowledge." https://www.wipo.int/tk/en/tk/.

INDEX

?E?ANX (The Cave), 117–18, 119

6th World—An Origin Story, 118
2001: A Space Odyssey, 115, 139–40

academia: anthropology of place and space, 18; atmosphere of dislocation, 149; exclusionary practices, 70; false Indigenous identities, 161n63; Indigenous engineering, 71; LaDuke, 129; Native anthropology, 26–29; peer review, 85; research, 73, 79; settler colonial erasure of Native presence, 19
Administrative Procedures Act (APA), 83
American Beaver and His Works, The, 100
American Indian Movement (AIM), 124
Ancient Society, 32
ankobthegen (ancestors), 35
Anthropocene: climate change, 37, 101–5; symbiotic entanglement in, 99
anthropology: Anthropocene, 102–3; climate change, 141; cultural, 15, 32–33; cultural politics, 148–49; ethnography, 100; Indigenous knowledge, 78; Indigenous studies, 29; of knowledge production, 14, 16–17, 73–75, 78–79, 83; Native anthropology, 26–28; other-than-human beings, 94; phenomenology in, 97; salvage, 34; science fiction and, 112–13, 116–17; of space and place, 14, 18, 41–42, 45, 57, 150; turns in, 77
Anthropology of Space and Place: Locating Culture, The, 57
Appadurai, Arjun, 122, 153
Ari, Waskar, 131
Arrival, The, 120
Arts of Living on a Damaged Planet, 104
Atalay, Sonya, 17, 79–80, 82

Bagone'giizhig (hole in the sky), 150–51
Basso, Keith, 18, 41, 57, 67–68
Bastien, Betty, 67
Baudemann, Kristina, 9, 35, 120
Becker, Nanobah, 118
Benedict, Michael A., 69
Benton-Banai-mba, Edward, 124
Berkes, Fikret, 69
Beyond Settler Time, 144
Bigjohn Jr., Cody, 46

Biolsi, Thomas, 153–54
Bisharat, George E., 57
bkanathmownen (speculative stories), 37, 111
Blackfoot Ways of Knowing, 67
Bodwéwadmimwen (the Potawatomi language): cartographic maps speckled with, 155; descriptive language, 62, 128; Hartford (*Byankik*), 40; phrases, 26; re-proliferation of, 8; retention of, 76; speaking, 122; teaching (*ke-'magéwen*), 17; ways in which travel is spoken about, 145
Bogosian, Vic, 89–90
Boone, Kyle, 48
Boyer, Dominic, 74
Braiding Sweetgrass, 17, 63, 67
Brown Spiers, Miriam C., 119
Bullard, Robert, 45
Bussler, Matthew, 80–81, 145–46, 148, 154
Butler, Caroline, 78–79
Butler, Octavia E., 115
Byankik (Hartford), 40

Caldwell, author's birth name, 23
capitalism, 48–49, 78, 106–7, 150
Carlone, Heidi, 75–76, 77
Carson, Rachel, 45
cedar, 66
ceremonies: artifacts of Midéwiwin ceremony, 51; Midéwiwin Lodge, 9–10, 15, 21, 26, 95–96, 108; naming, 9; Neshnabé futurity, 5; Neshnabék, 96; Ojibwe, 51; Pokagon Band, 126; Pokagon community, 169n37; Potawatomi peoples, 14; practices, 8; waters, 4, 10; Water Walks, 12–13, 133
Cerwonka, Allaine, 55
channelized waterways, 11, 89–90, 104, 105, 107–8
Chu, Seo-Young, 112, 115, 120
Clark, Arthur C., 139

Claspy, Everett, 13
Clifford, James, 98–99
climate change: anxieties about, 15–16, 103–4, 160n36; crisis research, 141; disproportionately affects Indigenous peoples, 103; experienced differently according to race, 18; Great Lakes, 11, 14, 48, 120, 142; how climate change is affecting communities, 101–2; Indigenous relationships to place, 37; Neshnabé futurity, 15; Water Walks, 13, 122
Collaborating at the Trowel's Edge, 80
Collins, Samuel, 116
colonialism: alternatives to, 10; blood quantum as colonial tool of erasure, 158n5; coloniality of anthropology, 117; colonial violence, 103; culpability of colonial states, 79; ending Indigenous peoples' relationships to ecosystems, 105; fantasies of white modernity, 38; Indigenous peoples and, 29; representational work and, 111; science fiction and, 112–13, 115–16, 118. *See also* settler colonialism
Colonialism and the Emergence of Science Fiction, 112–13
Comaroff, Jean, 22
Comaroff, John, 22
Common Knowledge? 76–77
community-based participatory research (CBPR), 78, 79
Coulthard, Glen, 83
counter-mapping, 38, 146, 148, 150, 153, 154
Creator, 125, 151
Crehan, Kate, 131
Crick, Malcom R., 74
Crutzen, Paul, 101

Dakota Access Pipeline (DAPL), 10, 34, 45, 46, 114, 121
Daughter of Dawn and Darkness, 15, 118

Dawes Act of 1887, 33
Day After Tomorrow, The, 15
Decolonizing Methodologies, 102
Decolonizing Methodologies: Research and Indigenous Peoples, 27–28
Deloria Jr., Vine, 66, 67
Dillon, Grace: Indigenous futurisms, 9, 31, 40; "reservation realism," 118; "slipstream" storytelling, 117, 119; "spiraling time," 121
Dimaline, Cherie, 15
dispossession: contemporary structures of, 42; corruption of place-names, 51; due to extractive industries and development, 51; ecological issues, 134; ecological regime change, 107; histories of, 43, 92, 107; during late 1800s, 11; reclaiming space, 149; settler colonial spatial techniques, 55, 58, 105; settler colonial violence, 9; settler expansion, 54
"distribution inequality," 44
diversity, 70
Doe-wah-jack (fictiious chief), 58–59, 140
Do Metaphors Dream of Literal Sleep? 112

Earth Politics, 131
ecological changes, 89–90, 93
ecological ethic, 68, 135
ecological integrity, 69
ecological issues, 133–34, 141
ecological management, 15, 67, 71, 78–79, 91, 138
ecological methods, 101
ecological regime change, 107
ecological revitalization projects: futurity, 105–10; Great Lakes, 120, 140, 142–43; Neshnabé futurity, 5, 13, 37, 110, 140–43; Pokagon Band, 8, 12; Potawatomi peoples, 12; stories, 141; Water Walks, 12, 14, 17–20, 141

ecologies: destruction of, 11, 12; "ecological ethnicity," 48; of Great Lakes, 22; milkweed, 62–63; Neshnabé, 37, 92; revitalizing, 10, 12, 36, 92–93, 106–7, 109–10; spirituality and, 94. *See also* traditional ecological knowledge (TEK)
ecologists, 105, 142
Eglash, Ron, 88
Elkins, James, 21
emerald ash borer, 69
Empire, 84
Environmental Protection Agency (EPA), 11, 50, 135
Envisioning Power, 77
Escobar, Arturo, 149
Eshel, Amir, 32
Estes, Nick, 45, 121
Evans-Pritchard, Sir Edward E., 74
Expanse, The, 114–15

Fabian, Jonas, 32
Falzon, Mark-Anthony, 23
Feld, Steven, 57
Ferguson, James, 56
Fictionalizing Anthropology, 98, 103
Foucalt, Michel, 74
Frankenstein, 16
Frelich, Lee E., 69
Future as Cultural Fact, The, 122
futures: coloniality of science fiction, 112–16; decolonial, 141, 143; demythologizing ideas of revitalization, 92–93; disrupting settler colonial futures, 8; imagining, 98–99, 139–40, 142; Indigenous articulations of agency, 103; in Indigenous-made science fiction, 118–20, 144; prophecy, 121–22; traditional knowledge, 65, 76; without caricaturing Indigenous communities, 7
futurisms: Indigenous, 9–10, 14–15, 19–20, 30–35, 38, 154–55; Neshnabé, 13

futurist, 4
futurity: activism as futurity, 128–30, 135–38; acutalizing in spaces, 126; ecological revitalization projects, 105–10; role of spirituality, 94; traditional knowledge, 84–88

Gallardo, Nancy, 46
Ganapathy, Sandhya, 107
Gedicks, Al, 49–50
Geertz, Clifford, 25
General Allotment Act of 1887, 54
Geography of Identity, The, 153
Ggaténma-êk (We Honor Our Ancestors) powwow, 92
Ggaténmamen Gdankobthegnanêk (We Honor Our Ancestors) powwow, 92
Goeman, Mishuana, 153
Goulet, Danis, 15, 118
Gramsci, Antonio, 130–31
Great Lakes: anthropology of knowledge production, 83; channelized waterways, 105, 108; climate change manifestions, 14; constellations, 151, 153; contamination, 50; ecological revitalization projects, 120, 140, 142–43; environmental issues, 44, 48; European imperialism in, 13; Indigenous ecology, 22; Indigenous eco-politics, 110, 141; Indigenous resistance to climate change, 11–12; insect damage, 69, 89; mitigating invasive species, 90; Native peoples origin story, 158n1; Neshnabé peoples' histories rooted in, 146; other-than-human relatives, 92; pipelines, 46, 140; place-names, 8, 153; Potawatomi peoples moving around, 5, 7; practices of place-making in, 37; reclaiming space, 38, 148, 154; resource extraction, 8; settler colonialism in, 20; Water Walks, 10, 12, 125–26, 135
Grossman, David, 32

Gupta, Aknil, 56
Gzémnedo ("creating spirit"), 95

Haig-Brown, Helen, 117, 118
Hardt, Michael, 84
Harjo, Laura, 39, 117
Hartford (*Byankik*), 40
Hegel, Georg, 22
Heidegger, Martin, 41, 97
Helmreich, Stefan, 100
Higgins, David, 116
Hirsch, Eric, 42–43
History of Magic in North America, The, 119
Hoffman, Walter James, 123
Holden, Jim (fictional character), 114
Homestead Act of 1862, 33
Hopkins, Rhonda, 63
Hoverboard, 118
How Forests Think, 94
huckleberries, 90–91
hydrofracking: contamination, 12; environmental issues, 134–35; Indigenous refusal of, 34–35, 130, 132; mitigating and surviving ecological destruction, 120, 142; proposals, 11; reservations, 46

Independence Day, 118
Indigenous activists, 46, 131–38, 142–43
Indigenous artifacts, 98–99
Indigenous ceremonies, 123, 126
Indigenous communities: access to natural resources, 106, 108, 148; climate change, 104–5; dispossession of, 7; environmental movements, 18; forest management and, 91; Indian Religious Freedom Act, 96–97; natural resource management (NRM), 101; possibilities departing from settler version of future, 36, 140; relationships to place, 37, 49, 59; "revitalization," 34; teaching and learning linked to earth, 17; tradi-

tional knowledge, 38; typically live in "expendable" areas, 11
Indigenous dispossession, 51, 54–56
Indigenous ecological knowledge, 13
Indigenous ecology, 22
Indigenous ecopolitics, 141
Indigenous experiences, 4–5
Indigenous futurity: contrasted with settler colonial structure, 30–35; ecological revitalization and political demonstrations, 5; Indigenous science fiction, 9; literature in, 130; "returning to ourselves," 40; traditional knowledge, 88; tradtional stories and, 99
Indigenous geographies, 39
Indigenous identity, 18, 54, 85
Indigenous knowledge: anthropological research, 74; appropriation of, 79; ethical frameworks, 63; ignored or co-opted by mainstream science, 37; insights through dreams or serendipity, 23–24; integrated into DNR science, 69; literature about, 67–68; methods and values shared with science, 71, 78; qualities of relationality and ethics of reciprocity, 84; social relationships to lands and waters, 144
Indigenous land, 48
Indigenous liberation movements, 10
Indigenous peoples: academic exploitation of, 27–29; asked to sacrifice their lands, 102–3; dissent, 12; erased or irrelevant in science fiction media, 113–15; global colonization of, 28; hegemonic discourse about, 27; temporalized by ethnographers, 32–33; violences experienced through settler colonialism, 20; working toward sovereignty, 19
Indigenous perspective, 42
Indigenous presence, 58, 146
Indigenous prophecy, 121–22
Indigenous representation, 76

Indigenous revitalization, 92–93
Indigenous rights, 83
Indigenous scholars, 143
Indigenous science fiction: Baudemann on, 9; estranges colonialism, 112; futurity, 111, 120, 141–42; futurity of, 14–16; imagining alternatives to present contexts, 12; relevance of Indigenous lives, 115–16; social equity, 116; "spiraling time," 120–21, 145; traditional knowledge blended with storytelling traditions, 118–19
Indigenous sovereignty, 86
Indigenous spaces, 149–50, 153–54
Indigenous studies, 19–20, 25–29, 45
Ingold, Tim, 97–98
Interstellar, 15, 120

Jackson, Andy, 40–41
James, Keith, 29
Jauss, Hans Robert, 119
Jemielniak, Dariusz, 76–77
jiibay kona (Milky Way as spirit path), 4
Johnson, Angela, 75–76, 77
Johnston, Basil, 94–95

Kanine, Jennifer, 106–7
Katesse, 7
Keene, Adrienne, 119
Keewaydinoquay (Margaret Peschel), 87
keno'magéwen (the earth demonstrates/shows us in the present), 17, 37, 63
Killers of the Flower Moon, 115
Kimmerer, Robin Wall, 63, 67
Kirksey, S. Eben, 100
Kirsch, Stuart, 84
Kohn, Eduardo, 94
Kosek, Jake, 91, 107–8
Kroeber, Alfred Louis, 116
Kroeber, Theodora, 116
Ktthémnedo (the Great Spirit), 73, 95
Kubrick, Stanley, 115
Kuwayama, Takami, 26–27

LaBine, Roger, 108
LaDuke, Winona, 45–46, 56, 129
Laing, Anna F., 149–50
Landes, Ruth, 14, 20, 21
Langdon, Steve J., 68
LaPensée, Elizabeth, 3–5, 118
Lawrence-Zúñiga, Denise, 57
Lea, Tess, 29
Lee, Annette Sharon, 151
Lefebvre, Henri, 42
Legends of Michigan and the Old North West, 52, 54
Le Guin, Ursula K., 116
Lempert, William, 31, 33, 119
liberal multiculturalism, 19
Littlejohn, F.J., 52, 54
Louis, Renee, 148
Low, John N., 13, 34, 41–42, 43
Low, Setha, 18, 57

Malott, Bmejwen Kyle, 37, 145–46, 148, 151–52, 154
Mandamin-mba, Josephine, 125–26
Mar, Banivanua, 58
Marcus, 64–65, 81–82
Marcus, George E., 22
Marlor, Chantelle, 78
Marrow Thieves, 15
Matthews, Maureen, 22
McGregor, Deborah, 14
McKinnon, Crystal, 153
McLean, Stuart, 98, 103
McLeod, Neal, 116, 145
Mdodosenik (sweat lodge stones used in ceremony), 150–51
Medak-Saltzman, Danika, 10, 111, 113
méndokaswen (ceremonial or spiritual doing), 37
Menzies, Charles, 79
Métis in Space, 118
Midés (members of Midéwiwin Society), 12, 96, 123

Midéwiwin Lodge, 123; ceremonies, 9, 15, 21, 26, 95–96, 108; Indigenous sacred knowledge, 23; LaDuke, 45–46; leader, 3; political activities, 18, 121, 124, 129–30; prophecy, 122, 142; research focused on, 20; Rhonda, 133–34; secrecy, 123; Water Walks, 121, 124–26, 130, 132, 142, 169n37; women responsible for cedar, 66
Midéwiwin Society, 13–14, 51
Mihesuah, Devon A., 28–29
milkweed (*nenwesh*): harvest and preparation of, 140; milkweed soup, 64; picking, 5, 39, 40–41; processing, 40–41; traditional knowledge, 62–63
Miller, Cary, 13, 18
Mining Capitalism, 84
Mishawaka myth, 52–54, 140
Mitêwâcimowina: Indigenous Science Fiction and Storytelling, 145
mko (bear), 92
mnedo (spirit beings), 15
Mnedowêk (entity that goes about causing change), 94, 141
mni wiconi (water is life), 133
mno bmadzewen (living the good life), 62, 121, 129, 150
mnomen (wild rice), 12, 34, 37, 106–10, 122, 141
Modern Prince, The, 130–31
Moore, Amelia, 101–2
Morgan, Lewis Henry, 32, 100, 101
Mzhigénak (Michigan), 8

National Environmental Policy Act (NEPA), 17, 46, 80, 82–83, 135
National Historic Preservation Act (NHPA), 17, 80, 83, 135
Native American Graves Protection and Repatriation Act (NAGPRA), 13, 80
Native Hubs, 149
Native to the Nation, 55

natural resource management (NRM): anthropology of knowledge production, 17; consultation with Indigenous communities, 101; cultural politics, 149; how non-Native community manages, 79; policy, 80; professionals, 90, 136; projects, 70; traditional ecological knowledge (TEK), 78; traditional knowledge, 66

natural resources: access to, 41, 54, 107, 148, 163n9; denial of access to, 141; exploitation, 150; extraction, 34; Native Americans alienated from, 91; professionals, 143; tree sap, 72

Negri, Antonio, 84

nenwesh (milkweed): harvest and preparation of, 140; milkweed soup, 64; picking, 5, 39, 40–41; processing, 40–41; traditional knowledge, 62–63

Neshnabé: activists, 132; artifacts of Midéwiwin ceremony, 51; concepts, 26; constellations, 151–53; cosmology, 3–4, 108, 157n8; culture, 13; ecology, 8, 92–93, 110; ethics, 67, 86, 137; fruits in diet and cosmology, 90; futurisms, 13; groups, 7; importance of movement and action in language, 128–29; origin stories, 126, 150; other-than-human relatives, 99, 105; participants, 48; perspective, 77, 93, 103; reclaiming space, 148; relationships to space, 44; stories, 97–98; traditional knowledge, 17, 62–63, 65, 67, 76, 88; women's traditional cedar roles, 66

Neshnabé communitites: anthropology of knowledge production, 16; author's research, 25; canoe-building in, 34; on climate change, 103; definition, 20; make space for themselves in the future, 120; managing natural resources, 79; Midéwiwin Lodge, 130, 134; scholarly work with, 22; traditional knowledge, 37, 69; Water Walks, 154; wild rice resources, 109; Williams on, 127–28

Neshnabé futurity: ancestors and future generations, 144; climate change, 15; ecological revitalization projects, 5, 13, 37, 110, 140–43; forward and backward in time, 35; ideas disseminated via "mainstream science fiction" media, 38; mitigating and survivng ecological destruction, 120; modernity invents primitiveness of non-European cultures, 30; possibility centered on ethical relationships with the earth, 5; reclamations of space, 9–10; stories, 110; storytelling and activism, 111; timeslip passages, 121; traditional knowledge, 36, 76, 140, 144; Water Walks, 122–23, 143

Neshnabék: ceremonies, 96; changes, 10; on climate change, 102; communitites, 17, 34; consider time as cyclical, 120; envisioning ecological future, 93; Madeline Island as site of Midéwiwin-practice, 50–51; migration, 108; Neshnabé futurity, 5, 15, 35, 121, 126, 129; prayers, 95, 124–25; prophecy, 121–22; sovereignty, 155; spatial contexts, 18; stories, 87, 90; traditional knowledge, 62–63, 88, 140

Neshnabé ke (Potawatomi homelands): author dwelling in, 93; decolonial futures, 143; the earth demonstrates/shows us in the present, 36–37; environmental issues, 18, 91; meaning of, 63; reclaiming space, 144–45; removal and remaining peoples, 8; restoration, 124; sacrificed to colonization, development, and tourism, 50; spaces for mobilizing futures, 9

Neshnabékwéwêk (Neshnabé women), 12, 25

Neshnabé peoples: bundles, 85; on climate change, 14–15; dispossession, 42, 59, 107–8; how Neshnabé relate to each other, 23; milkweed use, 40; place-names, 146; prophecy, 122; seasonal movements, 146; storytelling about futurisms, 35; water presentations, 133; Water Walks, 135; wild rice resources, 107, 108

Nietzsche, Friedrich, 75

Night Raiders, 15

nimkibneshi (thunderbird), 92

O'Brien, Jean, 54–55

Ojibwe: archaeologist, 17; constellations, 150–51; descendants of, 7; ethnohistorian, 54; identity, 108; language, 3–4; overlap with other Indigenous groups, 5; practicing ceremonies, 51; reality, 22

Ojibwe Sky Star Map Constellation Guide, 151

organicism, 130–31

other-than-human beings, 15, 93, 94, 103

other-than-human relationships, 100, 141

other-than-human relatives, 37, 92, 99, 105

Outlander, 120

Oza, Rupel, 149

Parable of the Sower, 115

Parajuli, Pramod, 46, 48

Pearce, Margaret, 148

Perception of the Environment, The, 97–98

Pigeon, John, 61–62

pipelines: bursting, 50; construction, 48; dispossession of Native peoples, 59, 140; Great Lakes, 44, 46, 47*f*, 120, 142, 154–55; Indigenous futurisms, 34–35; LaDuke on, 46; tribes protesting, 51. *See also* Dakota Access Pipeline (DAPL)

place: anthropology of, 14, 18, 42, 45, 150; environmental politics and ethnicity, 46; identity, 41, 57–58, 67; Indigenous conceptions of, 92; Indigenous connections to, 31; Indigenous loss of, 104; narratives of, 37, 42, 51, 59; Neshnabé conceptions of, 148; place-based "archives," 140–41; practices of place-making, 37; reclaiming space, 38, 144, 145, 150, 153, 154; "rootedness" in, 48–49; sense of, 121; settler sense of place, 56; social relationships, 14, 22; "spatialized power," 44; spatial meaning, 43

place-names: co-opting false narratives of, 146; corruption of, 51; Indigenous, 148; misappropriation of, 58; narratives of, 94; reinscribing original Indigenous place-names, 153; settler fictionalizations of, 54; stories attached to, 67–68; traditional Potawatomi overwritten, 11

Pokagon, Leopold, 7, 44, 158n5

Pokagon Band: anglicized surname, 7; archives, 86; author's enrollment, 5, 23, 25; ceremonies, 126; citizens living off reservation lands, 43; constellations, 150–51; ecological revitalization projects, 8, 12; environmental activism, 8; ethnic diversity, 158n5; foraging practices, 68; fractures between TCK students and teachers, 66–67; identity, 8; and Mishawaka myth, 52–54; Neshnabé futurisms, 76; photographs, 35; Pokagon Band DNR, 69–70, 89–90, 92, 106, 135; scholarship, 13, 34; spatial and social separation, 141; traditional knowledge, 37; Tribal Head Start school, 72; Water Walks, 10, 12, 133; and wild rice, 108–9

Pokagon community: author not as "in and of" the community, 25–26; author's archival work, 84; ceremonies, 169n37; constellations, 150–51; elders, 62, 67; federal refusal of tribe, 35; teachings and recipes, 40

Poole, Grant, 90, 135–37
Potawatomi: authors, 15, 118; author's identity, 23–24; experiences, 22; food, 40; histories, 146, 154; homelands, 5–8, 18, 37, 50, 63, 144–45; identity, 69, 73; nationalism, 13; placenames, 11; Pokagon tribal lands, 106; rights, 41; star knowledge, 150–53; stories, 87–88; territory, 5–8, 43–44; traditional knowledge, 26, 36, 37, 72, 140; traditional methods, 68; ways of knowing, 84
Potawatomi language: anglicized corruption of, 51; *bkanathmownen* (speculative fiction), 37, 111; *Bodwéwadmimwen* (Potawatomi language), 8, 128; *Gzémnedo* ("creating spirit"), 95; keno'magéwen (teaching or the earth demonstrates/shows us in the present), 63; keno'magéwen (teacing or the earth demonstrates/shows us in the present), 37; Manitou (evil spirit), 94; *méndokaswen* (ceremonial or spiritual doing), 37; *mno bmadzen* (how to live a good life), 121; *Mshéwaké* (land of the dead trees), 54; *mshiwakwa* (place of big trees), 52; *Mzhigénak* (Michigan), 8; *Ndowathek*, (place of harvesting), 58–59; *nenwesh* (milkweed or male plant), 62; Neshnabé futurity, 76, 111; Neshnabé ke (Potawatomi homelands), 36–37, 63; *Nokmis* (grandmother), 3; *thibékan* (Milky Way as spirit path), 4; *Zhabwagnak* (place of the sound of the drum coming through), 51
Potawatomi peoples: ecological revitalization projects, 12; identity, 20–21; migration, 108; misrepresentations of, 53; Neshnabé futurisms, 9–10; photographs, 35; practices and ceremonies, 14; practicing traditional ways, 122; stories, 141; territory, 5–8, 43; traditional knowledge, 17, 85, 109; *vivir bien*, 150
Potawatomi scholars: Low, 34, 85; Whyte, 12, 14, 16, 102, 104
Povinelli, Elizabeth A., 20
Power and Knowledge, 74
Price, Michael Waasegiizhig, 151
Primitive Man as Philosopher, 74
Purcell, Rhonda, 66–67, 72–73, 133–34
Pyne, Stephanie, 146

racism: against Aboriginal peoples, 153; "adverse racism," 29; assumptions about Indigenous peoples, 28; environmental, 45, 163n9; legal battles for resources, 49; Lorde on, 170n6; misrepresentations and misappropriations of Native cultures, 115; positioning Native peoples in the past, 32
Radin, Paul, 74
Ramirez, Reyna, 149
Red Earth White Lies, 66
Research Is Ceremony, 29
Reservation Dogs, 115
respatialization, 153
Rhonda, 61–62
Rieder, John, 112–13
Rifkin, Mark, 144
Risser, Paige, 52
"rootedness," 48–49
Routes: Travel and Translation in the Late 20th Century, 98
Rowling, J.K., 119
Rutherford Falls, 115

Saunders, Mykaela, 119
science: ethnographies of science education, 75–76, 77; Indigenous, 16, 67, 71; lack of Indigenous representation, 69–70, 72; mainstream, 68, 85; traditional knowledge and, 77–78, 82, 85; tradtional knowledge and, 73; Western, 16, 37, 63

science fiction: Clark, 139; climate change, 15; coloniality of, 112–16; effect on society, 112; imagining potential futures, 128; Indigenous, 15–16, 111, 112, 116–20, 121, 141–42; lack of Native peoples in, 104; mainstream, 38, 117, 142
Secunda, Benjamin, 13
Seeking Spatial Justice, 43
séma (tobacco), 39, 124
Senses of Place, 57
settler: anxieties about climate change, 103–5; channelization, 11; colonial futures disrupted by Indigenous nation-building, 8; colonial government, 107–8; colonial knowledge, 23–24; colonial projects, 102; colonial violence and dispossession, 9; expansion, 43–44; frameworks of territory, 7; futurity, 51–59; imagining future without Indigenous peoples, 13; logics of place, 51; narratives of place, 37, 154; narratives of place-names, 94; nation, 118; nation-building, 103; nation states, 29; society, 36, 140–41, 146, 149
settler colonialism: affects every aspect of Indigenous life, 30–31; ecological collapse, 141; eraure of Native presence, 19–20, 55–56, 150; Indigenous attempts to reclaim futures, 143–44; Indigenous movements against oil, 121; oppression, 153; speaking against, 27; as structure, 30–31, 54
settler futurity, 51–59
Shelley, Mary, 16
Sherman, Sean, 62
shishigwan (rattle), 72–73
Shomin, Sarah Jo, 46
Sibley, David, 149
Siksikaitsitapi (Blackfoot placed-based epistemology), 67
Silent Spring, 45
Silliman, Stephen, 80
Simpson, Audra, 20, 23, 143

Simpson, Leanne, 131–32
Smith, Linda Tuhiwai, 27–28, 102
Soja, Edward, 43
sovereignty: Aboriginal, 146; asserting, 145; data, 137; "este-cate sovereignty," 39; Indigenous, 19–20, 86, 148, 150; maps and, 148; Neshnabék, 155; rights to, 49; temporal, 144; tribal, 7, 34
"spatialized power," 44
Spiral to the Stars, 117
Standing Rock, 10, 34, 45, 121, 127–28, 133
Stern, Marc J., 82
stories: *bkanathmownen* (speculative stories), 111; colonial point of view, 112; constellations, 151–53; creation stories, 144–45, 150; ecological revitalization projects, 141; Indigenous storying about the future, 9, 35; milkweed, 40–41; Mishawaka myth, 52–54; and the natural world, 98, 99; Neshnabé futurity, 110; origin stories, 108, 126; other-than-human relatives, 92, 99, 105; place-names, 8; and places, 56, 59, 67–68; Potawatomi and settler stories, 146; scrolls, 85; short stories, 116, 118; speculative fiction, 37; of the supernatural, 97; sweet fruits, 90; "timeslip stories," 121; traditional, 5, 21, 73, 86–88, 119–20; traditional knowledge, 72
Streeby, Shelley, 34–35
Suvin, Darko, 112
Swain, Molly, 118

Taylor, D.R. Fraser, 146
Theories of Primitive Religion, 74
thibékan (Milky Way as spirit path), 4
This All Come Back Now: An Anthology of First Nations Speculative Fiction, 119
Thunder, Jim, 95
Thunderbird Strike, 118
Time Machine, The, 120
tobacco (*séma*), 39

Topash, Mary, 20–21
Topash, Tom, 20–21
Topinabe, Chief, 7
traditional cultural knowledge (TCK), 65–67, 78
traditional ecological knowledge (TEK), 65–66, 68, 78–79
traditional knowledge: acquistion, 26; author's knowledge of, 93; constellations, 151; as content, 63–64; futures, 65, 76; futurity, 84–88; ignored and stifled, 142; Indigenous futurism, 88; in Indigenous-made science fiction, 118; Indigenous ways of knowing, 24; informs Indigenous conceptions of the future, 38; lack of Indigenous representation in DNR, 69–70; methods and values shared with science, 71; milkweed, 62–63; mobilizing, 37; Native science, 14–15, 16; Neshnabé, 17, 62–63, 65, 67, 76, 88; Neshnabé communitites, 37, 69; Neshnabé futurity, 36, 76, 140, 144; Neshnabék, 62–63, 88, 140; new Native anthropology centered on, 27; Pokagon Band, 37; political movement grounded in, 137; Potawatomi, 26, 36, 37, 72, 140; Potawatomi peoples, 17, 85, 109; Purcell's knowledge of, 134; reclaiming, 17; self-determined practices, 39; social relationships, 67; stories, 72; traditional knowledge holders, 67, 85; traditional knowledge labels, 87; traditional knowledge systems, 68, 77–79, 82; in tribal schools, 72–73; waters, 144; Water Walks, 17–18, 138, 140; "ways of knowing," 62–63
Traianou, Anna, 75, 77
Tsing, Anna, 100, 104
Tuck, Eve, 23, 54, 143
Tuhiwai Smith, Linda, 27–28, 102, 122

Understories, 107–8

Vennum Jr., Thomas, 14, 21
Veracini, Lorenzo, 30
vivir bien, 150
Vizenor, Gerald, 33
Voigt Decision, 49
Vowel, Chelsea, 118

Wakening, 15, 118
Walking the Clouds, 118
Wall, Robin, 17
Wallace, Anthony F.C., 34
War of 1812, 10
War of the Worlds, 16, 113, 114, 118
waters: biodiversity, 105; bodies of, 144–45; contamination, 49–50, 80; drained for agriculture, 89; federal regulations, 82; hydrofracking, 134–35; identities, 41; Neshnabék sovereignty, 155; re-meandering, 90, 107–8; traditional knowledge, 144; water quality, 135–37; Williams on, 127–28
Water Walks: ceremonies, 12–13, 133; climate change, 13, 122; ecological revitalization projects, 12, 14, 17–20, 141; empirical data, 137–38; Great Lakes, 10, 12, 125–26, 135; hydrofracking, 135; Indigenous futurity, 5, 12–13, 14; LaPensée, 3; Midéwiwin Lodge, 121, 124–26, 130, 132, 142, 169n37; Neshnabé futurity, 122–23, 143; Pokagon Band, 10, 12; prophecy, 38, 121, 140; protesting Line 5, 46; resistance movements of, 93; resistance to settler narratives of place, 154; response to dispossession and environmental degradation, 10; responsibility of women, 124; rise of, 125–26; Three Fires Lodge, 123; traditional knowledge, 17–18, 138, 140
Weber, Max, 75
"webs of significance," 25
Weiler, Hans, 74–75
Wells, H. G., 16, 113, 114, 118, 120

Wemigwans, Jennifer, 86
Wesaw, Gerlad, 41
Wesaw, Jason S., 86
Wetzel, Christopher, 13
White, Richard, 13
Whitepigeon, Carey F., 15, 118
Whyte, Kyle Powys, 12, 14, 16, 102, 104–5
Wilbur, Matika, 115
Williams, Rebecca, 126–28, 129
Willow, Anna, 18
Wilson, Angela Cavender, 28–29
Wilson, Shawn, 24
Winchester, Marcus, 43, 86

Wisdom Sits in Places, 41, 67–68
Wiwkwébthëgen (bundle), 86–87
Wolf, Eric R., 77
Wolfe, Patrick, 20, 30
World Intellectual Property Organization (WIPO), 65
World War II, 34

Yang, K Wayne, 23, 54, 143

Zagbëgon (little sprouts), 72, 151
Zhabwagnak (place of the sound of the drum coming through), 51

ABOUT THE AUTHOR

Blaire Morseau is a citizen of the Pokagon Band of Potawatomi Indians and the inaugural 1855 Professor of Great Lakes Anishinaabé Knowledge, Spiritualities, and Cultural Practices in the Department of Religious Studies at Michigan State University. She recently released an edited volume featuring the collection of antique birch bark books written by nineteenth-century Potawatomi author Simon Pokagon titled *As Sacred to Us: Simon Pokagon's Birch Bark Stories in Their Contexts*. Her research interests include Indigenous science fiction, futurisms, traditional knowledge, digital heritage, and Native counter-mapping.